7/10/90

To Bob,

Thanks for saving
fishing pole and my life

Wish you the best,

Frank Summer

THE
LIVING RIVER

THE
LIVING

A Fisherman's Intimate Profile
Of The Madison River Watershed
–Its History, Ecology, Lore, and Angling Opportunities

RIVER

Charles E. Brooks

NICK LYONS BOOKS

WINCHESTER PRESS

Published and distributed by
WINCHESTER PRESS
New Century Publishers
220 Old New Brunswick Road
Piscataway, New Jersey 08854

Produced by
NICK LYONS BOOKS
31 West 21st Street
New York, New York 10010

PRINTED IN THE UNITED STATES OF AMERICA
10   9   8   7   6   5   4   3   2   1

Library of Congress Catalog Card Number: 84-62782

ISBN: 0-8329-0395-7 (hardcover)
ISBN: 0-8329-0381-7 (paperback)

Designed by Ruth Kolbert Smerechniak
Composition By Publishers Phototype, Inc., Carlstadt, N.J.

Art by Dave Whitlock

CONTENTS

ACKNOWLEDGMENTS

ALTHOUGH THIS BOOK WAS SUGGESTED BY AUSTIN HOGAN AND RESEARCHED AND written by me, there are a number of people who come into it, simply because they had prior interest, knowledge, and concern. Among these are those whose interest caused much of the research done herein. I append a bibliography, but I must here give credit to some whose influence was greater than a mere listing of books will show.

Howard Back's charming book created my first great interest in the area—and is the loveliest text that will ever be written about it. Ray Bergman's narratives of the fishing created a fever that brought me to live here.

Much of the information, however, was obtained from individuals and thus is an expression of individual opinion. Because these persons are diverse in background, education, and experience, and thus have different opinions—and memories—I have in many cases had to make a considered judgment about which opinion was correct. In some cases I struck a compromise. But without this information, freely given, the book would have been incomplete. Therefore, some information in this work must be considered unverified.

The same must be said about many of the written works. Writers and editors of history and science works are largely working with opinions. This in the case of history is because it is based largely on someone's opinion of what happened, and quoting several "authorities" as reinforcement does not automatically make something true.

Science is still advancing in many fields. Some of what we learned yesterday is outdated today, and some of what we learn today will be outdated tomorrow. To quote something in science as an absolute truth is risky.

So I have taken from my research what to me seems reasonably accurate, based on my own knowledge in some cases. But the conclusions reached and the opinions expressed are mine and I take responsibility for them.

This is *not* meant to be a source work but a readable account of a living river, and my thanks go to those below for their interest and information, and to many others, who though unnamed, are also thanked.

Robert W. Williams, Supervisor, Beaverhead National Forest. Virgil Lindsey, District Ranger, Ennis District, Beaverhead National Forest.

The Federal Power Commission.

Joel Shouse, Project Director, Blue Ribbons of the Big Sky Country.

Areawide Planning Organization.

Harry R. Cosgriffe, Natural Resources Area Manager, Bureau of Land Management, Dillon Resource Area.

Bud and Greg Lilly, guides and outfitters, West Yellowstone.

Dick McGuire, guide and outfitter, Ennis.

Ron Marcoux, Regional Fisheries Manager, and Dick Vincent, Area Field Biologist, Montana Fish and Game Department.

Howard Van Noy, Division Manager, Montana Power Company.

Dr. Dee C. Taylor, Professor of Anthropology, University of Montana.

Reference library department personnel of Arizona State and Montana State Universities.

Don McAndrew, Bozeman Area Conservationist and June Haigh, Ennis Area Conservationist, Soil Conservation Service.

John Varley, Fisheries Biologist, U.S. Fish and Wildlife Service, Yellowstone National Park.

R. A. Hutchinson, Park Geologist, Yellowstone National Park.

And the many friends and brother anglers who have shared their knowledge of the Madison River with me.

INTRODUCTION

The genesis of this book was a gathering at my home in August 1975. Among those present were Austin S. Hogan, curator of the Museum of American Fly Fishing, an old friend by way of correspondence; G. Dick Findlay, then Executive Publisher of *Fly Fisherman Magazine;* Dick and Lillian Nelson, two friends of theirs whose names elude me; my wife Grace; and an old angling pal, Koke Winter. We had just escaped an August snow-rainstorm that had driven us from the Federation of Fly Fishermen's end-of-Conclave barbecue at the Fenwick Fly Fishing School, a half-mile away, and were basking before a roaring fire in my living room.

The talk was about streams and fly fishing for trout. Sometime during the evening, Austin, who was also the first editor of the Museum's magazine, *The American Fly Fisher,* and remains this nation's foremost historian on fly fishing, made the point that no one had ever written a book on the *complete* fly-fishing experience, where all those things that make the sport so engrossing—the geology, geography, hydrology, biology, ecology, history, and other facets of the stream—had been explored and developed. We all think about and feel these things, he said, but no one has ever written extensively of them. Said he, Dudley Lunt and Robert H. Boyle have both written extensively on creeks or rivers, but Lunt's was on a salt-water creek and Boyle's on the Hudson River—neither fishermen's streams.

It was something I had been thinking about for several years, but I had not researched, or even seriously considered, such a project until Austin brought it up.

Man has always sought out, and lived along rivers; it is the major fact of his survival. He may have lived in caves for protection from the elements and from those creatures which relished his tender skin and succulent flesh, but those caves were almost always near streams. Those early men who dwelled in caves higher up and farther away often did not survive the trip to water.

Thus man's love of rivers is a primordial instinct, springing from the dual facts that all life was originally born of water and that survival has always been easier close to, or in it.

But where does a river come from? From volcanoes and air, from fire and ice, from dew condensed out of the atmosphere and from hydrogen boiling in the earth. There were rivers before there were seas—and the seas, now that volcanic and thermal activity no longer supplies enough moisture to replenish the rivers, does so by the process of evaporation.

The sea is not, as is so often written, the heart of the land as the rivers are its arteries. It is a reservoir, cradling and holding the waters so they may be cleaned, purified, changed and returned to the headwaters of the streams to complete the cycle and start the whole thing over again.

Rivers do not return to the sea; they return to their headwaters in the form of rain and snow to start their long run to the sea, nourishing and sustaining all life in the process. The sea is the child of the rivers and not the reverse.

Rivers are thus the life blood of the land, running over instead of through it; wetting, nourishing, tearing down and rebuilding, shaping and destroying, they are life itself in raw, living, always changing but never ending repetition. Without them, no other life can survive.

As it moves from the mountains to the hills to the plains to the sea, a river sings. It is a siren song, falling softly on the ear and heard gently in the heart of those fortunate few who are attuned to hear it. These are the anglers and to them is given not only the ability to hear the voice of the river in their hearts but knowledge of the tongues with which it speaks. Not all are so blessed, and there are those who live on the banks of a stream for all their lives and never hear the river's voice.

But the anglers, even though they live in the maddening press and crush of a great city, hear always in their hearts the song of the river; they alone are the ones who know the words and music. To them it is a song of peace and well being; it is a rhythm that puts all who hear it in harmonious accord. There are many who love rivers but do not hear its voice, but anglers have it always in their soul; it is for them the river sings, for them it is never silent.

It has been my privilege to hear the voices of many rivers: the sullen roll of the mighty Mississippi on whose banks I was born, the sucking chuckle of the lower Yukon, the thrash and slush of the Sacramento. But these are only incidentally fishermen's rivers; they are too mighty and too majestic. One cannot become intimate with them.

Give me instead the silken hiss of Alaska's Clearwater, the purling clatter of the Madison's South Fork, the riotous laughter of the Feather and the lulling, dappling murmur of the Firehole. And above all, give me the myriad enchanting voices of the Madison as it makes its way from tiny Madison Lake in a one-hundred-eighty-mile plunging run to the Missouri. I have heard its voices and fished its mingling currents for thirty years and I believe that gives me good and sufficient reason to tell its story.

For the story to be complete, we must go beyond the time of the river's birth, and we must often go far beyond its banks and watershed to find the sources of influence or change. Events that took place thousands of miles away at one point in history have had an impact on the river at a later date. And many things that seem insignificant can and have caused important changes in the river or its environment. As John Burroughs said, when one tugs at anything in nature he will find that it is attached to the rest of the world.

The clothing worn by trappers and Indians, and the food they ate might seem to have little to do with the river, but those animals whose skins clothed the early visitors to the Madison Valley, and whose flesh fed them, grazed and browsed the watershed—their numbers had a significant effect on the vegetation and any reduction in those numbers improved the growth of vegetation and thus the water holding qualities of the drainage basin.

The same is true with other things—the thermal features of Yellowstone not only warm the temperature of the Madison's major sources, they also enrich them, promote the growth of algae on which all other aquatic life depends, and thus affect everything in the living river. To know about a river, then, one must know about the thousands of factors that affect it, and it can be said literally that that includes everything.

I do not propose to go quite that far afield, yet I hope to show why it is that this most abundant of earth's inert compounds becomes a living, breathing thing when put into motion by forces of gravity. I hope that my readers will enjoy the trip, be better informed, and more able to defend and protect those things upon which the life of all of us depends, the living rivers. Without the circulation of fresh water down the arteries of streams to the ocean, and the water's return by evaporation and air movement to the headwater capillaries, all things on earth would soon cease to exist and the land would become barren. If the rivers die, so does the whole world.

The Madison River Watershed

Montana

N
E
W
S

To Livingston
Bozeman
Belgrade
Interstate 90
Gallatin River
Missouri River
To Helena
US 287
Interstate 90
State 287
To Butte
Jefferson River
To Twin Bridges
US 10
←34
US 287
Three Forks
Willow Creek River
Willow Creek Reservoir
US 191
County 289
33
Ennis Lake
Big Sky
Madis
32
31
Ennis
State 287
To Virginia City

Points of Interest

1. Madison Lake
2. Morning Glory Pool
3. Mouth of Iron Spring Creek
4. Biscuit Basin Meadows
5. Muleshoe Bend
6. Goose Lake Meadows
7. Ojo Caliente Bend
8. Mouth of Sentinel Creek
9. Mouth of Nez Perce Creek
10. Broads of the Firehole
11. Firehole Canyon—Firehole Falls
12. Firehole—Gibbon Juncture, Beginning of the Madison River
13. Grebe Lake
14. Virginia Meadows
15. Elk Park
16. Gibbon Falls
17. Big Bend
18. Nine-Mile Hole
19. Seven-Mile Run
20. Long Rifle
21. Cable Car Run
22. Holes 1, 2, and 3
23. Beaver Meadows
24. Baker's Hole
25. Quake Lake Slide
26. West Fork Madison
27. Snoball Creek
28. Wolf Creek
29. McAtee Bridge
30. Varney Bridge
31. "Channels" of the Madison
32. Mouth of O'Dell Creek
33. Beartrap Canyon
34. Madison Buffalo Jump

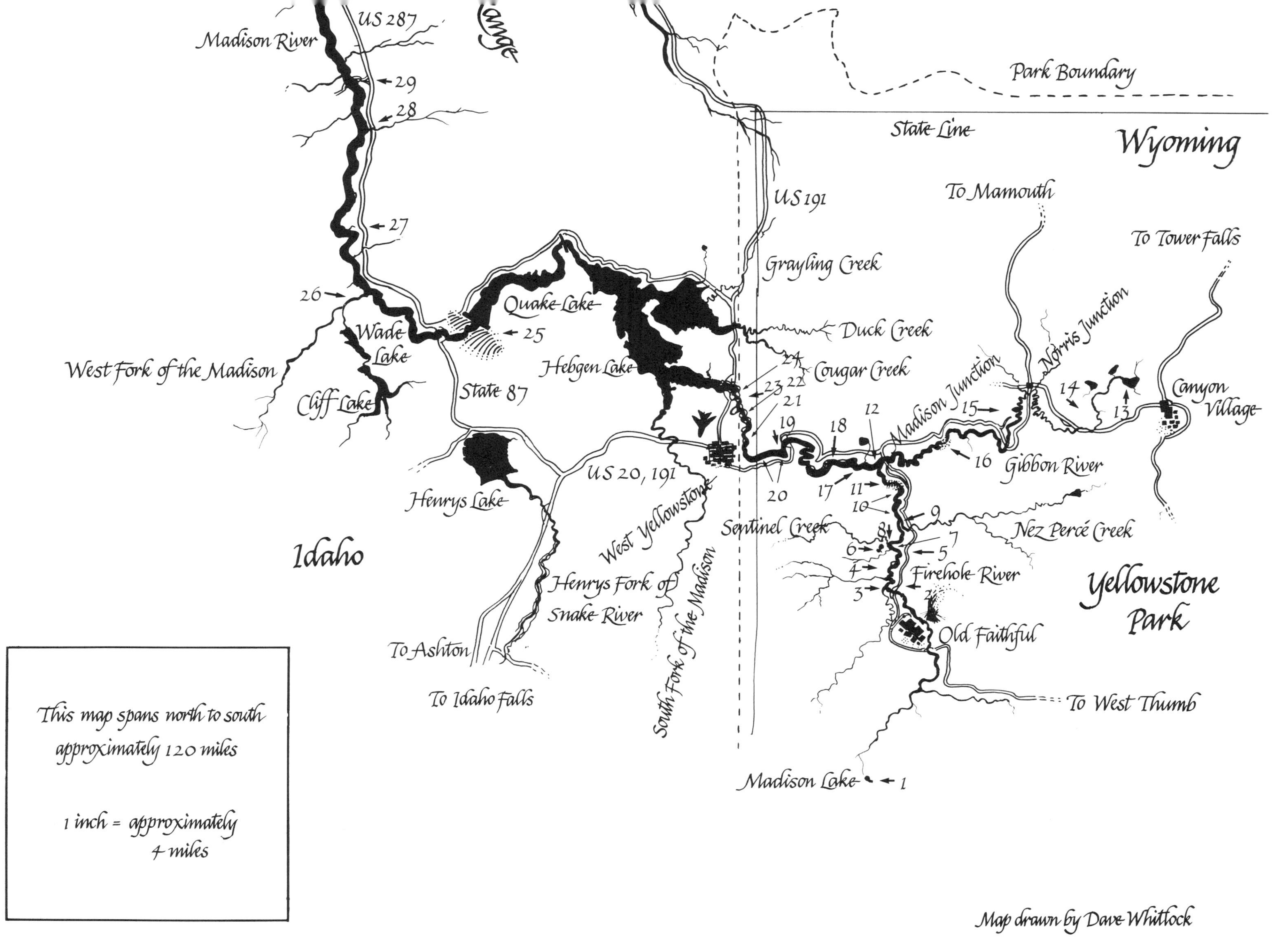

Wyoming

Yellowstone Park

Park Boundary

State Line

To Tower Falls

Canyon Village

To Mammoth

Norris Junction

13

17

Gibbon River

16

Madison Junction

15

Madison

12

18

Nez Percé Creek

Firehole River

Old Faithful

To West Thumb

9

5

7

8

11

10

6

4

3

2

Madison Lake 1

US 191

Grayling Creek

Duck Creek

Cougar Creek

24

23 22

21

19

20

Sentinel Creek

South Fork of the Madison

West Yellowstone

Henrys Fork of
Snake River

US 20, 191

To Ashton

To Idaho Falls

Quake Lake

25

Hebgen Lake

State 87

Henrys Lake

Idaho

ange

Madison River

US 287

29

28

27

26

West Fork of the Madison

Wade
Lake

Cliff Lake

Map drawn by Dave Whitlock

This map spans north to south
approximately 120 miles

1 inch = approximately
4 miles

FALL ON THE RIVER

WRITERS SPEAK OF AUTUMN AS A GOLDEN HAZE SPREADING OVER THE LAND. IN this high plateau, surrounded by mountain ranges through which the river cuts, the haze will be blue, for what reason even scientists disagree. The plateau is covered for the most part by lodgepole pines that have not seen fire for over a hundred years, but the blue haze does not seem to be of the forest. It is just there.

It spreads across the rolling interior hills in July and by September it veils the surrounding mountains. In July it is barely discernible, but as the late summer rains do not come the haze deepens and becomes like smoke in the fall.

Fall in this country can be full of color or it can be drab. If the rains hold off, the frosts come and the leaves and grasses and flowers change, each of its time and of its color, and the effect is lovely.

The aspens blaze in bright yellow among the darker trees, along the edge of the hills and up on the mountains' lowering faces. Along the stream the willows turn golden and red, illuminating the areas of tawny grass and mahogany fescue. Beneath the willows the currant and gooseberry glow in sullen red like late-night embers. The theme is carried further by the running vines of the strawberry spreading through culms of the golden grasses.

Along the higher banks and in the edge of the wood, ladyfern is demure in velvet brown, bracken still is glossy green, and hollygrape is purple. Below, on the benches, sagebrush is elegant in silver gray and is appropriately bordered by the dark reds of bitterbrush and mountain heath.

Where it slides otherwise unseen through the narrow valley, the stream is outlined by pale spikerush, sedge and saltgrass. The fall flowers grow and bloom beyond and in the edge of the willows. Paintbrush runs from pale yellow through scarlet, but only in warm recesses, it cannot stand much frost. The gentian may be gone, but windflower still nods in secluded nooks, and butterwort lies among the rocks in dry places, its tiny yellow flowers like drops of sunlight. Goatsbeard is at its most grandiloquent, but the winds of change will soon disperse it.

Mountain aster, or Michaelmas daisy, is an infrequent but cheery surprise that the unknowing confuse with fleabane. It is perhaps the loveliest of the fall flowers, but rare.

The tributaries to the river thin and grow silver, quickening while shallowing.

The river itself slows, becomes more deliberate. On cold mornings, it runs over the shallows with the look of jellied glycerin and the sound of rustling silk. The dace withdraws to his winter home, wherever that might be. The instars of the nymph become less frequent as all life slows with the chilling of air and water.

The animals are at their most visible. Muskrat, beaver, mink, and otter are busy along the stream, each preparing for winter in his own way. The coyote and lynx cross trails with amiable snarls; later they will not be so amiable.

The bear is at his most ingratiating. The tourists' handouts have been less than plentiful and he must work for the wherewithal of his winter fat. The mule deer is less shy—the frosts have made protein rich the herbs and forbs that are his mainstay; they are abundant now but soon the snows will cover them.

The elk string along the edge of the benches and up in pockets in the lodgepoles. Mating has not yet begun but will soon, and feeding, for the bulls at least, will cease for perhaps a month. So the golden grass falls steadily before them as they store up the energy reserves to carry them through their fasting.

The squirrels and chipmunks are everywhere, and are cheeky in their insolence: hard times are past, food is abundant, they liveth on the fat of the land. The hard-working and sober marmot works harder. He does hibernate as is thought, but also rises frequently during the winter to check on the weather and to snack on stored goodies; his appetite is that of ten.

Fall is harvest time for man but also for all of Nature's creatures. Summer is the time of blooming, but in the fall the crops are ripe and must be harvested; they will not be here another spring.

And I am doing, or attempting to do, my part, standing waist deep in the cold river, the strong current causing my waders to clasp me in an icy embrace as I swing a big weighted nymph into the deep, boulder-lined run.

There are big, sullen old browns here, and sprightly rainbows of two pounds, recently up from the lake, full of summer fat, zing, and cussedness. But they are safe from me today, because I am after food, and we do not find the trout as tasty as the remaining member of the family in my river. I am after the mountain whitefish, for smoking.

The river is big here, larger than most consider a trout stream to be. It is only fourteen river miles from its head at Madison Junction where it rises from the mingling of the Gibbon and Firehole rivers. Thus it is a full-blown river when it first appears.

At the point where I am fishing it is also a bold river, too bold for many who find its three-to-six-mile-an-hour currents too strong and its rubble-boulder bottom too rough for safe wading.

It is these very things that brought me first to fish it, back in 1948 when I was strong as an ox and just as smart. I still cherish these things about it, and more. Not only do the hidden boulders provide holds for unseen trout that are often much larger than one expects but the rubble bottom contains uncounted millions of aquatic insects, the most numerous of which are the giant stoneflies, *Pteronarcys* and *Acroneuria,** the largest of their kind. One may say that trout and stoneflies are intimately associated; where one occurs, the other also will be found. So says Richard Muttkowski in *The Ecology of Trout Streams in Yellowstone National Park* and it is invariably true.

The Madison River is a great and noted trout stream; for a number of years the outdoor magazines rated it number one in the country, whatever that may mean. There are those who believe it still is the best in the lower forty-eight states and of course some believe it is a better stream in Montana than it is where I am fishing it in Yellowstone Park.

Each to his own taste. There are as many "best" areas of this river as there are fishermen and methods of fishing. In the Park it is restricted to fly-fishing only and a limit of two fish of sixteen or more inches. In Montana any method of sport fishing is allowed and the limit is ten—pounds or fish.* Although the records indicate very few keep such a limit it may be that the opportunity to do so has a certain influence.

Of late there is considerable information which indicates that the popularity of the lower river is based not so much on the fish but on an insect, the so-called "salmon" fly, in reality the two stoneflies mentioned earlier. The records of the Montana Fish and Game Department reflect that 85 to 90 percent of the fishermen fish the river during June and early July, during the salmon-fly hatch, and that 90 percent of the fish are taken during this period. This would seem to show that the best opportunity lies in summer but the fact is that while the best per-hour catches are in the spring, the average size is larger in the fall. It is a wise fisherman who knows where his best opportunity lies.

The major sources of the Madison are the Firehole and Gibbon rivers. These both commence about eight thousand feet up in the south-central central Park area, and both begin in lakes. Both are small at their lake outlets and remain so for many miles. Not until they enter the area of their geyser basins do they grow appreciably, and much of their growth, particularly of the Firehole, is due to warm water from hot springs, geysers, and other thermal inputs that warm the up-to-now icy water while enriching it.

*This genera has undergone a drastic name revision, which is just now being brought out.

*See last chapter for changes in fish limits.

Elk grazing the Big Bend of the Madison.

At Madison Junction the two streams join in the narrow meadow over-looked by National Park Mountain and here the Madison proper begins a 150-mile run to the Missouri.

It is a meadow stream for the next ten miles, large deep pools and glassy glides, interrupted by occasional fast rocky runs through groups of lodgepoles that grow along the rocky benches. About ten miles from the Junction, the river begins a long downhill slide marked by a sharp breakover and an end, for a while, to meadow pools and glassy glides.

The first rocky riffle is almost three miles long and is a joy to visiting fishermen because it is right beside the road and easy to fish. It would be cruel to tell them that the six-to-eight-inch fish they are catching would only be a snack for those resident browns and rainbows farther down, in the deep rocky runs that I am fishing this fine fall day.

These runs, locally known as "behind the Barns" or by the casual, as the "Barn Pools," stretch for about three miles from the end of the riffle to the head of the Madison Basin; there the gradient slackens sharply and a section of flat marshy meadows known as Beaver Meadows stretch for three or four miles to the Park boundary, and beyond, to famed Baker's Hole.

From Baker's Hole the river slides around a long series of shallow bends and becomes esturial as it enters Hebgen Lake. This area is much preferred by tube-float fishing dry-fly fishers in the long summer mornings and eve-nings when twilight seems to last forever and the big browns and cruising rainbows prowl the flats gulping the tiniest of mayflies in the surface film. This sometimes exasperating and often very rewarding fishing is known as "gulper" fishing and has become a stylized rite, known to anglers country wide.

Below Hebgen Dam there used to be an eight-mile stretch of rocky pocket water famed far and wide as the Madison Canyon; where rainbows caught and kept averaged four pounds and reached eight. But in August 1959 an earth-quake of historic violence wrenched the mountains in this area, broke off the side of one mountain and dumped it into the river, creating a lake four-and-a-half miles long and 180 feet deep, wiping out one of the finest stretches of mountain trout stream in the world.

The adult of Pteronarcys californica, *or "salmon" fly, is about two inches long.*

It is this aspect of the middle Madison that causes it to be referred to as a "fifty-mile-long riffle."

Below the slide the Madison bolts out of the mouth of the canyon, spreads onto Missouri Flats and begins a sixty-mile almost uninterrupted run to Madison Dam and Ennis Lake. This is the stretch of the river that brings anglers from all over the nation, or even the world, to fish during the time of the "salmon-fly" hatch.

This part of the river is much of a piece—fast, of medium depth, rocky, and looking much alike on the surface. It runs through grazing land and is robbed occasionally of water for irrigation, but not to a great degree.

Just above Ennis the river slows down where the lower end of a very old lake once existed, spreads out, and becomes channeled. Some of the largest trout in the river will be found here, and knowledgeable local residents will catch them of trophy size in the fall.

Madison Dam is at the head of Beartrap Canyon. Here the river dashes foaming and raging through a steep, boulder-lined canyon that has become famous both for white-water boating and for the large fish in pocket pools behind huge rocks. It can be very dangerous either to fish or float.

Once out of the area, known locally simply as "the Beartraps," the river begins to settle down and accept the fact that it is, after all, only a major tributary of the giant Missouri. It flows through pasture and farm land, losing much of its speed, becoming warmer and more turbid. Coarse fish begin to replace trout as the dominant species although good trout will be found in the right places at the right time. It glides now instead of rushing, turns and twists, divides and rejoins, and becomes very much a lower-delta-type stream with low banks and a wide flood plain. The mountains are far away, and though this is the largest area of its watershed, it is the driest and contributes the least to the river's flow. Finally, it bumps into the Jefferson, long down from the Continental Divide and the Bitterroots, it too slowed and broadened. The two join and wander on a short distance, joining the Gallatin at Three Forks, where the three become one, the mighty Missouri. Three Forks was visited by Lewis and Clark on 27 July 1805, the first visit by white men, a visit not only historic but fraught with significance for the Madison. From this date, men would begin to exploit the river and never again would it be as it was before.

The Madison River flows through some of the most beautiful mountain scenery in the world, and the valley of the middle Madison, from the earthquake slide to Ennis, is one of the loveliest river valleys anywhere. It is broad, but not so broad as to diminish the mountains that flank it, or stretch across it, as at the north end of the Madison Basin.

The Henrys Lake Mountains, the southern spur of the Madison Range, flank Hebgen Lake and reach north to the Madison Canyon's western rim. On the other side, to the north, begins the Madison Range proper.

These are very satisfying mountains, looking as mountains should look, towering majestically aloof above the basin containing the lake. Along their bases the ground cover is bunch grass and sagebrush, gold and silver on such a fall day. The lower trees are aspen, which at this elevation always grow in pockets among spruce and fir. Farther up on the slopes the ubiquitous lodgepole takes over, blackening the slopes except in areas of old fire scalds, where alpine meadows furnish forage for deer and elk, and break the green-black of the sometimes monotonous stretches of pines.

The timberline is about nine thousand feet. Above here the slopes and scarfs and crags are pink and beige, composed of dolomite—magnesium—calcium carbonate—sedimentary rock, which plainly tells that those towering peaks were once the bed of an ancient lake, or perhaps of the inland seas.

They will be frosted with snow on the tops, along the ridges, and on the north-facing slopes the snow will trace in bands, outlining the different levels at which the rock originally formed.

Beyond Quake Lake, the Madison Range, reaching almost to eleven thousand feet, flanks the valley all the way to the region of the Beartraps. This rugged, serrated, and scenic range has some of the most distinctly shaped peaks of any mountain range, and this theme is picked up beyond Beartrap Canyon by the equally distinctive Spanish Peaks.

The Henrys Lake Mountains and the upper middle Madison.

On the west, the middle valley is enclosed by the Gravelly Range, a long ridge of rolling mountains, rounded hogbacks, sharp ridges, and large alpine basins, a completely different type of peak system from the Madison Range, and somewhat lower. This is fortunate. Our storms come from the west and the lower, gradually sloping Gravelly Range does not rob them of moisture as would a higher, more abrupt chain.

The valley has been grazed by cattle for over a hundred years, and before that by elk and antelope, which still exist here. The buffalo was rare and occasional in this valley for reasons we will explore later. The grass is not as lush as it might be, for the valley itself gets but little moisture. A foot of snow on the ground at one time is unusual even in severe winters. So it is good

Following page: *A section of the middle river and the Gravelly Range.*

grazing land in summer by virtue of irrigation, and good winter range due to lack of snow.

Willows grow densely along the tributary creeks and in places along the river itself. There are few beaver left; they were never plentiful except on the flood plain around Three Forks where the trapping of them began white man's exploitation of the river.

From Ennis Lake to Three Forks the river shows two distinct faces. The Beartrap section is about twelve miles of narrow, steep, twisting canyon water, with great boulders lining the stream. The river here is noted not only for the danger of its white water boating but the size and numbers of rattlesnakes that are found on its boulder-covered ledges. The fishing was once great but that greatness has faded. We will find out why later.

The section below the canyon looks and is less of a trout stream. Even before the water became too warm due to the silting in of Ennis Lake, the trout in this section were vastly outnumbered by coarse fish. But it was, and still is, a well-used fishery. The farmers and ranchers in the valley, and many of the people in Logan, Three Forks, and other villages are not primarily trout fishermen, and they like this section of the river just fine.

This has been a swift journey down the river, and we have made it just to get acquainted. Later we will take a more leisurely trip, stopping to fish many of the best places and exploring the most fishworthy tributaries. We will also explore the major sources to their headwaters, and fish them also. But first, there is a duty to be done, a task to be performed. We must learn the origins of our river—where it came from and why. I trust it will be a pleasant trip, but aside from that, it is a necessary one so let us commence so that later we will not be left wondering about it.

IN THE BEGINNING

A RIVER BEGINS AT ITS MOUTH; IT IS BORN THERE AND GROWS YOUNGER TOWARD its sources. A river begins at the sea, or on the banks of another stream or lake and cuts back toward the mountains, as a tree begins at its roots and grows upward. In the process of backcutting, rivers sometimes cut into and drain other rivers or lakes. This is called stream piracy when a younger river cuts into and robs an older stream. It is extremely raré.

Therefore, the Madison River downstream of Earthquake Lake is older than the river above there. It is also of somewhat different origin.

According to geologists, the Madison below the earthquake slide of 1959 began as a lake, separated from another lake by a range of mountains located about the area of the present Beartraps. The first lake formed in the area between the mouth of Beartrap Canyon and Three Forks, the second lake stretched from the head of Missouri Flats to just beyond Ennis.

These lakes formed fairly recently as geologic time goes, commencing in the Tertiary, fifty-five million to sixty-three million years ago. The events leading up to their formation and the creation of a river followed somewhat this order:

(a.) At the close of a long period of sedimentation extending from the pre-Cambrian to the Middle Cretacious, when the entire area was under the waters of the inland seas, an elevation of the underlying sedimentary rock took place and southwestern Montana became an elevated, rugged, and broken upland.

(b.) Subsequent erosion, long continued, reduced the upland to a peneplain.

(c.) Later, after an undetermined pause, great faulting and warping of these sedimentary rocks formed valleys and basins.

(d.) Volcanic activity was concurrent and intermittent with the faulting and warping. Lava and ash filled the valleys and basins on top of the sedimentary rock.

(e.) Erosion and subsidence deepened the basins and valleys. Water filled them and sedimentation continued into the Miocene, and these sedimentary rocks form what is now known as Madison limestone.

(f.) At the close of the Miocene, elevation again took place over an unknown period and created a plateau with basins and lakes.

(g.) Elevation continued intermittently into the Quaternary. Streams on the plateau became larger, wandered and backcut, eventually draining both upper and lower lakes.

(h.) A pause of undetermined length occurred in the uplifting process, streams in the area eroded their beds to "base level" (where a stream cuts more side to side than downward), wandered widely and deposited gravel over the entire area.

(i.) The land rose again, the streams downcut, and each successive lift created terraces and benches that may still be seen.

(j.) The Glacial Period (Ice Age), which may be still continuing intermittently, halted the downcutting. With later warming after its commencement, the valleys were gouged out, but only slightly in southwestern Montana. Canyons remained steepwalled. Downcutting continued after the ice vanished and goes on today.

During all the above, the mountains that surround the area and which were upthrust much earlier than the lake forming period, remained above the level of the lakes and rivers, forming both drainage slopes and barriers through which the river backcut. Backcutting continues in the present, for the river is growing longer.

These mountains, which still exist, extend back in time to the Paleozoic. The present Madison River, its valley and the last of the old lakes that underlie it, are less than twenty million years old, perhaps about thirteen million years.

Though the mountains exist just about where they have always existed, it would be wrong to think of them as the same mountains; the ones we see today are from a much more recent upthrust, which pushed them up to about their present elevation. This took place as recently as fifty million years ago, but the underlying rock that forms them, the base of older, much older, mountains, goes back over a billion years.

The mountains at the slide caused by the earthquake of 17 August 1959 were formed and in place at the time of the lake-forming period and even before. They were a barrier on their northwest side through which the river was a long time in cutting. To the south and east the mountains curved to join with others to form what is known as the Madison Basin in which present Hebgen Lake and West Yellowstone lie. This basin has caused some controversy among geologists. Was there a lake in the basin? They disagree. On the barrier mountains through which the river eventually cut and which formed the gap known as the Madison Canyon, they are in agreement. Although the mountains to the south and west are known as the Henrys Lake Mountains and the ones to the north and east are called the Madison Range, they are the same mountains and before the river cut through them they formed an unbroken chain.

But was there a lake in the Madison Basin before the river cut through? The area has been little studied; what study has been done is surface and superficial. Those who believe there was a lake, which filled from the waters of the Firehole and Gibbon rivers in Yellowstone Park, point to the fact that the soil of the upper basin is of an alluvial delta deposit material—volcanic ash, silt, and coarse obsidian sand. It is the sand that gives the strongest support for the lake theory.

Beyond any question the sand is from the volcanic plateaus in the Park; that is its origin and there can be no doubt of it. The lake people say its deposit over most of the upper and middle basin indicates the waters came here, spread out, slowed down and dropped the sand. There is little doubt of this. But those who do not believe there was a lake in the basin say the sand was dropped over such a wide area because of a sharp slackening of the gradient, causing the stream to wander and slow down. This does not convince the lake people who point to lack of any channeling. The argument is not very fierce; both sides admit they could be wrong.

The basin is formed by the mountains just mentioned plus the Washburn Range and the Yellowstone Central Plateau on the east, and the northern edge of the Madison Plateau, all in Yellowstone Park. During the early 1800s the basin was devasted by a forest fire and was known to the trappers who came into it as the "Burnt Hole."

The Central and Western (Madison) Plateaus of Yellowstone, above, hold the sources of the Gibbon and Firehole rivers. They are composed, for the most part, of rhyolite lava, at least on the surface. In some areas older basaltic lava shows, but these are small and scattered.

Though underneath the lava are rocks some two billion years old, these can only be seen, if at all, in the mountains surrounding the plateaus, since the mountains are much older.

The deepest canyons, even the Grand Canyon of the Yellowstone, have not cut completely through the rhyolite topping the plateaus; it is over two-thousand-feet thick everywhere and in some areas over eight-thousand-feet thick. Its decay and weathering* is responsible for all the colors one sees in the Grand Canyon, which run from red through deepest orange, all shades of yellow, and finally to white. The darker rocks one sees are, for the greatest part, relatively unweathered and lichen-covered rhyolite, or rarely, intrusive basalt.

*Some geologists believe the colors are produced by thermal action.

Underneath the rhyolite are breccia—broken rock from much older volcanic outpourings—then sheets of basalt, more breccia, then the shales and sandstones of the Mesozoic. Below these are the limestones of the Paleozoic. They lie *mostly* some ten to twelve thousand feet below the rhyolite. Yet it is they that are responsible for much of the mineral richness of the streams on the plateaus.

The rhyolite lava topping the plateaus was put down almost entirely during the Tertiary period of the Cenozoic, and during the latter third of that period. Thus, this volcanic outpouring was taking place here about the same time the lower Madison river was being born, some one hundred and seventy miles away.

But this was not the only period of volcanic activity in the area—such activity had been relatively constant since the latter part of the Cretacious. That earlier volcanic activity was extremely violent and it took place during and between periods of uplift, faulting, and warping. These caused some sedimentary rocks of much earlier periods to be thrust up into layers of much younger rock. Some Cretacious limestone lies only a little way down and even Paleozic limestone, three hundred million years old, is not too far from the surface in areas of earlier upthrust.

This violent activity—buckling, warping, upthrusting, and volcanic activity—has quieted to some extent but it is still going on. Many of the fissures caused by this activity were and are responsible for many of the thermal features in the area. Some of these fissures reach far into the earth and bring steam and hot water to the surface; some steam vents approach 300° F. at the surface.

The last *major* upthrust in the area is relatively old and while it cannot be dated precisely, its time can be estimated from events. This upthrust caused the lifting of the Central and Madison plateaus above the land to the north and west; it is marked especially by falls created in the Gibbon and Firehole. When white men discovered the area, these streams were barren of fish above these falls. Therefore, the upthrust occurred before the Madison River had backcut to join these two of its present sources. Had the Madison connected with them before the falls were formed, fish from the Madison would have been in the Firehole and Gibbon above where the falls formed. Since the original Madison River began forming less than sixty-three million years ago, and perhaps did not reach the Gibbon-Firehole junction until eight to eleven million years ago, the falls fault cannot be younger than the latter dates; but it can be much older.

At the time the river was coming into being, the area of Yellowstone Park was undergoing violent changes. Mountains already existed on all sides of the Park area, and they continued to be pushed up as the earth buckled and heaved. At times these mountains towered more than three miles above the interior valleys and basins. But periods of volcanic activity filled the basins over a period of thirty to sixty million years, to their present level; the so-called plateaus of Yellowstone are really nearly filled volcanic basins.

In the north central part of Yellowstone, the volcanic periods are recorded more clearly than anywhere else. There are at least six petrified forests there,* standing literally one on top of the other, with layers of lava between and over them. This arrangement makes dating of the various outpourings fairly simple and accurate.

It should be noted that all the forces that shaped the present surface of Yellowstone Park are still going on although at a reduced rate: upthrusting, faulting, warping, volcanic activity, erosion by water, wind and ice, cutting of valleys by streams, and building up of areas by hot springs and geysers bringing material to the surface. The only one of these not currently observable is volcanic activity. Geologists consider that it is merely quiescent, not vanished. Molten rock lies only a mile or so down in some areas and an outbreak could occur at any time, though there is no evidence that it will.

But the area is earthquake prone. Records show that a shake of at least 4.5 on the Richter scale occurs on the average of every two years within seventy-five miles of Madison Junction. Thus the potential for larger quakes and serious damage to the Madison and its sources not only exists but is an ever-present danger. The earthquake of 1959 measured 7.8 on the Richter scale, one of the most severe ever recorded on the North American Continent. The area is geologically unsettled and earthquakes of some magnitude occur every year; sometimes there are several in a single year. Some of these have caused and are causing changes in the flow and temperature of the Firehole and Gibbon rivers, and thus affect the Madison.

The quake of 1959 caused considerable change in the flow, temperature, and clarity of these two major sources, as well as causing the side of a mountain to break off and fall into the river, depositing eighty million tons of rock squarely across it, causing it to dry up below the slide and a lake to form above it. The river is still feeling the results of this quake; another of the same magnitude in the wrong place could be catastrophic.

A river has almost unlimited ability to heal itself, given time, and time means nothing to a river. Thus what man might consider as the destruction of a stream would only be a minor disruption to a river. Such disruptions are common, but ones caused by nature are seldom lasting enough to cause great change. Only man has the potential to destroy a river completely and he often does so without ever thinking that what he destroys was a living thing and will again live if left alone.

*Some estimate there are over twenty such forests.

THE SOURCES

THE SOURCE OF A RIVER IS EITHER THAT TRIBUTARY WHOSE HEAD IS FARTHEST from the river's mouth, the one that lies at the highest elevation, or the one that provides the largest volume to the whole. The Firehole qualifies on all three counts, and the Gibbon must be included because the head of the Madison River begins where these two join.

The Firehole furnishes 21 percent of the total volume of the Madison. It is the largest tributary of the stream and it lies at a higher altitude and farther from the mouth of the Madison than does any other. It is also a superb trout stream.

The Firehole begins in Madison Lake, a tiny snow-fed pond on that section of Yellowstone Park's Western Plateau known as Madison Plateau and this portion of the watershed gets an average yearly snowpack of three hundred inches—twenty-five feet.

The small basin in which the lake nestles has numbers of subalpine meadows and spongy bogs that hold water, keep it cool, and release it slowly. These keep the lake level and the flow of the upper river fairly constant.

Running out of the lake, the stream is a cold-water brook, rocky and shallow. It slides down the north edge of the canyon and begins to turn northwest against the base of the Continental Divide.

Although there are trails that reach its upper region in the dense lodgepole forest south of Lone Star Geyser, the river really does not come into view until just before it crosses under the highway near Old Faithful. It has become a cold, clear, swift-running creek, with numbers of brook and brown trout in its riffles and runs.

It tours around the mound of siliceous sinter built up by Old Faithful and its companion thermal features, and taking on volume, mineral richness, and warmth, becomes larger and more fishworthy. There are three-pound browns lurking in the root-guarded lairs and down-timber drifts behind the geyser area, but they are difficult to fish for. The stream is narrow and overgrown, there is little room to work the fly, and the twisting currents make trouble for either wet or dry fly, although both can be used with success by the patient angler.

In dry flies, high-floating hair-wings or grasshopper patterns offer the best possibility, and in wets one wants small, soft-hackled bright-bodied flies—Grey Hackle Yellow, Partridge and Orange, Grouse and Green, or even Royal Coachman tied with hen's hackle. Once you hook your fish, your chances of landing him are slim—these wise old lunkers know all the moves and the location of every rock, snag, and limb.

Beyond here the river slides through a widening meadow and exhibits many of the characteristics of a meadow stream, although there are no deep pools. This is a very pleasant place to fish even though the fish are mostly small, twelve inches or under. On rare occasions in the fall you will hit one of seventeen inches but they are scarce and spotty in their occurrence.

Below the bridge at Morning Glory Pool (a thermal feature) the river skids and glances down a series of shallow rapids with pools at the foot of each. There are many small fish here and some larger ones. Also, for the first time the trout seem more interested in hatching aquatics than they do farther up. Small caddis and mayflies *(Baetis)* are the usual fare.

There is perhaps a mile or more of this water before one reaches the mouth of Iron Spring Creek and the Little Firehole at the head of Biscuit Basin Meadows. These two nearly double the volume of the river, and lower its temperature, which has been steadily climbing due to the thermal input of the Upper Geyser Basin (which has over one thousand such features).

Iron Spring Creek (known locally as Iron Creek) and the Little Firehole are holding streams during spells of hot weather. I have counted over two hundred trout of two pounds or more in Iron Creek in August and have seen trout there of over six pounds. This is a mostly shallow, crystal-clear stream and the large fish are in it only to escape the high temperatures of the main river. They are wary beyond belief and any angler who can hook two over sixteen inches in a single day qualifies as an expert.

In Biscuit Basin Meadows the river becomes a typical meadow stream, winding, deep along the banks, and with a glassy surface. There are no pools as such although there are places over five feet deep. But the glassy surface is deceiving; there are strong currents throughout and one has only to cast a fly with a long line upon them to see how unbelievably tricky they are.

Nevertheless, when the temperature of the water is below 76° F. this is one of the finest dry-fly stretches in the country. There are more aquatic insects of greater variety than anyplace in the river up to now.

Mostly the insects are small—*Siphlonurus* and *Ephemerella* mayflies are found in short stretches but the major mayfly is *Baetis.* Caddis are more plentiful and

This big loop in Biscuit Basin Meadows of the Firehole is small-fly-big-trout water—for the expert.

both *Brachycentrus* and *Rhyacophila* are abundant. Midge and blackfly abound and how the anglers curse when the trout are rising to these tiny dipterous creatures.

The fish are somewhat more browns than rainbows, and both are extremely wary, especially when they are up near the surface. One must take advantage of all concealment, keep the backcast up out of the tall meadow grasses, and often take "an attitude of becoming reverence before the fish." Even then, and with the exact right fly, one needs a little luck.

Once you have fished here, even without success, you will find yourself coming back often because the surroundings are so lovely, the water so good, and the opportunity so great. You will find yourself escorted on occasion by elk or buffalo, neither of which pose a threat except to your backcast—I once hooked a two-thousand-pound bull buffalo here on a size sixteen Adams on the backcast. He broke me on the first jump, but I was using 4X.

If flowers are your passion then this area in June or September will thrill and delight you. There are over six hundred varieties of blooming plants in Yellowstone Park and many of these are found on the banks of the Firehole and Madison. They carpet the banks in a riot of color—reds, yellows, and blues prevailing, in a hundred varieties. Lupin, larkspur, musk and mallow, geranium, forget-me-not, phlox, primrose and flax, spurge, foxglove and columbine, harebell and thistle, they come in turn, play for a while—and then depart, leaving the field to the next bloomer. They must be seen to be believed. In August and September the gentian turns the meadows to royal blue and paintbrush stands among it in blazing scarlet. When the flowers are in mass bloom I know of no place more lovely than the riverside in Yellowstone.

In contrast, the birds are not many and of drab color, although one will occasionally see the bright scarlet and yellow of the western tanager. In early spring the sandhill crane sets the air ringing with his raucous halloos and in the fall geese, ducks, and swans appear. But by and large, in summer the birds cannot compete with the flowers.

From Biscuit Basin the river runs a few miles through the lodgepole forest, a stretch of runs and riffles, pleasant to fish if you keep your backcast out of the trees. It is an excellent stretch for the high-floating dry or small wet and though most of the fish are small one cannot relax completely because as sure as you do a two-pounder will blaze out from under the bank or up from an unseen pothole and smash your leader like thread.

Below the Iron Bridge—now closed to traffic but which once carried the broad-tired wagons plying the Fountain Freight Road—the river dashes down a long set of rapids and into the head of Muleshoe Bend at the top of Midway Geyser Basin. In spring, the pockets in the rapids deliver fine rainbows to the big stonefly nymph, but after the first of July your chances are better with the dry fly; there is no more reliable stretch of dry-fly water anywhere than Muleshoe Bend and rainbows of seventeen inches are not rare for the skilled angler.

This quarter-mile-long, tight curve, is dry-fly water at its best. The holds are beneath undercut banks, in weed beds or potholes in the bottom. The currents are diabolical. Hatches are frequent but of short duration and more often than not it is midge or blackfly and not mayfly or caddis, and they are hatched and gone before one has the right fly.

The middle of the bend is edged by a fifty-foot-high bank; the highway is on top and one can park at the turnout and wait for the rise. This convenience makes Muleshoe Bend one of the most popular stretches of water on the whole river.

Along the bank, especially on the highway side, there are spouting hot springs, steam vents, and other thermal features. These sometimes spout off with sound and fury and startling suddeness, scaring the angler out of his boots.

Beyond here is a long shallow riffle for half a mile or so; it holds mostly small fish but is much fished by the casual angler. It is convenient to parking areas, the bottom offers good footing, and the broken surface tends to make the fish less wary. There are many, and many kinds of, insects as in most riffles. Most prevalent are caddis, several genera and species; there are some mayflies, damsel and dragonflies, blackfly, and perhaps others. Thus, unless there is a hatch on, choice of fly for the fisherman is not critical.

Excelsior Spring pours in a flood of steaming water at the lower end of the riffle, and the next half mile of water is warmed by this and by other factors; the stream here is almost continuously shallow, and not fishworthy.

But Goose Lake Meadows is eminently fishworthy. This is a much-favored stretch, even though the banks are boggy much of the time, and one must proceed with caution. This holds true while wading. The bottom is uneven and there are potholes, some of which are two or more feet deeper than the surrounding bottom. In areas of slower flow these have been filled with silt and stepping into one can cause some trouble.

But the size of the fish that one may encounter and the quality of the water make it all worthwhile and it is unusual not to meet several other anglers on this stretch.

Above the lower iron bridge at Ojo Caliente Spring there is a long stretch of broken water, runs, rapids, cascades, and a low fall that, while attractive, is not as easy to fish or so productive as the water above or below it.

Ojo Caliente Bend is a quarter mile or more of mostly deep, weed-filled pockets with clear channels in and among them. The insects here are mostly very small: midge, blackfly, and small mayfly. *Chimarrha* caddis are present also, and are taken well in the fall. However, unhappily for the angler, the main food item taken by the fish is the small black snail.

This section of the river becomes warmer than any place else and the temperature in a very hot August *may* reach 84 to 85° F. This causes most fish to migrate to cooler water. Some go into Sentinel Creek at the lower end of the stretch but most go downstream a mile or so to below the mouth of Nez Percé Creek.* This area, commonly known as the broads of the Firehole, is

*This stream is locally pronounced "Nezz Purse" and not the French pronunciation "Nay Pair say."

Lower Muleshoe Bend of the Firehole, a classic piece of dry-fly water.

about three miles of water that is varied throughout. Mostly the bottom is fairly even but there are channels here and there that are more than twice the average depth. There are deep stretches by the grasses of the far bank, some short fast riffles, and a run or two of more than average speed and depth.

The highway is right beside the river, there are turnouts and picnic areas, and frequently elk are in the river, making this perhaps the most populated spot, excluding the major thermal areas.

The river now begins to trot and then to gallop. It hobby-horses down chutes and runs, dodging huge boulders in its bed. The bed becomes more broken, wading more difficult; mayfly nymphs become less important while caddis larvae increase in abundance. There are spots where the giant stonefly nymph, *Pteronarcys,* will also be found.

From the area of Muleshoe Bend there has been a steady change in the kind of trout in the river. Above Muleshoe to Old Faithful, brown trout predominate; above Old Faithful, brook and brown trout are about equally divided. At Muleshoe Bend, however, rainbow form more than half the population. And the farther downstream one goes, the larger the percentage of rainbow until here, just above the head of Firehole Canyon, they become the dominant species—in some places, the only species. The apparent reason is the warming of the water.

Above this stretch the three major thermal basins—Upper, Midway, and Lower Geyser basins—spill 82,500,000 gallons of water daily into the river, water ranging from 50° F. to over 200° F. Because of this both the *National Geographic Magazine* and Ernie Schwiebert have called the Firehole the strangest trout stream in the world. I guess that makes it official.

There is another unique feature to the Firehole. The bottom is bedrock, rhyolite lava, for almost the entire length of the river. It is very broken and uneven and silt and gravel have filled in many of these deeper areas. Although some of the silt is from normal erosion, the undamaged watershed and deep meadows flanking the stream preclude much damage of this kind.

But the thermal features put many tons of dissolved minerals into the stream daily. Much of this is calcium bicarbonate, the most valuable single mineral for building underwater life. Phytoplankton use it as do all other creatures, although most obtain it second-hand by devouring creatures rich in this body-building mineral.

The solid that precipitates into the river is mostly of a siliceous nature; the soil throughout, from Old Faithful to just above the canyon, lies on top of a caprock formed mostly of siliceous sinter. This is the whitish and grey material one sees in all the geyser and thermal areas. It is virtually insoluble and very erosion resistant. Some travertine—porous, stained limestone—deposited by hot springs, is found here and there but largely the major solid mineral above the rhyolite is some form of silica.

The watershed of the Firehole is covered mostly by virgin lodgepole pine. Neither it nor the deep grass meadows flanking the stream have been seriously damaged by fire within the memory of man. No matter how fast the snow on the watershed melts, or how heavy the rain, I know of no one who

The density of the lodgepole forests of the Firehole watershed must be seen to be believed. Some of these trees, no larger than a man's forearm, are over one hundred years old.

has ever seen the Firehole muddy. It does get over its banks; it becomes the color of strong tea; but it does not become muddy.

The lodgepoles shut out most sunlight. Little of anything grows beneath them and the ground is dry and dusty, seemingly not good for holding water. But it is deceiving. By deep affinity, every speck of dust draws water to itself. The dryness of rotting logs absorb water and grow sodden. Where there are piles of needles and bark from the centuries, the water from a torrential rain will not escape. These porous masses suck up moisture like huge sponges, and the life-giving water stirs to new vigor the process of decay.

The living vegetation sucks in and holds the rain. Millions of bucketfuls are required to soak up and turn black the bark on the numberless trees. Tons upon tons of water are retained by the thirsty needles. It takes a long sustained rain before the trees begin to drip heavily.

It takes many more tons of water to uncurl the leaves of the meadow grasses; the leaves, shrunken to conserve moisture, expand and grow heavy in a rain. The sod, two or more feet deep, absorbs countless tons of moisture; the roots of a single culm will contain over a quarter mile of water-holding stems and root hairs.

The channels of the earthworm spread the water everywhere, as do the tunnels of the voles; there are millions of these conduits as well as those of ant and beetle. The moisture penetrates ever downward, constantly being absorbed by the dry soil below until it reaches the fissures running to the ground water-table or to the top of the caprock. Only that which reaches caprock moves downhill to the stream to replenish it. It takes a mighty torrent of water to raise the level of the Firehole.

An inch of rain or its equivalent in snow puts 113 tons of moisture on each acre of a watershed. What happens to it after it falls or melts determines the quality of life in that watershed. Three things happen to it; flyoff (evaporation); runoff, which reaches a stream and moves away; and sinkin, where the water sinks down through ground cover, soil, and rock to the water-table. The condition of the watershed determines the amount of each. Generally, the higher the rate of sinkin, the better for everything.

Grass lands will absorb over twenty times as much water as bare soil; some forests will absorb over an inch of rain an hour for long periods. And the ability of a forest to delay water reaching the ground, and to spread it slowly throughout the subsoil by channeling it along its roots is one of the major and most important flood-reducing factors.

When watersheds are clearcut of trees, damaged by *major* forest fires or by road building, the values of flyoff and runoff are increased, that of sinkin reduced. The water is simply hustled more rapidly out of the area where it fell. The greatest water-conservation and flood-control policy is a natural one: keep the raindrop where it falls by promoting sinkin. It is not only the cheapest and most sensible; it is the most beneficial to everything and everyone. And the chief weapon in the battle is natural vegetation. This is why the streams of Yellowstone Park, including the Firehole, are almost immune to serious flooding.

From the top of the canyon the river drops rapidly, several hundred feet in a short space of miles. There are swift runs, rapids, cascades, and falls through most of the canyon; there are some deep ledge pools and an abundance of pockets in the white water, which hold some very fine trout. But the canyon walls are steep, the rock crumbly, and one risks serious injury getting to or from the water.

From the mouth of the canyon, the river spills happily out into a wide airy meadow, wanders and meanders until it joins the Gibbon, where it loses its identity and becomes the famed and noted Madison.

The Gibbon River, the other major source of the Madison, rises on Solfatara Plateau at 8,000 feet. It commences in Grebe Lake, a beautiful isolated trout pond that also is loaded with grayling. Since Grebe is almost entirely fed from melting snow, it is a very cold lake. The river running from it is icy—a small, twisting, tortuous brook, winding and dodging through a dense lodgepole forest to Wolf Lake, two miles away. Here the river, upon leaving the lake, flirts with the edge of the plateau, approaching, then turning away, coming to the very edge, retreating as though shy or afraid. Finally it gathers itself, tumbles over the edge and plunges downward through a tiny crooked canyon and spreads into Virginia Meadows under the Norris Canyon highway bridge.

It is tiny here. There are places where one can jump across. It is very winding and still icy. Brook trout and grayling dwell in the bathtub pools and under the grassy banks. It is a delightful small stream to fish with light tackle. The fish are wary and must be treated with respect but they are not overly discriminating in choice of fly. For the most part, wet flies in size twelve with bright body colors—Grouse and Purple, Heckham and Red, Grizzly King, Parmacheene Belle and others of similar dress—will work as well as the most accurate imitation. For dry flies the Goofus Bug, hair-wing variant, or Brown Spider will give hours of angling pleasure for the bright fish come to them willingly.

After Virginia Meadows there is a short trip through the ever-present lodgepole forest, then the river slides into view again at Norris Junction. The meadows at Norris are Virginia Meadows all over again. The stream is a little larger, and the fish also, but not plentiful. This area is constantly besieged by hopeful but generally inept anglers who do not catch many fish, but frighten all of them into hiding.

The river detours around the strange, sinister, and weird-looking Norris Geyser Basin with its dead trees, steaming vents and sulphurous smell. It picks up volume and enriching minerals, and the temperature warms—but apparently the river is not tainted by this witches' brew. However, it again chooses to hide itself by retreating back into the lodgepole forest for a pair of winding miles.

At Elk Park it has become an ideal trout stream in size and appearance. There are deep pools, glassy glides, long shallow runs with an occasional very short faster stretch, the banks are undercut and waterweeds flank the deeper channels. It is a stream for an easy approach, quiet stalking, and careful delivery of the fly. The trout caught here are mostly rainbow, much fished for, very wary and discerning in taste. Those over fourteen inches require considerable wooing before they allow themselves to be duped into taking your fly.

Two miles away, again through the lodgepole forest, and one comes to Gibbon Meadows, a larger version of Elk Park. These two areas are the haunts of many wild creatures. Canada geese are present in numbers in spring, larger than the barnyard fowl, arrogant in their assurance that the land and water is theirs. They are condescending to the tourists, strutting and posing, showing off their families for the tourists to take pictures of.

A deep pool and following run in Firehole Canyon. There are big fish here but caution is required to prevent injury in getting in and out of the Canyon.

Preceding page:

The lower broads of the Firehole normally have more than these two fishermen working the waters.

The Cascades of the Firehole at the head of Firehole Canyon. Here the river leaves its meadow-basin area and tumbles many feet in a short space of miles to join the Gibbon and form the Madison in National Park Meadows.

A stag party in Elk Park on the upper Gibbon.

Sandhill cranes whoop and halloo and stride through the meadows, reminding one of the appropriateness of the name, Ichabod Crane. Coyotes skulk around the edge of the meadow, on the lookout for an adventurous crane chick or a fat gosling.

Elk Park and Gibbon Meadows are courting, mating, and calving places for the elk. The calves are born in May and June, before the tourists come. They are secretive and seldom seen, lying back among the dark of the lodgepoles while their dams crop the newly greening meadow grass. In the fall, the air rings with the piercing challenges of the mating bulls as they gather their harems and defend their territory. The young bachelors skulk and hide in the pods of lodgepole, peering covetously out at their more favored brethren. Harem bulls and frustrated bachelors can both be dangerous so one keeps alert in Gibbon Meadows and Elk Park in the fall. But do not avoid them; the fishing is excellent and the presence of the elk adds to the charm of the angling experience.

The river enters the canyon beyond Gibbon Meadows and begins a riotous tumble down the escarpment of the plateau. It has many feet to fall but it chooses to do so in a series of runs and plunges, pausing at the foot of each rapid and cascade to gather itself for the next plunge.

Beyond Beryl Spring, a beautiful but smelly thermal spring, the Gibbon gathers itself for the leap over Gibbon Falls, the barrier that blocked fish migration from the Madison when the Gibbon was formed and joined the parent stream.

The canyon below the falls is fairly steep and severe in places but it soon widens and disappears almost entirely a mile or so before the Madison proper is reached. The stream in the canyon is a large, clattering fast-water brook, with riffles, runs, rapids, and cascades succeeding each other one after another. It is largely a pan-fish stream, though now and then an old lunker that has spawned in the stream will stay because he has found a place to his liking. This will usually be in the deeper areas, behind a large boulder, under the frequent drifts, and rarely in one of the pools at the foot of a swifter stretch.

A mile or more before Madison Junction the river comes out of the canyon into a broadening meadow valley, becomes deeper, quieter, and meandered. In the fall, running spawners from the Madison will be found here, in the potholes, under the weeds and undercut banks. Insects are more plentiful here and the structure is different from the upper river.

In Gibbon Meadows and upstream, the predominant aquatic insects are several species of caddis, *Rhyacophila* and *Hydropsyche* mainly. There are some few dragon and damselfly nymphs and a scattering of the smaller mayflies. In the meadows where it joins the Madison *Brachycentrus* caddis also appear, some smaller silt-dwelling mayflies of *Ephemerella* are found and dragonfly becomes more numerous. The river, lying as it does, at the junction of two major highways, is heavily fished, and except for spring and fall, one's chances are not great here.

The Gibbon and Firehole have not eroded their valleys appreciably above their respective falls; the only signs of long-continued erosion is in the canyons just before they join the Madison. This leads geologists to believe that the canyon stretches are not part of the Firehole and Gibbon proper but extensions of the Madison, which backcut to the fault line several million years ago. The general belief is that the Firehole and Gibbon are young rivers, much younger than the Madison, probably less than a million years old, possibly only twenty-thousand years.

The waters of the two sources, while similar, are far from identical. The Friehole is the richer stream, ranging from sixty parts per million of calcium

Following page: *The Gibbon River sliding into the head of Elk Park. A lovely piece of water but difficult.*

A royal stag—seven points per side. A bull elk of this conformation will weigh eight hundred pounds. He is safe to approach this closely only when his antlers are in velvet and still growing, as here.

bicarbonates at Old Faithful to about one hundred and twenty parts per million at the top of Firehole Falls. The Gibbon ranges only to about fifty parts per million at its falls. These are average readings. When the rivers are high with runoff in the spring, the readings will be only about half what they will be in late fall when the streams are low and more of their volume comes from the minerally rich springs, geysers, and other thermal features.

The richness of the streams and their year-round warmth prior to the 1959 earthquake caused the insects and fish to grow rapidly. But both streams have suffered from a series of quakes measuring from 3.5 to 6.5 on the Richter scale between 1973 and 77. The Gibbon ran heavy with silt for months after the 1959 quake, and for some weeks after each of the quakes in the latter years. But its temperature seemed unaffected.

Not so with the Firehole. The stream was never silted appreciably but its temperature has fluctuated, dropping a few degrees just after the 1959 quake, then climbing almost constantly until now. Prior to the major quake of 1959 the top daytime temperature* recorded on any stretch of the Firehole was 75° F. at Ojo Caliente Bend in 1958. In July and early August of 1975 temperatures of 83 to 84.3° F. were found in the same area. The fish have become inured to the high temperatures, which are thought to be fatal to

*For which I can find any record.

most trout. But growth and reproduction have been affected. Also, it is uncertain how much higher temperatures the trout can stand without a major fish kill. Only time will tell. But rising temperatures have killed many species of insects.

Though both streams are still excellent trout streams, it is amusing to note that neither of them, and not the Madison above Hebgen Lake, meets health standards for drinking water. The thermal features put minerals, including more than allowable traces of arsenic, into the river and it is this that some biologists object to. But I have been drinking the water and occasionally eating the fish since 1948 and I feel, along with the late Arnold Gingrich that "If the water is good enough for trout, it's probably too good for me."

I took my first trout ever of over three pounds in 1948 in the Firehole in Biscuit Basin Meadows and this has remained a charmed spot for me ever since. I had come to fish the river in late August; it was my second visit. My first was as a tourist ten years earlier.

I fished the last two weeks of August and caught only one fish, a sixteen-inch rainbow. The river abounded in larger fish. One could see two-pounders any day lying on the bottom in plain sight, apparently asleep. Even three-pounders could be seen, usually up near the surface in feeding position. But not on my flies.

On the first of September I quit fishing and spent the day stalking and studying the fish. I marked down several feeding places occupied by large fish that could only be seen when they rose to take the fly from the surface. I found some of these places by using a trick that now seems a little unethical.

During the winter, when tying flies, I had tied several on bits of toothpick rather than on hooks. When I located spots that looked fishy but where fish could not be seen (and therefore, could not see me) I drifted one or two of my toothpick flies over the spot, unattached. I raised several good fish, including one brown that came clear of the water while taking the decoy. He looked as big as a suckling pig.

The next day I returned to the same spot and started casting from below, dropping the fly a little short of the actual lie of the fish. On the first cast the number 16 Adams was taken by a fish of about a pound. I didn't strike. I saw instantly, as the fish rose, that it was not the one I was after. My reflexes were pretty good in those days and I just froze until the yearling had returned to his holding spot and ejected the fly. Then I replaced it with a new one.

The second cast brought up the lunker. He was hooked, played hard but unexceptionally, and landed. He weighed three pounds, nine ounces. I took a couple more from other prelocated spots, trout of one and two pounds. But they were not in the same league with that first one.

This technique still works in the same location, and others but I seldom use it anymore. I somehow feel guilty about it. I have a friend who performs the same stunt using live grasshoppers as decoys. He catches—and releases —more big trout than anyone I know. I feel guilty about him, too.

The Firehole is one of the pleasantest of rivers to fish; access is easy because the highway parallels it for all of its fishable length. From Old

Faithful down to the head of the canyon, it runs through a valley or rather a succession of basins, the chain of which have the appearance of a valley.

These basins are volcanic sinks, filled in thousands of years ago nearly to their tops with volcanic ash, tuff, and glacial till. Over this is a layer, almost completely covering the tuff and till, of siliceous sinter spewed out by the hot springs, geysers, and other thermal features. This comes to the edge of the river almost everywhere; it is especially noticeable just above the first iron bridge on the Fountain Freight Road. For the most part the soil above this caprock is thin, the exception being along the river banks where in some places the soil and silt have a thickness of several feet. These are pockets in the almost impermeable caprock and they hold water as well as soil; thus they are usually boggy or marshy and some few, though they have grass growing on top, have the consistency of quicksand underneath.

The basins are now meadows. At the head and foot of each and on stretches in between, the lodgepoles stand dense and black. These shallow-rooted trees are about the only ones that can grow in these areas. The siliceous caprock or the rhyolite lava is never more than a few feet down anywhere along here.

Though the lodgepole is shallow-rooted, which adapts it remarkably for living in shallow soil over cap or bedrock, it is also remarkably equipped to survive in such places. The root systems interlace each other as well as crevices in the underlying rock. The tall, slim, almost limbless shaft that gives the tree its common name is tough and extremely pliable, like a giant fishing rod. The top hamper of limbs and needles is small and sparsely needled. These features, plus the denseness of the stands in which it grows and which have to be seen to be believed, make it effectively resistant to wind and storms that would uproot other shallow-rooted trees.

I mentioned earlier that I took my first trout of over three pounds in the Firehole at Biscuit Basin Meadows. I took my last trout of such size also from the Firehole at Ojo Caliente Bend, some three years ago.

Nick Lyons had asked me to send him some pictures for the dust jacket of *The Trout and the Stream,* showing me netting a five-pound brown. In the short time alloted I was unable to fill the order. But I did take a nice three-pounder in the deep water next to the little island at the lower end of Ojo Caliente Bend on a grasshopper pattern. I sent pictures of this but you will not see them on the dust jacket of the book. After making up a sample jacket, the printer managed to lose the slides.

The Firehole, as mentioned earlier, was barren of fish above Firehole Falls when the river was discovered by white men in the 1830s. It was stocked first in 1889 with brook trout, most of which promptly fled upstream to cooler water above Old Faithful.* Some few escaped into the cooler tributaries and still survive there.

In 1890, a more suitable trout, the brown, was stocked and prospered marvelously. In 1897 a woman named Mary Trowbridge Townsend caught a

---

*The stocking records are much mixed up, and there are at least two versions of what trout were stocked where in the first stocking of the Firehole.

The first wagon in history into the upper Firehole Basin (Old Faithful area). A road survey crew led by Park Superintendent P. W. Norris, 30 August 1878. National Park Service Photo

gorgeously colored "Von Behr" (brown) trout of four pounds in the Firehole and wrote a charming account of the fishing in "A Woman's Trout Fishing in Yellowstone Park," which was published in Volume 20 of *Outing* magazine.

Also in 1897, an Englishman, Sir Rose Lambart Price, made an extended trip through the Park and spoke glowingly of the fishing in the Firehole. Price was intrigued by stories that it was possible to catch a trout from a lake or stream and, without moving, cook it in a nearby thermal feature. Fishing Cone in Yellowstone Lake was the normal locale for stunts of this type but Price missed his chance there and decided to make up for it while fishing the Firehole just above Nez Percé Creek.

Wrote Price: "I had not had time at Yellowstone Lake to try from the fishing cone there, to catch and boil a trout without removing it from the hook, or touching it with the hand, and here was a chance of performing so unique a feat. . . . More line and a longer cast to take me beyond the water already flogged, and flop, whirr, I am well stuck into a game pounder. . . . However, I got him under control at last. Fortunately the cast was a strong one, and working him up to the edge of the crater, one strong pull on a short line dropped him into the boiling water and the feat was accomplished."

Writings on the Firehole fishing were scarce in these and the following years. Although the railroad had reached within fifty miles of the Park by 1885, it was still a two-day ride over a bumpy, rutted wagon road from either Mammoth or West Yellowstone to the Firehole.

In 1910, a man using the pen name Kla-how-ya (Orange Perry Barnes) wrote a small but charming book, *Fly Fishing in Wonderland* about fishing in the Park. The book is less than fifty pages but it is a lovely thing, full of pleasant reminiscence, description, and charming quotes. About the fishing, including the Firehole and its tributaries, he wrote: ". . . taking climate, comfort, scenery, environment, the opportunity to observe Wildlife, and the quality of the fishing into consideration, it has no equal under the sun." This is still true.

When the railroads reached Gardiner on the north, and West Yellowstone, in the early 1900s the number of annual visitors doubled but still did not reach 25,000 per year until 1915 when automobiles were first admitted. So, in the 1880s and 1890s the number of sport fishermen were few. But commercial fishing was beginning to take a terrible toll. Commercial fishing in a National Park? Yes, and even hunting was allowed until 1883 when laws prohibiting it were passed but not enforced. For all practical purposes, there was no game and fish laws in Yellowstone Park prior to 1894. But commercial fishing went on until 1919.

There were three hotels in the Firehole area after 1886 and these employed several men to catch trout to feed their guests.* It was not unusual for these men, five or six of them, to take one hundred to two hundred trout each per day, supplying the hotels and selling the surplus. After this was stopped the sport fishing became fantastically good and remained so for years.

In the 1920s the limit was twenty fish and many limit catches would average four pounds a fish. And in those days, keeping a limit was the thing to do,

*This was completely illegal but was one form of commercial fishing practiced.

This type four-horse-drawn stagecoach commenced running from the Staley Springs–West Yellowstone area in 1886 to the hotels in Fountain Flats and near Old Faithful. The horses were stabled and stagecoaches housed in barns along the Madison in the section now known as "behind the Barns," or "the Barns holes." Picture circa 1898. National Park Service photo

Three limit catches from the Firehole, circa 1900 when the limit was twenty-five fish. Photo courtesy of the Haynes Foundation

even if the fish were wasted, which many were. The limits were reduced to fifteen, ten, and in the 1940s, to five but only after it became apparent the river could not supply a limitless number of fish.

In the early 1960s a strong and determined research program was launched, the amount of fishing pressure determined, and the catch totalled. As a result of this study, in 1968, the Firehole, Gibbon below its falls, and the Madison in Yellowstone Park were restricted to fly fishing only, and the limit set at two fish of sixteen inches or longer. The fishing has improved and is still improving.

Stocking of all trout in already stocked streams was discontinued in Yellowstone in 1955. Prior to that, the Firehole and Gibbon had been repeatedly stocked—the Firehole with brook, browns, and rainbows (first stocked in 1923), the Gibbon with those species, grayling, and black bass! The bass did not survive.

The main street of West Yellowstone, circa 1927. Practically all of these buildings have since burned down. Photo courtesy Walt and Nora Stewart

This old White "stretch-out," an elongated limousine, ran visitors into the Park as late as the middle forties. Picture circa 1916. Photo courtesy Dutch and Donna Spainhower

The Yellowstone Special. This, the first passenger train into West Yellowstone, came in June 1909. It "made up" in Ogden, Utah, in the evening and delivered the passengers to West Yellowstone the following morning. This train ran well into the forties before auto travel put it out of business. Photo courtesy Walt and Nora Stewart

The first "hotel" in West Yellowstone, circa 1909, and the first two guests to reside there. Photo courtesy Walt and Nora Stewart

This is how the wealthier visitors got from the depot in West Yellowstone to Old Faithful and Norris. Circa 1915. Photo courtesy Dutch and Donna Spainhower

The road from the West Yellowstone area along the Madison and Gibbon rivers to Norris, 1912. National Park Service Photo

A dog-powered snowmobile of the 1920s, all set for a winter trip up the Madison and Firehole. Photo courtesy Dutch and Donna Spainhower

The forerunner of today's motor home. The first such vehicle ever in Yellowstone, 1923. National Park Service Photo

The first permanent buildings in West Yellowstone, 1923. The one advertising fresh fruit and dusters was the original Smith and Chandler Indian Traders. Their stores still exist, one in West Yellowstone. Photo courtesy Walt and Nora Stewart

The depot in West Yellowstone when train travel was at its peak. How would you like to locate your bag in that bunch? Circa 1931. Photo courtesy Dutch and Donna Spainhower

These two streams are unique in many ways; their year-round temperatures and their mineral richness both result from the thermal features that pour their flows into them. The fissures that cause these thermal features reach down thousands of feet, through the overlaying lava beds and down into cretacious limestone. Water seeps from the surface down into the limestone beds where it is heated and returned to the surface. Ground water is acid; it is a powerful solvent and the hotter it is the more it dissolves. Limestone is especially vulnerable and great quantities of dissolved limestone are brought to the surface and run into the Firehole and to a lesser extent, the Gibbon, as calcium bicarbonates. In *Streams, Ponds, and Lakes,* Robert E. Coker says that calcium bicarbonate is readily soluble; it is formed from carbon dioxide and water acting on calcium carbonate (limestone); these materials build the bulk of *all* aquatic organisms, animal or vegetable, and the quality of a body of water is dependent on the amount of such materials in it.

One of the ways that this shows in the Firehole and Gibbon is in the number and kinds of snails that inhabit them. Formerly the Firehole also supported multitudes of crustaceans, but these have diminished with rising temperatures.

The streams have remained largely undamaged by man. A spill of chlorinated water from the swimming pool at Old Faithful in the 1950s caused a fish kill in the Firehole; in the late 1960s road building caused turbidity and some silting—but prompt action by the then Park Superintendent Jack Anderson put a stop to this. The Gibbon, because of its narrow canyon, with the highway paralleling it through the canyon, has suffered more from road building but to all appearances has recovered from all such indignities.

At present it appears that the streams are in more danger from nature than from man. The forces that built the area of Yellowstone Park are still going on and are having an effect on the Firehole and Gibbon. The recent series of quakes have silted the Gibbon and increased the flow of thermal features into the Firehole, causing a temperature rise that is at a critical state for the survival of both trout and aquatic insects. What the future holds in that direction, only time will tell. We must wait and hope.

If I've appeared to give more attention to the Firehole than to the Gibbon in this chapter, the emphasis is intentional. Since the Gibbon is only about one-third the size of the Firehole, its influence on, and potential for mischief to, the Madison is thus much less. Another reason is the fishing. To say that the Firehole provides better fishing than the Gibbon would depend on the definition of "better," and each individual is entitled to make his own judgment as to what better means to him.

The Firehole is the more difficult fishing. Research indicates that only 18 percent of all who fish it catch fish, and only 5 percent catch fish of sixteen or more inches. It is the most difficult stream to fish with success in all Yellowstone Park, and to me this makes it a more desirable stream to fish, since for many years the fishing, to me, has been more important than the catching.

Our get-acquainted trip on these rivers is over. I hope it has been rewarding and informative and I hope it will give you a better understanding of the Madison, whose character and quality depend much on these two sources.

HISTORICALLY SPEAKING

MAN, BOTH RED AND WHITE, GOT INTO THE MADISON RIVER VALLEY BY WAY OF the river's mouth, near the present Three Forks, Montana. The exact date of the first intrusion by man is a matter of some conjecture.

Man's presence in other parts of Montana, not too far from the Three Forks area, can be placed about 200 to 600 B.C., and there is evidence from other parts of the state that indicates man was hunting elephants in Montana as early as 10,000 B.C. But he cannot be placed in the Madison Valley with assurance much earlier than 1500 A.D.

At the Madison Buffalo Jump, now a state park, some few miles south (upstream) and just east of the mouth of the Madison, there is abundant evidence of man's presence several centuries ago. The site was used as a place to drive buffalo over a cliff to kill them by several tribes of Indians for at least five hundred years. The first tribe that can be identified was the Salish (Flathead), an inoffensive and peaceful people.

The Salish were driven from the area sometime around 1700 by the Shoshoni, who had obtained horses somewhat earlier and were expanding onto the Great Plains. The Shoshoni route to the plains was mainly to the south of Montana and by 1800 one branch of the tribe had been established for some years in the Wind River area of Wyoming.

The Indian who made his presence felt most strongly in the Three Forks area was neither Salish nor Shoshoni, but the hard-riding, aggressive Blackfeet. The Blackfeet came into the area as a result of the same thing that led white men to explore and exploit it—the fur trade.

In the 1780s, British traders of both the Hudson's Bay Company and the infamous Northwest Company had established posts in Canada as far west as Lake Athabasca, four hundred miles north of the present Edmonton, Alberta. The area to the south as far as the North Saskatchewan River was the home of the Blackfeet and in their dealings with these people, the Northwesters set in motion actions that were to have far-reaching consequences.

The Blackfeet confederation was a loose arrangement of the three major tribes within it. These were the Siksika (Blackfeet), Kainah (Blood), and Piegan. The largest and most aggressive tribe was the Blackfeet.

The Blackfeet had already some horses when, in the late 1780s, the Northwest Company traders gave them guns. The purpose was to obtain their loyalty, and thus their furs, and to aid them in driving out other tribes who were trading with the rival Hudson's Bay Company.

At first, the plan worked. Shortly after they were provided weapons, the Blackfeet attacked a trading camp of the Hudson's Bay Company, killing many Indians who had come to trade, several white members of the Company, and driving the entire group from the area.

Flushed with the success of this operation, the Blackfeet looked around for other worlds to conquer and saw their future to the south. Here, in the relatively flat, unwooded country, their horses and guns could be used to great advantage, and there was one other attraction. To the south there were many buffalo.

The southward movement began *about* 1789 and proceeded slowly. By the time the Lewis and Clark expedition reached Montana and crossed it, the Blackfeet occupied most of the area north of the Missouri River from the Milk River on the east almost to Glacier National Park on the west. Except for occasional forays by hunting parties, they had not penetrated seriously south of the Missouri, nor did they ever.

There is a great misconception about the dangers that faced Lewis and Clark at the time their expedition was penetrating north of Nebraska. Most people seem to think the area was swarming with savage Indian tribes. It wasn't. The tribes we think of as occupying the area had not reached it yet. Except for the peaceful Mandans of North Dakota, who long had friendly relations with whites, and the agricultural Hidatsa to the north, there were no *permanent* Indian tribes between northern Nebraska and the western edge of Montana along the route of the expedition.

The tribes generally thought to be in the area were forced into it later by pressure of the expanding white population in the east and south. The first pressure in the area came from the south.

The Mexicans, pushing up from Santa Fe in the 1700s, put pressure on the Pawnee and Arapaho, and these tribes later forced the Cheyenne out of northern Kansas and Colorado into Nebraska and Wyoming. At the time Lewis and Clark came up the Missouri, the Cheyenne had reached the southern Black Hills. Later, the arriving Sioux would push them west to the base of the Rockies. The Sioux had earlier forced the Cheyenne out of Minnesota and Iowa into the area where they came into conflict with the Pawnee. The Sioux themselves had been shoved out of their lands farther east by the Chippewa (Ojibway) who had been thrust out of their lands by the Iroquois, who had been furnished with guns by the British and Dutch about 1680.

The name Sioux itself is of Chippewa origin, from a Chippewan word, Nadowessioux, which was shortened by the French to its present form. The French understood the word to mean "snake" or "enemy." It is likely that it meant neither. When Indians talked to others who did not speak their language well, they also used gestures. In conjunction with the name Sioux, the Chippewa used two gestures—one a sinuous wiggle of the hand and forearm, the other a drawing of the forefinger across the throat. The same motions were used by western tribes when speaking of the Shoshoni. In both cases, the sign meant "devious" or "untrustworthy," not snake or enemy. Another sign used to designate the Sioux was a turning of the outstretched palms up, then down, then up; again the meaning was "devious."

There were three dialects used by the seven tribes of the Sioux Nation: Dakota, used by the most easterly tribes; Nakota, used by northern Sioux and Assiniboin; and Lakota, the dialect of the western tribes—Ogalala, Teton, and others. In all dialects, the words meant the same thing, "friends."

The Ogalala and Teton and their subtribes were the ones who later caused the whites so much trouble, although they were still east of the Missouri at the time of Lewis and Clark. Among the subtribes of the Ogalala and Teton were the Sans Arc, Two Kettle, and Hunkpapa. Sitting Bull was of the latter tribe. Crazy Horse was an Ogalala.

There is a tendency to confuse the Teton with the area of the Teton Mountains in Wyoming. There is no connection between them; the words do not have the same roots in language. The Teton Mountains are named from the French *teton* ("tay tonh") meaning breast or teat, and that is the meaning applied to the mountains. The Sioux *teton* ("tee tahn") is the Lakota word for "prairie dwellers."

The only warlike tribe actually in the path of the Lewis and Clark expedition between St. Louis and western Montana was the Arickaree (Uh-rik'-uh-ree) also known as Arikara and Rees. This was an offshoot of the Pawnee, a subtribe so unsociable and hostile that their own tribe forced them out, and all other tribes refused them shelter. They comprised less than three hundred persons and their small number and warlike ways caused their annihilation in less than a century. At the time of Lewis and Clark, there were probably less than a hundred of them dwelling to the west and south of the Mandan Villages. They may have been the tribe that fired on the expedition from the river bank.

Prior to the arrival of Lewis and Clark at the Mandan Villages the Crow Indians had split off from the agricultural Hidatsa (Minnetaree) who lived north and west of the villages. The Crow were hunters and horsemen, and they migrated up the Missouri and then up the Yellowstone to south of present-day Livingston, Montana, although they did not reach that area until about 1830. They posed no threat to the westerly trip by Lewis and Clark but did lie in the path of the return trip by Clark's group, which detoured to explore the Yellowstone from about nine miles downstream of Livingston to its mouth.

Lewis and Clark first saw the Madison on 27 July 1805, but their visit had little impact, for they did not explore the river either coming or going. But the area made a definite impression on one of their party and this young man was to lead the first trappers group into the area, although not until he had contributed considerably to the knowledge of the areas south and east— Jackson's Hole, Yellowstone Park, and the Bighorn Mountains.

Historians who have written of John Colter as the discoverer of Yellowstone Park have generally considered him a man of uncertain impulse and vague motivation, and some say that he snowshoed through the Park and Jackson's Hole in the winter of 1807–08.

If any of this is true, there is no proof of it, and there is no direct evidence that Colter was ever in Yellowstone. There is proof, however, that Colter was an exceptional backwoodsman of thoughtful good judgment, who probably did discover the Yellowstone Park area.

Colter joined the Lewis and Clark expedition on 15 October 1803, at Louisville, Kentucky, and stayed with it until it returned to near the Mandan Villages. There are numerous references in the expedition's journals that imply that he was one of the most trusted woodsmen and hunters in the group.

He left the group on 5 August 1806 to join two other men trapping on the upper Missouri. The leaders agreed to release him from his contract on the basis that no other member of the party would ask for the same consideration. As a token of the esteem in which he was held, he was given powder, lead, and other articles necessary for survival in the wilderness.

In the spring of 1807, while on his way to St. Louis by canoe with a load of furs, Colter met Manuel Lisa, the first prominent fur trader of the era to explore west of the North Dakota border by land, as opposed to by sea. When he discovered the range of knowledge of the area possessed by Colter, Lisa persuaded Colter to join him in establishing a post at the mouth of the Bighorn River.

From this post, Colter was dispatched in the fall of 1807 to reconnoiter to the southwest, contact Indians in the area, and arrange for the trading of furs. Here all direct knowledge of Colter's trip ends. From this point on what we know is second-hand and hearsay.

This hearsay has it that Colter returned with stories of high, jagged mountains (the Tetons) large lakes (Yellowstone and Jackson) geysers and hot springs that smelled of brimstone (sulphur). His companions laughed and dubbed the region Colter's Hell, by which name it was known even after hundreds of trappers had visited the region and Colter's description had been verified.

The evidence that Colter discovered Yellowstone Park is thus indirect but convincing. He described mountains and lakes never seen by whites before; they are there. He described thermal features never seen before in this country; it is totally unlikely he could have invented them. There is no doubt that Colter was in the Yellowstone Park–Jackson's Hole area in the winter of 1807–08, even if we cannot prove it.

Colter later gave the information about his trip to William Clark to augment a manuscript map of the area that the latter worked on from 1806 to 1811 and which was printed in 1814 from an engraving by Samuel Lewis. Unfortunately, Samuel Lewis took unwarranted liberties with the hand-drawn map, changing the shape of lakes, the direction of one outlet, and the location of mountains. This led to Colter's being discredited until Clark's manuscript map came to light some years later.

In the fall of 1808 and spring of 1809, Colter went back to the Three Forks area with another trapper and on one of these trips he had a run-in with the Blackfeet and Crow who were having an altercation over the hunting. Colter was severely wounded in the fracas. Nevertheless, he led the first large group of trappers into the area in the winter of 1809–10. This group, led by Andrew Henry and Pierre Menard, arrived at Three Forks on 3 April 1810 and were to leave a permanent mark in the region, even though the Blackfeet drove them out. In spite of this, Colter returned once more to Three Forks. His companion on this trip was killed, Colter was captured, stripped and made to run for his life. Stark naked, he ran for miles over a rocky, cactus-covered plain, outrunning all but one of the Indians. This one hurled a spear at him, then fell exhausted. Colter seized the spear, dispatched the Indian, then made his way back to the trading post over two hundred miles away. He left the region soon after.

Colter's run for life in the Three Forks area, in 1809, by an unknown artist. National Park Service Photo

Raynolds Pass, discovered by Andrew Henry in 1810, but named for Captain W. F. Raynolds who mapped it in 1859. Madison watershed to the left, Henrys Fork to the right. This low pass only rises a few hundred feet above Henrys Lake Flat and the Missouri Flats.

Andrew Henry and his group, which then included Colter, were driven from the area in the fall of the same year they arrived. Henry led the party *up* the Madison, thus becoming the first white men to see the river above its juncture with the Missouri. The group traveled up the river to the head of Missouri Flats, near present Quake Lake, over Raynolds Pass, down along the shores of Henrys Lake and down the Henrys Fork (of the Snake) to near the site of present St. Anthony, Idaho. They erected a fort there, soon abandoned it, and returned by a southerly route to the trading posts in Wyoming. The opening of the Madison River to exploitation and settlement had begun.

Even before the coming of the white man, the valley of the Madison above Beartrap Canyon had never been a favorite area for Indians. The reason was simple. The broad plains at the head of the Missouri held many buffalo, but there were never more than a few above the canyon. Elk also grazed the lower valley, and plants and roots considered necessary by the Indians also grew more profusely. There was room to maneuver and escape if attacked by a larger force. The upper middle valley, in essence a choke-bored funnel trap, with narrow canyons at either end, was not much used by either Indian or buffalo.

As far as the plants are concerned, the idea that the Plains Indians scorned their use as articles of food is a myth. Joseph W. Blankinship, in *Native Economic Plants of Montana,* notes that the Plains Indians in Montana used over seventy native plants as food, fifty for medicine; eight were used in the household and fifteen for war and hunting purposes. I have been able to identify twenty-eight of the food plants in the Madison Valley upstream of Beartrap Canyon; the area downstream is much more diverse in flora and undoubtedly many more of the seventy are found there.

Though the various Indian tribes occupied the area for three hundred years before the arrival of the white man, they left little trace of their occupation of the land and their presence had even less impact on the settling of the land by whites.

After Henry and his men departed the region in 1810, it was several years before trappers returned to the area. There were several reasons. Fur trade west of the Mississippi had been fought over by the various nations claiming the land—England, France, Spain, and after 1789, the United States. Then, just as the Americans were getting well started, the war of 1812 threw things into an uproar that lasted several years. This war forced John Jacob Astor to abandon his trading post at Astoria on the mouth of the Columbia; looking around for new territory, he and his American Fur Company lighted on the Rocky Mountains.

Astor was by all odds the greatest fur trader in history. He started in the business in the early 1790s with twenty-five dollars in cash and seven flutes and went on to become this country's first millionaire. When he died in 1848, he left his eldest son, William Backhouse Astor, an estimated $30,000,000. By perserverance, good business methods, sharp dealings, and bribery Astor managed eventually to take over a near-monopoly of the Rocky Mountain fur trade before he retired in 1834.

The record does not show which of the various competitive companies next sent men to the Three Forks area. David Thompson, who had been in the Mandan Villages as early as 1798 (La Verendrye was there in 1738–43 but established no lasting dealings with the Indians), moved west as the agent for the Northwest Company but it is not known if he established a post at Three Forks, although from 1809 to 1814 he was active in northern Idaho.

Wilson Price Hunt visited Jackson's Hole in 1811 and was in southeast Idaho and perhaps northern Utah but left no record of being in Montana. The next recorded mention of trappers in the north Rocky Mountains was of Donald McKenzie who established a camp at Bear Lake, Utah, on 10 September 1819 from which trappers operated for several years, trapping as far east and north as Jackson's Hole and the edge of Yellowstone Park. Thus trappers were once again nibbling at the headwaters region of the Madison River.

For a number of years trappers had been around the region of Yellowstone Park; but except for Colter none entered the area. The reason was the same for which the Indians avoided the place. Yellowstone Park is located on a massive upland plateau surrounded on all sides by towering mountains— Teton on the south, Absaroka on the east, Beartooth to the north, the Gallatin range down most of the west. No matter which direction you go from the area you go down, and sharply. The average *interior* elevation in the Park is 6,500 feet; no place is lower than a mile above sea level. It is covered by snow and ice from November until May, and many of the steep mountain passes are full of snow until mid-July.

Compared to adjacent areas, the hunting was not good, and it did not provide as good beaver trapping as many areas nearby. Because of these facts, trapping did not seriously begin in the Park until 1832 although a group of trappers did visit it in 1826 and one of them, Daniel F. Potts, wrote a letter from Sweet Lake (Bear Lake) Utah dated 8 July 1827, to his brother Robert, of Philadelphia. The letter was published 27 September 1827, in the Philadelphia *Gazette* and that is a remarkable fact.

There was no regular intercourse or trade between Bear Lake and St. Louis. No railroad had yet entered Pennsylvania, much less reached its western border. Steamboat traffic had not yet commenced on the Ohio River. Yet we have a letter traversing over 2,700 miles, most of it barren of habitation and trails, in eighty days, an average of better than thirty-three miles per day.

Potts was in the area with a very large group of men from the Rocky Mountain Fur Company, formed in 1822 by William Ashley and Andrew Henry. This group was to generate more famous mountain men than any other, and they were to leave a very large impact on the history of that part of the country.

Among these were Jim Bridger on his first trapping trip at age nineteen, Thomas Fitzpatrick (Broken Hand), Hugh Glass (*The Saga of Hugh Glass*), David Jackson (Jackson's Hole), Etienne Provost (Provo, Utah), Jedediah and Thomas Smith (Peg Leg), and the Sublette brothers, William and Milton.

One of them was a man named Manuel Alvarez who was to become the first white man to see the Firehole River, although not until some years later. In 1833, Alvarez led a band of about forty trappers, of which Jim Bridger *may* have been one, from Ft. Hall on the Snake River in Idaho, up the Henrys Fork, over Rea's Pass, across the Madison Plateau, and into the Upper Geyser Basin. Our record of this is second-hand; Warren A. Ferris, another trapper, got the information from Alvarez and set it down in *Life in the Rocky Mountains (1830–1835)*, not published until many years later. Alvarez is identified by some historians as the same Alvarez who became U.S. Consul to Santa Fe in 1842.

Among trappers of the era, there were three kinds of operation. Brigades employed men to trap and tend camp and paid them a salary as well as furnishing them with food, supplies, and equipment. Free trappers provided their own supplies and equipment, which they bought from the same companies to which they sold their furs. In effect, they were contract trappers. The last group were the individual trappers who trapped in groups of two or three and carried their own furs to market. There were few of the latter.

There was intense competition and rivalry among the different groups. There were often deadly fights over territorial rights—or, occasionally, just for the hell of it.

The free trappers sneered at the brigade men, who employed camp tenders and carried bacon to tide them over when game was scarce. The free trappers had a contemptuous sobriquet for the brigade men—"mangeurs du lard" (pork eaters) they called them, and scorned such aids, depending entirely on their rifles to keep them fed. Some came near to starving because of this, as did brigade trappers on occasion.

Osborne Russell speaks of his group being caught in a gameless area in 1835 while on their way to Yellowstone for the spring trapping. The group left Ft. Hall on the Snake in April and soon found that the snow between there and the Tetons was unusually deep. There was no game to be found, and for ten days the group, consisting of ten trappers and seven camp tenders, had nothing but roots to eat.

On the eleventh day, they killed a bear early out of hibernation, butchered it in frantic haste, cut the meat into very small pieces and filled four three-gallon kettles with just enough water to avoid scorching. After what Russell describes as the longest wait for a meal in history, the senior member of the party pronounced the meat "fit" and the seventeen starving men fell to and ate twelve gallons of meat, nearly three quarts each.

Russell is the outstanding recorder of the area's fur traders-trappers of the 1830s. His *Journal of a Trapper (1834–1843)* is the finest on the period I have read. It is rather surprising also. At this time, education such as Russell and Warren Ferris, mentioned earlier, possessed, was rare. There were *no* public schools as such, no tax-supported educational institutions, no school boards, state or local, anywhere in the United States. Schools were private, or rarely, cooperative, where parents paid for the books, erected the building and the teacher "boarded round." Less than 10 percent of the population had the equivalent of a grade-school education in the 1830s.

Russell gives this picture of the free trapper (which he later became) of the period: his outfit was austere, and consisted of two horses, two blankets, a flintlock rifle, one pound of powder, four of lead, melting and pouring ladle, bullet molds, a one-quart and a three-gallon kettle, hatchet, axe, seven traps, awl, and flint and steel. This was the basic outfit for a spring or fall trip of two to three months. If the trapper felt particularly inclined toward luxury, he might carry seven pounds of flour, two pints of sugar, four of coffee, and of course, tobacco.

The dress of the trapper was likewise standardized, being the five-piece buckskin outfit of moccasins, leggings, pants, coat, and cap. The winter coat came nearly to the knees, cut off to just below the hips; belted at the waist, it became the summer shirt. Hatchet and knife, and pouch for flint and steel and dried moss hung from the belt. The cap was a buckskin skullcap, the fur cap was almost never worn, being subject to vermin. In times of extreme cold, the trapper would throw a bearskin or sometimes a blanket, over his shoulders.

The pants, coat, and leggings were fringed, not for decoration as is generally thought, but to promote drying after a soaking. A fringed outfit would drain and dry in half the time it took an unfringed suit to do so.

The skins were tanned with a mixture of deer brains, tallow, or grease, and water well worked into the skin. Then the damp skin was broken—made soft by working, pulling, and stretching—then smoked over a smudge. I did much of this as a boy in the Ozarks. The finished product was fawn yellow to smoky grey, depending on the exact process and what wood was used in the smoking. After repeated wettings and being soaked in sweat and grease, the outside of the clothing became a dull, smooth russet, the color and appearance of rusty sheet iron.

The trappers seldom made their own clothing—it was done by Indian women. Crow women were considered the best tanners and made the best clothing. Blackfeet women were next, although not much dealing with this tribe took place. Shoshoni women made most of the clothing for area trappers, on a rather standardized trade basis.

One raw deer skin would trade for two pairs of short moccasins, unsoled. Three skins would exchange for leggings and pants. The long (winter) coat and cap required five skins. A suit of such buckskin would last two seasons under hard usage. Most trappers carried three to five pairs of extra moccasins, since this item got the most wear and was considered the most necessary.

The trapper's diet was almost entirely meat, and boiled meat at that. Ribs and loin of a fresh killed animal or the hump of buffalo, or the tail of a beaver might be roasted but everything else was boiled; salt and pepper were the only seasoning. The salt was more than likely obtained from nature, for salt springs, oozings, and outcroppings abound in the northern Rockies.

The hunting knife was the only tool for eating. A piece of meat was speared from the pot and caught between the teeth; one hand pulled the free end away and the knife sliced between hand and lips. Until nearly 1850 the knife had no guard or fancy trimmings; nine times out of ten it was a short-bladed butcher knife, known in the trade as a "Green River." The late Townsend Whelen, one of our greatest outdoorsmen, used such a knife for over fifty years. He called it "Seeds ke dee," Absaroka or Crow dialect for Green River.

The rifle was the most important piece of equipment, more so even than the horse. When trapping first began in the Rockies, the rifle was probably a Revolutionary War musket or the standard Kentucky muzzle loader, most likely the latter.

These were *long* rifles, of sixty-six to over eighty-five inches, and of light caliber. In those days, a rifle was not called by its caliber, however, but by its gauge—i.e., the number of balls of bore size that could be made from a pound of lead. Thus, the weapon would be referred to by a number that had only a bare relationship with caliber. "Killbar's* a 90," a hunter would say affectionately of his favorite weapon. The number meant that a pound of lead would make 90 balls for said rifle. This was a very light weapon of about .38 caliber, satisfactory for animals up to whitetail deer in size but in spite of its owner's feelings, totally inadequate for bear, especially the grizzly, which on occasion, absorbed nine to a dozen balls from such weapons and still wreaked havoc upon their owners.

The presence of the grizzly and the buffalo called for more powerful weapons, and since these men traveled by horseback, for shorter ones, also. The result culminated in the plains rifle, of which the Hawken was far and away the most popular. The Hawken rifle was not an advance in hand-held firearms; it simply used known principles to produce a handier weapon with a great deal more killing power. The rifle became known, because of the care with which it was made, as a totally reliable weapon.

The Hawken was short, compared with other rifles of the period. Seldom did the barrel exceed thirty-six inches or the total length fifty-six; thus it ran some *feet* shorter than other, earlier rifles. Though each one was built to the

*Pronounced "Killbare"; the broad a was not used by frontiersmen or trappers. The modern misunderstanding of "bar" for bear is the result of Daniel Boone's famous misspelling of the word. The trapper would no more say "bar" than "bahth."

exact specifications of the buyer, it could be said that by the mid-thirties the average Hawken used by trappers and mountain men was fifty-three inches overall and of .53 caliber, but they ran from .48 to .75 caliber. It was a flintlock weapon; though caplock rifles were in use, they required an extra loading component and an extra loading step—not popular features when a man traveled alone for months, or was fighting for his life.

The accuracy of the Hawken combined with its much greater striking power gave the trappers ascendancy not only over the grizzly but over the Indian as well. A single ball would do the job formerly requiring several, and after the advent of the Hawken, Indians, including the aggressive Blackfeet, were less inclined to dispute the right of way with a group of trappers.

If the trappers ate fish or fished at all, it was rare enough to be unusual. The only mention of it in any writings I have seen was in Russell's *Journal*. It was on the Fourth of July, 1839, that Russell and his companions were camped on Jackson Lake on their way to and through the Yellowstone area. Nearby was camped a brigade of French trappers. Russell and his friends wished to show the "Frenchies" how real Americans celebrated their Independence. They killed elk, mountain sheep, and a buffalo, caught twenty "salmon" trout from the lake, and served up a meal of three kinds of meat, fish, biscuits, and coffee—a proper celebration, all agreed.

Russell lists, in an appendix to his *Journal*, the following animals, with an excellent description in each case: wolverine, wolf, panther (cougar), marmot (pika), porcupine, badger, groundhog (marmot), blacktail deer, elk, buffalo, and beaver. This is a nearly complete list of animals presently in the area. Missing are the pine squirrel and the moose. The pine squirrel is scarce, and small enough to be overlooked—but a moose? Especially by men who lived on wild game and whose very existence depended on it? But Russell is not the only one of the period who fails to mention this giant deer. No one does.

The reason was simple. There were no moose in the area until about the mid 1850s when some were seen in Jackson's Hole, and a few years later, in Yellowstone. The conjecture is that they pushed up along the Missouri River, up the Madison, into the Park and down into Jackson's Hole sometime between May 1805 when Lewis and Clark first observed them at the juncture of the Milk and the Missouri on their westward journey, and the early 1850s when they were first seen in Jackson's Hole. This is *only* conjecture; no one really knows where they came from into the area, or when.

Trapping for beaver in the area began to decline in 1835 and was literally gone by 1839. The reason was the ascendancy of the silk hat in London, replacing the long-favored beaver item. Some trappers continued to trap beaver into the mid-forties, but the price declined from a high $5.00 a pound (about $7.50 per skin) to less than $1.50 per pound, while the prices trappers paid for supplies remained at early 1830 levels. Coffee and sugar still sold for $2.00 a pound but on occasion cost over $20.00 a pound. Lead cost as much as $5.00 a pound, and the cost of a rifle zoomed from less than $60 to over $150 from the mid-thirties to 1840.

The trapper, like the Indian, was a bird of passage. He left little lasting

This young bull elk, in velvet, is more interested in filling his stomach than in the photographer. He has many pounds to put on before the fasting time during the rut.

evidence of his trip, did little damage to his environment, and is remembered more as an explorer than an exploiter.

The Indians of the period and of the area also left little mark, either upon the land or upon history. Their mode of life would preclude either. Theirs was a philosophy of "do it the easy way," and they never were concerned with leaving a record of their passing. Also, they lived lightly on the land, and not long in one place.

Although we often speak of the Plains Indians living in villages, this was only a temporary state. They did have sizable areas where they spent the summers and the winters, and to which they regularly returned, but in general they were seminomadic.

This was the result of their preference for hunting—and the shocking amount of meat required to supply their needs. A group or clan of two hundred persons would devour, if they were available, an average of forty buffalo per month, and in times of plenty, twice that number. They did not hunt every day; that would have been work, and inefficient. Instead, they hunted only when food was running low.

If there was a herd of buffalo nearby, that was fine. But such was not usually the case; a ride of several to more than fifty miles to find sufficient animals was the norm. When the buffalo, from fifty to over two hundred animals in some cases, were slaughtered, a messenger went back to the camp and brought it to the game. It was easier and far more practical to do this.

The things that made it so were the horse and the tepee, of which the National Geographic's *Indians of the Americas* says "a simpler, more graceful or more practical portable dwelling was never devised by man." The tepee, made of from twelve to twenty-eight buffalo hides, could be taken down in minutes, folded and strapped on the back of a horse, the twenty to thirty lodgepoles strapped on the sides, and in an hour a whole village would be on its way to a new location.

While the women were bringing the home to the hunter, the men would rough dress the buffalo. If the hides were not needed, the animal would be propped on its back, the hide split down the center and around the legs and pulled down; the meat was then removed in sections easily unjointed. First the forequarters, then the hindquarters and rump were chopped loose. Next the flank was peeled up and forward and detached from the brisket, the ribs were

This bull moose is not eating grass as it appears here. He is picking out the coarser weedy forbs and herbs.

chopped from the backbone, and the job was done. Only the head, the bare spine, brisket, and entrails remained lying on the hide. The tongue and liver would be taken as delicacies.

Some trappers who dwelt with the Indians noted that at times an Indian could strip a buffalo in this fashion in fifteen minutes; thus, what appeared to be the insurmountable task of butchering a hundred or more animals would take only a couple of hours, and was usually accomplished before the women arrived.

The women cut the meat into strips and sheets for making jerky.* The ribs and hump would be roasting at the same time, as would the thigh bones, the former for eating at once, the marrow from the latter to be mixed with the pounded dry meat and berries for making pemmican, perhaps the finest preserved food ever invented.

The buffalo was literally an industry with the Plains Indian. The hides made tepees, robes, blankets, and epishemores (saddle blankets). The marrow of the large bones went into pemmican, the smaller bones made spoons and ladles, as did the horns, which also made cups. The shoulder blade made a shovel for cleaning around camp and for digging roots. Green hides were stretched over frames for boats and shields, or cut into strips and braided into ropes, and the droppings made the finest fire material.

During the latter days of the beaver trade, a large trade in buffalo robes began; these were much in demand in the East and Middle West for sled and carriage robes. The same traders who bought the beaver did a brisk trade in robes, and the traders of the day had a saying, "Ten cups of sugar equals one robe, ten robes equal one pony, three ponies equal one tepee." The preferred robes were made by Crow women and brought more in trade than those of other tribes.

Because of his way of life, the Plains Indian required a large territory over which to hunt, and it was this that brought them most often into conflict with the whites. But the conflict did not become serious in Yellowstone Park and the Madison Valley. These were not choice hunting areas and were yielded virtually without struggle.

---

*From the Spanish *echarqui*—dried meat. It has nothing to do with jerk or jerking and the terms, jerked meat or jerking meat are an aberration better discarded.

RETURN
TO THE RIVER

AT MADISON JUNCTION, WHERE IT BEGINS, THE RIVER IS ALREADY LARGE BY trout-stream standards, but it is not majestic. It runs intimately with its landscape and with splendor. Its immediate prospects are open and friendly.

The elk, in spring and fall, crop the rich meadow grasses, aided in this by the Canada geese, both greater and lesser, which nest here. The buffalo and the moose are occasional visitors and if the bear is allowed, he will be seen along the stream of evening, when the bullbats roar and thunder in their booming dives.

The osprey soars above the scarp of National Park Mountain, foraging here though his nest is far away; the odds are that he will be robbed of the fruits of his labor by the bald eagle before he reaches home. Because the river contains over one hundred parts per million of calcium bicarbonate, it is a chalk stream, some say the largest in the world. The mineral richness and the temperature favor green plant growth and the river is full of waterweeds, *Potamogeton, Chara, Eleocharis,* and *Myriophyllum*—muskie weed, stonewort, needle rush, and milfoil, to the layman. By whatever name, they attest the richness of the water and furnish hiding places for insects and trout.

The bottom is mostly sand-silt over bedrock and the insects will be small. Caddis is number one in rank and total weight. *Ephemerella* mayflies live in shallower sections where the bottom material is coarser, and dragon and damselfly nymphs prowl all but the deepest pools.

The meadows stretch more than half a mile, curling away from the walls at times on either side to give a feeling of airy openness. On the north side, the

A splendid dry-fly stretch below Madison Junction. But that white shirt and hat aren't the best camouflage.

lodgepole-covered slope leans back against the shoulder of the mountain, but on the south the wall is abrupt; it is the edge of the Madison Plateau, broken off by uplift and not yet carved by the river.

The water is typical meadow stream: deep glassy runs and glides, and one great pool at the elbow of Big Bend, where the river, having swung over to the south wall, now comes back and returns to the highway, threading its way along the foot of the north slope.

This is good dry-fly water most of the season. If one waits for the hatch, disappointment may overtake you; the mayfly hatches are sparse and irregular and the caddis hatch mostly after dusk and on into the night. But high-floating "shotgun" flies—Brown Spider, Hairwing Variant, Brown Bivisible, and Whitcraft—will bring many fine trout to investigate when the naturals are quiescent.

Then in July, the meadows bring forth grasshoppers and high sport is to be had for two months, dropping these big imitations along the grassy banks or onto the grass and shaking them off into the water. Do not be surprised if a trout comes clear of the water in his eagerness to get the fly when you are practicing the latter method.

The most successful nymphs are dragon and damselfly imitations. They must be sunk to the bottom and twitched along in imitation of the natural. The water will be deep and the current strong even when the surface is glassy. A sinking line is nearly always required.

When the river comes to the highway, it does so at a rocky breakover and a downhill stretch of half a mile. This stretch is shallow except for a quiet spot on the inside of the bend on the far side. An eight-pound brown has been taken from this deep pocket but you must cross over to fish it.

The shallow riffle contains only small fish except when the browns are spawning in the fall. It is rubble-bottomed and quite swift. At its lower end, there is a pocket meadow stretch, another long riffle, and then a deep, fast rocky run that holds good trout and that is heavily populated with the giant stonefly, *Pteronarcys californica,* as are the two riffles just mentioned. The best fly is an imitation of this huge nymph, Whitlock's Black Stone, Troth's Terrible Stone, Montana Stone (my own pattern) or a huge black Wooly Worm, size four, 4XL.

It was along this stretch one frosty September day that Ernie Schwiebert and Gene Anderegg harvested over thirty trout of two to six pounds, as Ernie relates in his fine book *Nymphs.* It is not that productive except when the fall fish are running to spawn but a good fish or two is a possibility any time.

Just at this point the river is squeezed between Mt. Haynes on the south and Mt. Jackson across and upstream a bit, forming the gap known as Madison Notch. The pika will chirp and whistle and cheer you on from the talus slope that slides down to the river here.

Below, the river makes a big sweeping curve alongside the highway, a deep, broad section filled with giant boulders big as sports cars. This is the famous Nine Mile Hole, meaning, in the terminology of the local anglers, that it is just nine miles in from the west entrance to the Park.

This is a truly excellent piece of water, which always contains trout of one to three pounds, but it is difficult to fish. The great boulders cause deep pockets, cross currents, and swirls; the channel swings about in the stream bed because of these influences; there are hummocks and bars of fine material and beds of weeds. All these make for capricious currents and the broken surface causes distortion of vision, leading one to misjudge the depth and step in over his waders. But these are the things that make it a home for fine trout and a challenge to the thoughtful angler. Years ago a local angler achieved momentary fame for his skill—and his greed—by taking and keeping fifteen trout that weighed a total of seventy-four pounds from this piece of water.

From the tail of this deep run, the river drives through a dense patch of lodgepole hard into the shoulder of the plateau, breaks around to the right and enters a large marshy area. There are many good holds and lies here but the area is dangerous. There are many, many places along the bank where one can simply vanish from sight into a silt-and-water-filled pocket that is as treacherous as quicksand, which indeed it resembles. I do not fish this area and I would advise all to give it a pass. A friend of mine stepped into one of these holes once and went in over his head; water and silt filled his waders and except for a small willow that grew within reach, he would have lost his life.

The willows are plentiful here and perhaps there are some beaver. There are myriads of waterfowl, trumpeter swans, Canada geese and puddle ducks, all of which nest and spend the summer and fall. One can observe and study them from the safety of the highway shoulder, but only the reckless will invade the area, which stretches to the highway bridge a mile or two below the beginning of the marsh.

The long stretch of glassy weed-filled water below the bridge, known as Seven Mile Run, is one of the finest pieces of dry-fly water in the world. The constant weed beds, potholes in the bottom, and huge logs and drifts along the right bank host a multitude of fine trout but they are trout that require some catching. If you do not catch them, do not say they are not there. These are the most difficult of fish and even if one hooks them, chances of landing anything over a pound are slim.

I once sent a couple of lads from France, Pierre Affre and his friend, Edouard, to fish this place. Both are splendid casters and fine fly fishermen who have fished the chalk streams of France and England and who know the necessity of stalking wary fish. Pierre reported that they saw at least a dozen of three pounds or more, but were able to raise only fish under two, and they landed only those of a pound or less. His estimate was that it was the most difficult and challenging water that he had ever fished. This is the major reason one sees so few fishermen along this stretch; it takes only a little while to discover the difficulties. Most anglers one sees are fishing from the left bank, the highway side, and the fish are from the middle to the far bank.

The famous Western Green Drake, *Ephemerella grandis,* hatches here, sometime between mid-June and mid-July, but its appearance cannot be predicted accurately and its season is short. More plentiful is its smaller cousin, *Ephemerella lacustris,* Pale Morning Dun, which also hatches in numbers along

Following page: *Seven Mile Run on the Madison in the Park—here the largest chalkstream in the world.*

Muleshoe Bend and Goose Lake Meadows of the Firehole. Some *Baetis*, Blue-Winged Olive, are seen, especially in the fall, and *Brachycentrus* and *Rhyacophila* caddis hatch on into September.

The end of this stretch is quite marked. There is a break in the bedrock bottom and the gliding, weed-filled runs give way to a wide shallow riffle about three miles long. The highway departs the stream bank and does not return.

The riffle is the delight of the neophyte and one will see them often along the head of the reach. They catch mostly six-to-eight-inch trout but this seems to please them.

The area just above the breakover is an excellent spot for watching wildlife. The river will often be full of ducks and geese, the magnificent trumpeter swans glide majestically over the smooth surface, and otter families play and cavort here more frequently than elsewhere. Elk graze on the far hillside, buffalo may be seen at times, and on misty mornings a moose may stride powerfully along, heading for the more plentiful willows downstream in the Beaver Meadows.

The birds seem more numerous. Gray and Steller's jays, Clark's nutcracker, and hairy woodpeckers are most abundant although because of his size the raven is most obvious. The osprey works the water and the bald eagle works the osprey.

The marsh hawk plies the blue, working in quartering sweeps across the open hillsides, calling plaintively in a mewing voice. Seagulls skim over the water; they are probably farther from the ocean in Yellowstone Park than anywhere else. At times the nocturnal loon will appear briefly and vanish; grebe are somewhat more visible; and the kingfisher will streak along the far bank, piercing the shade of overhanging limbs with a flash of blue light and a racheting chatter.

There are smaller birds, finches and hummingbirds, but such tiny creatures are seen only if you are actively looking for them. They prefer areas away from the rush and bustle of the highways, which in Yellowstone flank the streams much of the time and are filled with lines of cars the summer long. About two-and-one-half million people visit Yellowstone yearly, two million between June first and mid-September, just under 20,000 persons per day. Thus many of the creatures in the Park may be seen only in areas away from the road. The fisherman, if he will take the time to look up from the water, has the best opportunity, and the presence of the wild creatures adds much to the fishing experience.

About a half-mile before the highway reaches the west entrance, a road turns off to the right and runs narrowly and inconsequentially through the lodgepoles, over a little hill, falling around a curve and across the flat to the river, which comes into view on the right in the stretch known as Cable Car Run. Here begins three miles of the finest fast-water nymph fishing anywhere, although the dry fly can be used on those very rare occasions when the fish show themselves.

This section as noted earlier, is known as "behind the Barns," or as the

"Barns Pools," which they are not, being deep, very swift, rocky runs with boulder-rubble bottoms. The name "Barns" comes from the fact that in the days when the auto bus replaced the stagecoaches that used to haul the Union Pacific passengers from the depot in West Yellowstone into the Park, the old stables and barns that once housed the horses and coaches were remodeled to handle the buses. They are gone now, both buses and buildings, but the name remains.

The "holes" are prosaically named Hole Number One, Hole Number Two, and Hole Number Three, the one I was fishing in the opening chapter. The name hole comes from the fact the river deepens suddenly from the long stretches of knee-deep riffle, and the bottom drops away into deep boulder filled channels, four to five feet deep in places.

Fishing a floating line in Hole Number One on the Madison in the Park is not the best way to go. You must get down to the fish in these fast runs.

The trout lie behind the boulders that break the racing flow of the current; the depth and broken surface make them feel secure, and they do not have to move far to dine. The bottom of this entire stretch contains millions of *Pteronarcys* and *Acroneuria* stonefly nymphs, the largest of their kind in North America.

From my own experience, I've seen only brown and rainbow trout, sculpins and whitefish in this stretch, and this is perturbing because suckers exist naturally in the river below Hebgen Dam, and were reported from this very stretch some forty years ago. Yet in thirty years of seriously fishing here, I have never seen one, nor have any of my friends or angling companions. My several biological studies, done by the U.S. Fish and Wildlife Service, which manage the streams in the Park, make no mention of suckers here, nor does the booklet *Yellowstone Fish and Fishing* by biologist E. Phillip Sharpe. Since these are thorough and official documents, I wonder about the suckers.

The little longnose dace is a sometime resident of this area; it prefers shallow, swift, gravelly stretches and is fed upon by the trout. The only specimen I have ever seen was in the belly of a two-pound brown some years ago. However, their presence may be responsible for the effectiveness of the Spruce streamer, which takes some very good fish from these waters as do the Brown and Green Marabou Muddlers.

This is my favorite water. It is just ten miles by road and one or two miles along the stream from my home. I have met more knowledgeable anglers along this stretch of river than anyplace else I've ever fished. Its appeal is partly in knowing that knowledge of the water is required, and that the huge *Acroneuria* and *Pteronarcys* nymphs are present at all times.

These nymphs have caused some controversy among entomologists. One group says that *Acroneuria* is a two-year species and *Pteronarcys* a three-year species; another group says they are three and four-year species. The difference is partly one of attitude, partly one of fact. The attitude of the two and three-year believers is that we are talking only about the life of the *nymph* in the stream; the other group insists that the aquatic life spans runs from when the eggs are laid until the adults emerge. On the latter basis, the species have three and four-year life spans, because the egg will sometimes take from six weeks to eleven months to hatch. There is no known cause for this, but it happens, and it varies by stream and place. I have studied these large insects rather closely for about fifteen years and my studies support the latter theory.

This entire stretch is fast, powerful water, running three to six miles an hour over very rough bottoms. It is not dangerous to wade but it is difficult. A wading staff is an excellent piece of equipment to have along here.

The river moves through the widening meadows in sweeping curves, and there are islands and channels that must be explored. This is the living river at its liveliest, carving away at bed and bottom, moving its channel from place to place, removing material here, depositing it there, growing and changing like a teenage child. Part of its fascination is that one must constantly relearn its holds and lies to be aware of where the fish are.

The meadows flanking this stretch are loaded with wild mint; in spring and summer the tangy smell pervades the area. It is refreshing to chew, and on occasion I gather a large clump to put in my desert water-bag creel, well dampened to keep the mint fresh and crisp for the sour-mash juleps I relish.

More and more, the willow begins to appear, spotty and in clumps, as the river approaches the upper end of the Madison Basin. There are beaver holes along the bank, but in such areas of fast-moving water, this admirable creature does not build dams but carves caves out some feet back from the river edge, with tunnels leading from the river. Near the bank edge, he will drill an escape shaft from the tunnel to the surface, and these pose a definite threat to the welfare of the angler. I have fallen in them a thousand times.

In August of 1974, I fell into what I hope was my last one, injuring myself so badly that I wound up in the hospital for a month. During the time I was there a rather amusing incident occurred that might give some insight into how nonfishermen regard anglers.

The hospital was in Ashton, Idaho, about a mile from the Henrys Fork and not over twenty from the famous Railroad Ranch fly-fishing section. During my stay in the hospital, many friends and correspondents fished the river and during the middle of the day when things slowed, someone invariably would say, "Let's go see Charlie."

They would come in groups of three or four, in full regalia, waders dripping slime and algae through the halls, nets dangling, hats a-bristle with flies, and plop into my room like a group of deflated Michelin tire men. Then they would stay for three or four hours, regardless of visiting rules, before departing for the stream.

For about two weeks this parade of strange-looking and oddly accoutered men traipsed through the hospital. Finally, this drew a reaction.

I was sitting in a chair one day while a young nurse's aide made up my bed. By her expression, I could tell she had something serious on her mind, and after a while she turned to me, with a questioning look and asked, "Mr. Brooks, don't you know any *real* people?"

My advice is quite serious to the visiting angler: beware of those beaver holes. They are fortunately few along this stretch, but the next water, the Beaver Meadows reach, is boggy, marshy, and loaded with tunnels and escape holes. Go warily in this section. Keep your eye on the trail along the bank and not on the lovely water or it is all Wall Street to a rotten apple you will go crashing into one of these deadly traps.

The pools of the Beaver Meadows are wide and deep, connected by narrower, swifter sections that are more productive although the fish are not so large. The largest one will get in these faster sections will be about three pounds; the deep pools have surrendered trout to eleven pounds, but such fish are not plentiful.

The river winds like ribbon Christmas candy in this area; there are oxbows and channels, islands and cutoffs, and the river has the appearance of a typical basin delta stream, which hydrologists describe as braided.

The main aquatic nymphs are dragon and damselfly, small silt-dwelling mayfly, and tiny caddis. The mayfly is often *Tricorythodes*, that strange little creature that will hatch, molt, mate, and die all within the same half hour. If you can arrange to be at the exact spot on the stream at the exact right time, rigged for dry-fly fishing, you can have a furious few minutes during which every fish in the river appears to be active.

This is a most attractive stretch of river, one of the few areas where the mountains can be seen in all directions, close enough to be clearly discerned in detail but far enough away not to give a closed-in feeling.

To the east the rounded peaks of the Washburn Range stride away to the north. Though Mt. Holmes, Dome Mountain, The Crags, and Crowfoot Ridge appear a solid chain, they are all well separated; and passes are low and open, attesting to the truth of Jim Bridger's remark to an Army survey team in the 1850s that one could cross from Targhee Pass to the Yellowstone without having to cross any mountains.

Targhee Peak is to the west; it is the highest peak in the Henrys Lake Mountains, where I live. These are serrated peaks for the most part—except for Baldy—jagged and ledge scarred. Lionhead, Sheep, and Coffin stretch away to form the southwestern flank of the Madison Canyon. Beyond, the subranges of the Madison Range—Tepee, Hildgard, and Monument Ridge— run northeast by north to form the spine between the Madison and the Gallatin rivers. The Gallatin Range, a high lofty ridge, comes down to the edge of the Madison Basin, finishing an encirclement that is complete except for the narrow winding gap of the Madison Canyon.

The tall meadow grasses make the area into a waist-high green sea in spring, when the willows also are the same rich green. In the fall, the willows are brilliant yellow, like splashes of sunlight among the tawny grasses. Beyond, the sagebrush silvers the benches; behind them the lodgepoles stand black and dense. Over all loom the mountains, like giant ice-cream cones, white on top, pink and beige down to the timberline.

The buffalo and elk are busy adding to the coat of hard tallow that will see them through the winter. The moose is here year around; they and beaver will

A herd of buffalo to gladden the eye of the Indian or trapper. It is not safe to approach these animals on foot closer than this.

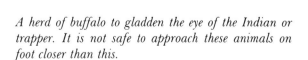

be found cheek by jowl throughout the northern Rockies, for their needs are mutual. The grizzly roams and lives here in spite of the town and highway only a few miles away. No fisherman has ever been harmed by one, and they are usually quietly gone before the angler is aware of them.

Coyotes lounge on the faces of the sloping benches, ducks flap and quack in the pools, the spotted sandpipers flit and bob along the stream edges. I have seen the downy chicks of this bird trotting fearlessly through the sagebrush a half-mile from the stream, no bigger than a fuzzy ping-pong ball, completely at ease and going about their business with total confidence. Such sights often remind me how great it is to be a fisherman.

The end of the Beaver Meadows comes just at the Park's west boundary, at famed Baker's Hole, a deep, gliding, curved meadow pool, the lower end nestling into the encroaching lodgepoles. It is a tremendous trout factory, and the home of monstrous trout. There is a USFS campground on the banks of the Hole and camper's children swim and cavort in the pool by day. Still, as the orange disk of the sun slips behind the shoulder of the mountain and the long summer twilight settles upon the land, bringing out the myriads of mosquitoes and driving the tourists to cover, the big trout will commence sipping inconspicuously along the bank, and one's prospects are actually enhanced by the daytime activities, which have kept the trout from feeding.

The water slides out of Baker's Hole, around a curve, under the 191 highway bridge and slips into the estuary of Hebgen Lake. The length of this estuary is always some miles, due to the shape of the basin floor, but its actual length is dependent upon the level of the lake, which is low in fall, high in spring.

The estuary is the playground of the "gulper" fishermen, that silent and secretive (some say shifty) breed of men who gather in the dawn and twilight with their giant inner tubes and tiny flies to join in this exasperating, frustrating—and highly satisfying—form of fly fishing, nationally known, and practiced almost exclusively here.

The canal-like section of placid, secretive Duck Creek in the Madison Basin. The usual fall haze obscures the mountains.

Do not expect a gulper to tell you about his form of madness, nor to offer any information on the fishing any more reliable than the chant of a Florida swamp-land salesman. These fellows have a lodge, complete with a code, password, secret grip, and a stylized line of misinformation that may even be copyrighted. Some of them are my good friends; I would, and have, loaned them my car, my rod, my waders, and extended the hospitality of bed and board. I would not believe the finest of them on a stack of bibles Dwight Stones couldn't leap over if they are talking about gulper fishing.

The Madison has three major tributaries feeding into Hebgen Lake; of course, they ran into the river before Hebgen Dam was built. They are dissimilar streams and one of them, Duck Creek, is the strangest trout stream in my experience.

The Duck is a different stream for most of its length, from its beginning where the waters of Gneiss, Campanula, and Richards creeks come together to form the Duck in the flat upper reaches of the Madison Basin. It runs through a bunchgrass meadow, so calm and placid, so quiet and still that it seems to have no character at all, and all anglers I have known, myself included, have misjudged it terribly. It is a very fine trout stream but one that takes some knowing.

Gneiss and Campanula creeks come in from the east on a ring of water that is totally unique in my experience; I know of no other stream in this country or others where a stream or streams form a complete circle. Richards Creek joins the circle on the south and Duck Creek glides away to the west, sole nominee of the waters.

It is a very winding stream, with almost no gradient at this point, and this combined with its sand-silt bottom, creates a stream that appears uninteresting. Do not be fooled. The Duck is a startling trout stream. It has produced browns to eight pounds and contains many rainbows two pounds and larger.

Duck Creek is not rich water, compared to the Firehole and Gibbon, and the Madison itself, but it is not poor water, either. It averages about forty parts per million of calcium bicarbonates and thus is classed as medium rich. It is cool and stable, seldom topping 66° F. even in a very hot summer, is well supplied with oxygen, and though its insect structure is limited, it is sufficient to maintain the fish in excellent flesh.

Mostly, the aquatic insects are small, but two exceptions are dragon and damselfly nymphs, both large and preferred food by trout. I have caught browns here stuffed to the gills with dragonfly nymphs and have become so bemused by two-pound rainbows stalking my Light Assam Dragon nymph across the mud flats that I forgot to strike when they finally pounced on it.

The smooth-water section lies in the Park in deep grass meadows, the banks willow-lined and undercut. The willows are seldom close enough to the banks or dense enough to create problems for the angler. The water has long stretches of shallows; it slides around the heads of the bends, and there on the outside will be a dropoff of three or four feet and the clear water will appear suddenly black.

The trout lie here, in a pecking order of size and caste—a smaller brown trout will crowd ahead of larger rainbows and occupy the choicest areas. Which of these fish one catches depends largely on the choice of fly and how quickly it drops over the edge of the ledge.

Dry flies for most of the season should be small and a caddis imitation is better than a mayfly. Most of the better hatches will be between dusk and nightfall.

In late July and August the grassy meadows are alive with grasshoppers. These creatures range to over two inches long, dusty tan to dark grey in color, with orange wing liners. When they start up out of the grass with a fierce rattling crackle, your heart will jump, but there are no poisonous snakes in this angler's Eden and you may walk and fish at ease, looking only at the lovely water and watching for the big fish that come to your Dave's Hopper or other bold imitation. They seem to know that you mean them no harm and that you wish them well, to be released to go and grow larger and beget their kind so that when you or your children come again, the charm will still hold.

Just below the Park boundary there are huge beaver dams and one small

Duck Creek at its glassy, difficult best—or worst—where it exits the Park.

man-made affair that is seldom closed. The deep, algae and insect rich water here holds huge brood fish, browns as big as cocker spaniels and smaller but more plentiful rainbows. These fish pour out of the ponds in spring and fall, running to spawn in the rocky narrows of Gneiss and Campanula creeks, which ordinarily hold no fish of catching size. They run to a lesser extent in Richards Creek, but far more of them remain there; it is a truly excellent small trout stream with many good holds and lies in deep pockets, beneath under-cut willow-covered banks and under the frequent drift piles.

Richards Creek rises in Richards Springs, dammed by beavers long ago trapped out, leaving one of the loveliest backwoods spring ponds anywhere. It lies deep in a dense lodgepole forest that has not seen fire since the early 1800s when it was part of the area known by trappers as the Burnt Hole. It is pure hell to get to overland and you never get there up the creek itself because you are constantly coming upon spots so fishy that no angler, however stouthearted and determined, can possibly pass them by.

You will possibly see the secretive grizzly back in these dense woods along the creek; moose are frequently encountered, and buffalo and elk will graze peacefully in the meadows. The cheeky pine squirrel or chickaree and the bold Clark's nutcracker will spur you on your fishing rounds with their noisy admonitions until you leave the deep woods.

The beaver ponds on the Duck have beaver, ducks, and other waterfowl, and there are now many houses built and being built in this scenic basin area with towering mountains looming wherever you look. This stretch along Duck Creek is one of the few pockets of private land between the National Forest and the National Park; it is choice—and expensive. But no lovelier area to live in can be found anywhere.

Where it slides under the 191 highway bridge and wanders off toward Hebgen Lake, the Duck is deceptive, resembling any small, pretty, gravel-bottomed, riffle-and-run trout stream. But it is no more out of sight than it changes back into its still, stealthy, gentle character.

It flows in winding fashion through a narrow little valley that is occasionally boggy and marshy, dotted with willows. On the right a high bench of sagebrush and pasture leads off to the north and Grayling Creek. On the left, the bench is covered densely by the ubiquitous lodgepoles along the northern base of Horse Butte. The fish from Hebgen are often in this stretch and if the water level of the lake is propitious, one can get into a really big trout of an evening.

It is more than a day's fishing from the highway to the lake—in airline distance only two miles, but due to its winding nature, more than twice that along the stream. In summer the mosquitoes will all but carry you off, and occasionally a moose will bar your way, questioning your right to be in *his* willow patch. Ducks are plentiful, their presence having given the stream its name, and Canada geese are frequent, grazing in the pastures on the north bench.

Elk and deer both browse and graze in the area and come of evenings to drink from the stream. The osprey and his nemesis, the bald eagle, will both be seen, the whistle of the redtail hawk will be with you as he glides and soars so high in the blue as to be indiscernible unless your eyesight is equal to his. Seagulls and shore birds; curlews, avocets, killdeers, sandpiper, and snipe have their haunts in this area; grouse will flush at times; and coyotes are almost insolent as they perform the necessary balancing of nature.

There are dirt roads that leave the highways and go down to the stream.

Richards Springs, perhaps the loveliest backwoods pond ever created.

The highways are 191, under which the creek runs, and 287, a quarter-mile beyond, which turns off left and goes along the shore of the lake, to Quake Lake and then Ennis. If the weather has been dry, these dirt roads furnish safe but rough passage to the lower Duck. If it has been raining, however, forget it. Many's the angler who has had to send to West Yellowstone for a tow truck when caught by a thundershower on the benches of the lower Duck.

The second tributary of the river, the South Fork of the Madison, rises some fifteen miles to the south and west of the Duck and runs in a looping curve, northeast and then northwest to enter Hebgen Lake in a deep mile-long estuary known as the South Fork Arm. The source of the South Fork is in the Henrys Lake Mountains, which form the Continental Divide and the border between Idaho and Montana, thus the river commences just six miles along the mountains south of my home. It crosses the highway from West Yellowstone to Idaho Falls (191) four miles from the former and three from my house. It is the closest major trout stream to where I live, and one would think that I would spend much time here, but I do not, even though it harbors many trout and large ones. An eleven-pound brown was taken on a dry fly from the deep pool under the old airport-road bridge and an eighteen-pounder came out of the estuary some years ago.

The fellow who caught the latter fish was a local angler, and he carried it up and down all the streets of West Yellowstone until finally people began to rib him about it. But he quickly squelched his hecklers with that old Chinese proverb: "Man who catch big fish *not* come home through alley."

From its source near the old Johnson mine to the mouth of Mosquito Gulch (how aptly named!) the South Fork is a tiny clattering mountain brook, pretty but not fishworthy. After the influx of Mosquito Creek, it becomes, for a ways, a charming mountain creek of riffles and pools, in a typically lovely mountain setting. This is an immensely popular stretch; there is a state campground here and angling pressure drives the larger fish downstream to deeper water.

The next few miles is dramatically different water, of willow marsh-swamp origin. It is extremely winding, almost impossible to reach in most areas, though the road is nearby, and one must proceed *in* the stream to move either up or down. Under the willow-root mats on the outside of the bends are caverns, deep and mysterious; since the other side will usually be shallow enough to wade easily, one tacks along from side to side like a sailing ship, keeping to the shallow side and fishing the deep.

It is difficult work, and even if one hooks a fish every few casts the odds are always with it. One cannot hold the more sizable ones away from the roots, and some of the smaller ones cause panic by darting out, hitting the fly, vaulting into the air and dropping through the overhanging limbs.

The fish are brown and rainbow, with now and then a whitefish. Grayling were native once in this stream, as they were in the entire Madison drainage below the falls of the Firehole and Gibbon, but they are rarely seen these days. But if this charming and beautiful fish has almost disappeared, this is balanced by the virtual disappearance of the mountain sucker, which were also native to these waters.

The rarity of the grayling and its willingness to take the fly, as well as its beauty and succulence as a pan fish, add to the charm of the fishing, and here in the South Fork, with bighorn sheep present in the nearby Henrys Lake Mountains, one may experience, as did Robert Service, in *Spell of the Yukon:*

> *The summer—no sweeter was ever;*
> *The sunshiny woods all athrill;*
> *The grayling aleap in the river,*
> *The bighorn asleep on the hill."*

The winding willow-lined character of the South Fork is maintained for most of its length. The spring-fed bogs and marshes keep the level and temperature constant, the most prolonged runoff barely tinging the crystal clarity of this icy stream, and the many secure holds under the willow roots all combine to make it home for many fine large trout. The willows crowd so closely and densely along the banks that one's backcast must of necessity be kept up or down the stream, and the curves are so close upon one another that the cast must be short.

The river is seldom over twenty feet wide most places, so the short backcast is not the handicap it might be elsewhere. A greater handicap is the size of the insects, small caddis and mayfly. Hook size fourteen is normally as large as is used except in the estuary and the last mile before it, and leaders of 3 and 4X are necessary. This is a major factor favoring the fish, and lending tenseness and excitement to the fishing. At any time a brown of unbelievable proportions can take your fly and vanish back into his root-lined cavern before you're aware he's there. And there is almost no way one can be assured of getting him to come out. I have played them for nearly an hour, my rod under water and most of my person immersed only to have them make a downstream run among the haystack tangle of roots and limbs, weave my line and leader among them and break off, leaving me unsure if I still had a fish, or a tough root or limber limb. But if your frustration threshold is high, by all means come and challenge the trout of the willow sections of the South Fork.

About a mile before it enters the estuary of the South Fork Arm of Hebgen, the river slips out of the willows into a broad meadow, widens and slows up. It retains its icy temperatures and crystal clarity but becomes somewhat easier to fish, and one does not have to fight the willows, which on the regions upstream are a veritable witches' forest of tangles.

The meadow section receives heavy play from both local and visiting anglers; the dirt road that has been paralleling the river from Highway 191 downstream makes a big curve out of the lodgepole flat and comes out on the grassy knoll above the meadows. Fish from the lake frequently come up this far to feed and the insect hatches are more plentiful and reliable. Almost every evening in summer there will be a hatch and a rise, and although many of the fish will be small ones, one cannot count on it completely. Al McClane once wrote of taking a number of four to seven-pound fish from this stretch and a local angler named Glenn Goff once showed me a catch of sixteen trout averaging four pounds each, which he and three friends had taken here in a few hours on the locally popular Goofus Bug.

The estuary, flanked by a high bank on the right, is a popular spot for bait fishermen whose chairs and poles and beer coolers will be much in evidence. But twilight usually finds them gone, and the fly fishermen will be busy plying their subtle trade although in the fall there will be little of subtlety about it.

At this time, really big fish circulate from the lake through the estuary and the streamer fishermen catch them on big 2/0 and 3/0 streamers, Dark Spruce, Spuddler, Green and Brown Marabou Muddlers and big tarpon-sized bucktails. They do not often catch many fish, since none of such size are resident here, but the ones they do catch are nearly always "braggin " fish.

The South Fork divides easily into four sections for the angler. The upper section, from Mosquito Gulch to the old airport-road bridge, is about three-and-a-half airline miles long, but the stream is more than twice that length. The first half-mile below the state campground is beautiful, gravel-bottomed, riffle-and-pool mountain stream, a delight to fish. But the rest of this section is willow-beaver swamp, and is best fished after the middle of July.

The insect structure of this upper piece of water is totally different from that of the rest of the stream, due to current speed and the nature of the bottom, which is gravel-rubble. Downstream, the bottom is sand-silt and this is not the preferred habitat of many aquatic insect species. The upper section holds stonefly nymphs, large caddis, good-sized mayfly and few blackfly, whereas downstream, blackfly, midge, small caddis, and tiny mayflies predominate. The pool-riffle design gives trout ideal feeding and holding places, and before this stretch was overrun with visitors, it was possible to see and count two hundred or more fish of one and two pounds on any good day.

The fish have not been caught out—it is almost impossible to do that on a good trout stream and the South Fork is a fine one. The fish have been *driven* out, downstream to bigger water and better, more secure hiding places.

The second section of the stream runs about four miles from the old airport-road bridge to highway 191. The latter two miles runs through private property, the Madison Fork Ranch, an old and honored guest ranch for the more affluent. This property has been maintained with care for the environment for over fifty years and this concern has helped to maintain the quality of the fishery both above and below.

The South Fork is not a navigable stream by any definition and thus both the banks and bed of the stream belong to the ranch owners, and trespass is forbidden. Only the upper two miles of this stretch is public water.

There is a large National Forest campground just below the highway, excellently located, with spacious camping areas among the lodgepole forest, and easy access to the stream just at and below the camp. This is a particularly good area for both the fly fisher and the animal lover. It is a major crossing point for moose moving from the upper to the lower river, and every spring, on one or other of my trips to town, I will see a female moose, that homeliest and best of wild mothers, leading her gangling, knobby-legged calves across the highway to the willow cafeteria downstream.

Pine squirrels pester the campers for tidbits, gray jay (whisky jack, Canada jay, or camp robber) and the Clark's nutcracker will literally swoop down and take food from the picnicker's lips. Most any day the observant can see the osprey at work, while deer will come to the stream at nightfall, as will his larger cousin, the wapiti or elk. Porcupines and skunks love a campground in the trees, and bears will make an occasional foray to raid the garbage cans; even that shy creature of the deep forest, the pine marten, can be seen peering 'round a stump or log, his weasel's face a picture of interest and curiosity.

Grouse are cyclically abundant. Ruffed and spruce, or Franklin's grouse, are local, but the larger and more prolific blue grouse seldom descends to this 6,700-foot elevation. When the grouse are prevalent, both lynx and coyote will be also, and when the grouse mysteriously vanish, as they do regularly, the two predators turn their attention to muskrat and beaver, or leave the country.

From the campground, the river pursues its winding way, the lodgepole forest on the bench to the right, the meadows of the Madison Basin opening up to the left, and the willows, if anything, becoming thicker and more tangled. It is about four miles to the estuary, but three times that around the bends of the river. This is the most winding stream I have ever seen, including the many mouths of the Yukon, and a good angler could not fish all of it in less than two weeks.

Except for the willows along the bank, and a short meadow section, the South Fork lies in a dense lodgepole forest; its watershed is 80 percent covered by this and it has not been touched by fire for over a hundred years. Some clearcut logging has been done, about 1955 to 1960, but only a small percentage of the watershed has been affected.

The yearly precipitation averages sixty inches of moisture in the upper watershed and thirty inches in the lower. Snowpack averages three hundred along the divide and down to the state campground area; below here, two hundred inches of snow is normal.

The undamaged watershed releases this tremendous amount of moisture slowly. The bogs and swamps along the watercourse swallow most runoff, and the stream is fed by hundreds of springs, which originate a few yards from the stream, with temperatures in the low fifties. The water level and temperature are thus more constant on this stream than in any other tributary of the Madison.

The marsh-swamp springs are acid; rain and snow water percolating down through decaying vegetation picks up carbon dioxide, creating carbonic acid. The South Fork has little limestone in its lower reaches, so it seldom tops forty parts per million of carbonate minerals and thus is not as rich as other tributaries in this area. The temperature seldom goes higher than the low sixties, the water is always saturated with oxygen, and this stability makes up for any mineral shortages. It is a truly excellent small river and its constancy of volume has a very beneficial effect on the Madison despite three dams below the outlet of the South Fork.

There is a small group of summer homes located in the National Forest just above the old airport-road bridge, another group on private land across from the Forest Service campground, and a couple of ranches flanking the stream. For the most part, these have affected the stream only slightly. At present no significant erosion or pollution is caused by these and since most everyone who lives along the stream does so because of the total environment, it does not appear that there is any future danger to the river from man.

Grayling Creek, the third of the major tributaries in the Madison Basin, rises back in Yellowstone Park at about 7,700 feet; thus, in a fifteen-mile (airline) run, it drops 1,200 feet before entering Hebgen Lake. The last three miles lie in the floor of the basin and are of very low gradient; the stream here is very meandered, a typically braided delta stream.

The upper ten miles is mountain-type stream entirely; a survey in the late sixties notes a 25:1 ratio of riffles to pools. This survey also noted there were practically no fish in this ten-mile stretch and gave as probable cause angling and predator pressure that had caused the fish to move downstream to deeper water and more secure holds. There is a low falls about two miles from the lower end of this stretch and the stream above here is literally barren.

From this little unnamed falls down to Grayling Falls, about three miles, there is an increase in the numbers of fish but they are still far from plentiful. Angling pressure on this section has almost ceased and the fish are slowly making a comeback.

Below Grayling Falls, the creek runs quickly out of its canyon and onto the floor of the Basin. All but the last three miles, lying between highway 287 and Hebgen Lake, is on private land. The public-land section runs in several winding channels that come together to form one just as it enters the Grayling Arm of the lake. It should be remembered that all of these tributaries' entry into the lake are greatly affected by the level of the lake. In times of drought there will be several miles of mudflat from the erstwhile shoreline to the edge of the lake. Such a drought had been expected for some years by area climatologists. It came in 1977.

The Grayling contributes a natural form of pollution to the lake. It cuts through rich deposits of nitrate and phosphate, and the resulting "fertilization" settles out quickly into the Grayling Arm of the lake, causing an intense algae growth. In summer this is dense enough to cause a smothering effect and the chances of a good fish entering the river from the lake is far less than at other times. Far more deleterious effects came in the summer of 1977.

In the fall a good run of browns go up as far as Grayling Falls, but due to private property beyond the highway bridge, one has to intercept this run in the willow flats. The fishing here has problems—sometimes boggy banks, the crowding willows, many dead willows in the water, and the fluctuating level of the lake. These are too much for the average angler, who is more likely to seek easier and more open waters, leaving the lower Grayling for the patient and solitary.

The proximity of the highway, some noisy resorts, and the flat, open area result in their being few animals in this section; the birds are mostly shorebirds, gulls or willow tits. This is also one of the few areas where one will see small garter and grass snakes and leopard frogs. The cold, long, and intense winters strictly limit reptiles and amphibians in the Madison Basin. Just what factors favor their existence here I do not know.

The climate in Yellowstone Park along the Madison headwaters, and of the Madison Basin, is different from that of the surrounding areas; it is, in fact, a microclimate. It has longer, colder winters, shorter, cooler summers, and considerably more snow.

The cause is the mountain ranges that ring both the Park and the Basin. These are the highest in the area, and each consists of a single series of peaks in a long ridge, ranging roughly north to south. They might be described as tall but thin, and these two factors cause the severe climate between the Henrys Lake–Madison Ranges on the west and the Absaroka–Wind River Ranges on the east.

The weather fronts come from the northwest, from the Gulf of Alaska. When they reach the mountains, these fronts—or air masses—are thrust sharply upward, causing the air to be quickly cooled. Warmer air rising from the interior basin-plateau areas is chilled by mingling with this much cooler air, moisture is condensed and precipitated out, and at the same time, the cold air settles into the basins. There is no long "slide" down gradual slopes that would allow warming, and the area averages some ten degrees cooler than surrounding areas. The snowpack is much heavier.

The snowpack for the headwaters of the Firehole–Gibbon averages three hundred inches, as do the inward facing slopes of the surrounding ranges. The floor of Madison Basin averages two hundred inches, whereas the middle Madison Valley averages from one hundred inches in the upper end to less than twenty at the head of Beartrap Canyon. From the mouth of Beartrap Canyon to Three Forks the snowpack drops off to practically nothing.

The temperature ranges are similarly different. At Riverside, a gauging station on the Madison in the Cable Car Run section, a Park Service weather station, recorded a temperature of 66° F. below zero in 1933. The coldest ever recorded at Three Forks is 40° warmer. Three Forks is about one hundred and twenty miles north, but is some 2,600 feet lower. However, temperatures just on the west side of the Madison Range are so much warmer than those of the Madison Basin that it is difficult to comprehend. I have left the Basin in winter to fish the Madison above Ennis and found temperature differences of 40 to 60°. In summer when it is 78° in the Basin, it will be nearly 100° at Three Forks.

Though we are largely concerned with the Madison watershed, it should be noted that these temperatures and moisture differences occur no matter which direction one goes from the Basin–Park area—it will be warmer and drier, whether winter or summer. The area is the first to be snowbound in winter, the last to be snowfree in spring, and this, more than any single factor, caused its late discovery and exploration.

The impact of people on the area, though considerable, is more esthetic than physical. Old Faithful sees about 2,000,000 visitors a year, but careful planning keeps them in a blacktopped area near the geyser. This area is largely covered by impervious siliceous sinter, much of which still shows through in open areas; thus degradation of the watershed is slight. Street and highway runoff is detrimental if it gets quickly into a stream, but the mount built up by Old Faithful and other thermal features channels this runoff into a meadow area between the river and Iron Creek. It has nearly a mile of meadow to percolate through to reach the latter stream and is consequently purified to the extent of being harmless.

Three-quarters of a million cars annually pass by the main intersection at Madison Junction, and many visitors linger in the area. Runoff from the highways carries some hydrocarbons and tetra ethyl lead into the stream but at present these levels are not damaging. But lead is long lived and it may build up in the meadows around the junction to a point that stream channeling could cut into deposits of sufficient virulence to cause damage to insects and fish. This is not presently considered likely, only a possibility.

The large campground of nearly three hundred spaces at Madison Junction is an immensely popular spot, and from mid-June to mid-August it will be jammed. The area in and around the campground has been severely degraded. This comprises perhaps forty acres, about one-eight-thousandth of the watershed. It is probable that the present level of use and degradation will remain relatively constant; there is little likelihood of its being lessened.

The area of Madison Basin is subjected to considerable impact from people, but largely this is due to the proximity of Yellowstone Park, and, to a much greater extent, Hebgen Lake. Since there are three lakes along the river, a full treatment of them will be taken up in the next chapter.

DAMS AND LAKES

HEBGEN LAKE* LIES AT THE FOOT OF THE MADISON BASIN, ITS DAM ACROSS THE head of Madison Canyon. It is a large lake, some sixteen miles long, four miles wide at its widest, and eighty-one feet deep at the dam face. It impounds, at full pool, 386,000 acre-feet of water; thus it is quite deep on the average. It belongs to The Montana Power Company.

Hebgen Dam was commenced in 1909 and completed in 1915. Inundated by the gathering waters were the main channel of the Madison and the confluence channels of the South Fork, Duck, and Grayling creeks, and a dozen lesser streams whose channels form a dendritic pattern on the present lake bottom. Also flooded was the village of Grayling, composed of a post office and a few other buildings.

Whether there was any opposition to the dam at the time of its building is not recorded. There were several miles of prime trout stream, and some thousands of acres of grazing land that would be flooded—but opposition to such projects in those days was almost totally absent.

If the dam were to be built today there would be a nationwide uproar, and the flooding of that trout stream and those grazing acres would be treated as an ecological disaster of catastrophic proportions. However, since the dam was completed over sixty years ago, we can now look at the evidence calmly and determine if any measurable catastrophe has occurred.

The trout-stream mileage has been irreplaceably destroyed as a *trout*

*Named for the engineer who designed and supervised the building of the dam that created the lake.

stream—or *streams*—since some miles of the Duck, Grayling, and South Fork also lie under the waters of Hebgen Lake. This would cause proponents of trout streams to cry havoc, but what about the lake? All trout fishermen do not necessarily care to fish in streams; a great many prefer lakes.

Then there are other benefits to the vacationer—swimming, a national pastime; boating, water-skiing, and a stable shoreline on which many homes with a lake front and a mountain backdrop can be and have been built. On the basis of taking something from some while providing something else for some others, more people have benefitted from the recreational opportunities provided by the lake than have been deprived by the loss of the stream mileage. I may be drummed out of the ecological protection society for such remarks, but I deplore stupidity and obsessive reaction to change as much as I deplore a "the public be damned" attitude. Both are archaic and neither is useful.

The grazing land now flooded by the lake was covered by five to ten feet of snow in the winter; thus it was *summer* grazing land only. One cannot ranch in this country without having a viable winter range and none exists or has ever existed in the Madison Basin. All cattle and horses summer grazed here have to be driven or trucked elsewhere come late fall. It was and is being done but there was and is more summer graze in this area than needed to balance the available winter range. The loss of this grazing land, then, was not a large economic or ecological factor, when the dam was built, or now.

As far as scenic beauty, few lakes more beautiful than Hebgen exist anywhere. Its location is superb, its size, shape, and clear blue waters are a joy to the eye. Certainly it is not a trout stream, and for those who love streams, as I do, a lake cannot replace one. But a trout stream is not a lake, and for those who love lakes, the Montana Power Company has created a beautiful one, and one whose total benefits outweigh the benefits destroyed by creation of the lake.

The lake and dam were not intended for the local production of electrical energy. It is a storage facility to provide a regulated flow of water to dams and generators on the Missouri River many miles away. In past years it has been operated with only the thought to provide water when needed to keep electrical supply and demand in balance. This has resulted in some temporary damage to the Madison River fishery and to the banks and flood plain when water was held back or released at the wrong time. The Montana Power Company is not wholly responsible for these damages—they were operating as a matter of course and not in defiance of the laws of man or nature. There was no public outcry or governmental agency to draw attention to such damages.

The Montana Department of Fish and Game was beginning, in the 1960s, to assess some of the damages caused by this legal but thoughtless operation of the dam. It had no legal standing at the time and sought to have the power company cooperate in its own best interest. The company, as do nearly all such companies, resisted any changes in its operation, and there did not appear to be any way to alter its thinking.

Then, in 1970, a heavy winter snowpack, wetter than usual, followed by a wet, early spring, caused a heavy runoff at the time when Hebgen Lake was at full pool. This resulted in a large release of water from the lake. Severe damage to the flood plain below Quake Lake occurred, a portion of the highway there was washed away, some private property was damaged, and the spring spawning run of trout was destroyed. The total damage was estimated at $3,000,000.

Several state agencies, private-property owners whose land and buildings were damaged, and guides and outfitters whose income was reduced because of the overabundance of water, banded together and threatened to sue the Montana Power Company for criminal negligence for releasing extra water when the river was already at peak flood stage.

The suit was never filed but the threat—and attendant publicity—caused a definite change in the company's policy. It now cooperates and coordinates water releases, whenever possible, to accommodate the Fish and Game and other state departments. This arrangement has cost the company no money, and only some minor inconvenience. It has benefitted both the fish and the landowners, in that the former face only normal high water at spawning time, and the latter are safer from flooding. In short, all parties have benefitted from more intelligent operation of the dam, and no party has suffered.

Disregarding its role in producing essential power for electricity, Hebgen Lake has produced other benefits than the ones already discussed. The Madison River, because of the input of thermal features from its two major sources, the Firehole and Gibbon, has on occasion become too warm for best trout growth and reproduction. Below Hebgen Dam the cold water pouring from the tailrace chilled the water to the extent that the stretch from the dam to Ennis Lake, about sixty miles of river, was held at almost optimum temperatures until the forming of Quake Lake. The water coming from Hebgen is still cold, but now the water reaching the Madison is off the top warmer layer of Quake Lake and this has caused a raising of the temperature of the river.

Another benefit of Hebgen not widely known is the fact that it forms a reservoir for brood fish to replenish the streams leading into it—Grayling, Duck, the South Fork, and the Madison itself. In the spring and fall these fat fish pour out of Hebgen and up these four streams. And not just any four trout streams but four of the best and most beautiful trout streams in all America. Yet, without the brood fish of Hebgen, they would not be nearly so well supplied with trout, and the spawning runners are large fish and in splendid condition. Many remain in the streams after completing their reproductive duties, and keep the head of sizable trout at excellent levels. The very reputation of these streams is founded on the riches in the depths of Hebgen Lake.

The richness of the lake is legend, and the streams feeding it are responsible for it. However, there can be too much of a good thing. I mentioned earlier that Grayling Creek cut through beds of natural phosphates and nitrates, which it gave up in the estuary to the lake known as the Grayling Arm. In ordinary years these minerals caused only an enrichment of the lake water that resulted in much algae growth. Normally, this growth is not only harmless but beneficial.

But 1977 was not a normal year. A severe shortfall of snow in the surrounding mountains produced drought conditions that led to a considerable drop in stream levels and a warming of the water. Grayling Arm is a baylike body of water that enters Hebgen Lake through an opening which the late Vint Johnson appropriately called The Narrows, by which name it is still known. This restricted flow, drought conditions, and warming of the water produced ideal conditions for algae "blooming" and bloom it did with disastrous results.

The blooming algae released a toxic material allied to saxitoxin, the poisonous product of the famous and deadly "red tide"—the microscopic organisms known scientifically as *Gymnodinium brevis,* which have been responsible for enormous fish kills in the ocean. But the fresh-water algae's toxins are not harmful to fish, only mammals; over one hundred animals died in the summer of 1977 from drinking the water of the Grayling Arm. Among these were about forty head of cattle and fifteen dogs, as well as other creatures. The neurotoxin put forth by the blooming algae was so virulent that one-fiftieth of an ounce would produce death in three minutes, and one-millionth of an ounce had a fifty-fifty chance of producing paralysis and death. For reasons not clear, it is not so deadly to humans.

As far as is known, this did not happen in previous drought years, including the 1930s, which were severely dry. At that time, Grayling Arm became nearly dry; thus there is a possibility that the water dropped so much and so rapidly that the algae had no chance to bloom. But this is only conjecture, for the record is bare of any facts regarding algae bloom and resulting poisoning of the waters in that period.

However, there is much evidence that blooming of algae occurs on nearly all lakes where there are shallow benches or gently sloping shores. But this blooming is seldom toxic. Scientists who have dealt with the problem can find no factors that can help them predict at what point the bloom becomes toxic, or what the causes are that produce a toxic condition.

The resorts around the shores of Hebgen Lake have grown, like Topsy, without plan. Yet because most were built *on* the landscape instead of into it, little ecologic damage has occurred. Where some older resorts have vanished or have been torn down, little evidence of them exists; the land has returned almost to its former state. The ones that remain are somewhat rustic, and fit into the area unobtrusively for the most part and provide comfortable if not luxurious accommodations for some thousands of vacationers each summer. These are mostly boaters, swimmers, water skiers, and boat fishermen who cause little damage to the shore or surrounding areas. So little in fact, that if all habitation was forbidden and removed tomorrow, within five years most areas would return to a wild condition.

One area where such return would take much longer is the Rainbow Point area of Horse Butte, a knobby peninsula between the Madison and Grayling arms. Permanent, year-round homes have been built here, and have caused a greater impact on the land. But there are not many of them and most home-owners have changed the landscape as little as possible. All in all, Hebgen Lake and its environs have not suffered greatly at the hands of man.

The ranches on two sides of the lake are fairly well cared for; again no thoughtless or unnecessary changing of the landscape has been done and if it were not for the fences and buildings, one would note practically no change.

One change that has taken place is the conversion of sagebrush land into pasture and hay land. This has resulted in an insufficiently appreciated resource. Waterfowl by the scores of thousands populate Heblen Lake in the fall—ducks, geese, and swans, many of the latter the rare, beautiful trumpeter swan. Both swans and geese graze on the adjacent land.

I have walked the shores of Hebgen many a fine fall day, delighting in rafts of ducks numbering many thousands, geese in the shallows and on the sandbars in groups of fifty to five thousand, and even flocks of several hundred swans. Most of the geese are Canadas but on rare occasions blue and snow geese set the air ringing with their sharp honking, which at a distance sounds like the barking of dogs.

Neither ducks or geese are much hunted here, and snow geese and all other large white waterfowl are totally protected, lest trumpeters be taken for them and illegally shot. To my knowledge, no such tragedy has ever occurred, and most local people get pretty "riled" up at even the thought. This area, because of Yellowstone Park and the Red Rocks Wildlife Refuge in nearby Centennial Valley, is responsible for saving the trumpeter from extinction. At the time the Red Rocks Refuge was founded, there were only seventy trumpeter swans in the entire country. In these two areas, 90 percent of the remaining United States population of trumpeter swans live and nest. They are regarded, both locally and nationally, as a national treasure and now number over five thousand.

Fishing in Hebgen Lake is considered good. By those with much skill in lake fishing, it is considered excellent. The lake hosts, in order of numbers, or abundance, brown trout, mountain whitefish, rainbow trout, brook trout, and cutthroat trout among the game fishes. Nongame species, again in order of abundance, include Utah chub and mottled sculpin. The chub are non-native and were introduced by bait-fishers in the 1930s. They are considered trash fish and a detriment.

In the spring the rainbow and cutthroat run out of the lake to spawn, followed in the fall by brook, browns, and mountain whitefish. Some 60 percent of each species return to the lake; some 17 percent do not survive spawning or the winter; and the rest remain in the streams, keeping both size and numbers up.

At present, except for one small cloud, the horizons of Hebgen Lake are clear. The cloud is in the form of a proposed ski resort called Ski Yellowstone to be built on the north side of the lake not far from Grayling Arm. Though the resort planners have protested that the lake will suffer no ecologic damage because of the resort, many concerned people are skeptical, having heard such protestations before. Certainly the watershed will be somewhat degraded; you cannot replace sod and ground cover with cement, asphalt, and wood without doing some damage, nor can you build a ski run or runs without destroying some ground cover. But there are other considerations. Runoff from streets and parking lots will pollute the lake if such water reaches it largely unfiltered. And then there is sewage, a considerable amount of it if the resort reaches its planned size.

If the resort is planned and built with all ecological safeguards, it will have little impact on the lake. The fear here is that most safeguards will be bypassed or eliminated because of money. There is a feeling the planned resort is not sufficiently funded and that shortcuts will be taken. Also, there are those, and I am one, who believe the resort cannot be made economically viable in competition with present nearby resorts—Big Sky to the north and Storm King and Teton Village to the south. We fear the area may become a resort slum. Since this cannot be proven until it happens—if it does—it appears Ski Yellowstone will become a reality in the near future. It is something to be watched.

A few minutes before midnight on 17 August 1959, a mighty earthquake wrenched the mountains and uplands of southwestern Montana with historic force. It measured either 7.1 or 7.8 on the Richter Scale, depending on your source, and its epicenter was alongside the east end of the Grayling Arm of Hebgen Lake, centered beneath the junction of highways 191 and 287 just north of Duck Creek known as Duck Creek Y. This location is eight miles north of West Yellowstone and twelve miles southeast of Hebgen Dam. The fault scarp, which dropped the earth as much as thirty feet in some places, ran roughly parallel to the lake to well beyond the dam.

At West Yellowstone damage for a quake of such violence was minimal. The town sits on a bed of alluvial gravel, sand, and silt over a hundred feet deep. It would be difficult to design a system better able to absorb the shock and earth motion of a major quake. There was much interior breakage of glass, glassware, dishes, bottled goods, and so forth, which created a mess—but external damage was slight.

Highway 191, running north to Bozeman, was broken in several places and shifted some feet one way or another. The junction was dropped eight feet. Damage was considerable but not extensive. Highway 287, which runs along the lake—or did—was extensively damaged. Great sections simply broke off and dropped into the lake. Other sections slid downhill some feet or yards and others were covered by landslides.

Hebgen Lake, which lies with its long axis roughly northeast–southwest, had its bed tilted sharply northward. The bedrock beneath the dam dropped 9.74 feet. The opposite, upper end of the lake raised about twelve feet. The north shore dropped into the lake near the dam, and one resort and several homes went with the land. On the south side, homes that once stood on the shore are now some hundreds of feet back from the water. The tilting of the lake bed and dropping of the dam caused huge amounts of water to slosh six to ten feet over the top of the dam and send a seismic wave several feet high rushing down the Madison Canyon like a tidal bore. This happened four times.

The waves destroyed and washed away several summer cabins and part of a resort in the upper canyon. When they reached the Rock Creek Campground near the canyon mouth they would have posed a deadly threat to the one to two hundred persons camped there except for one thing. When the waves arrived, the campground no longer existed.

At the instant of the quake, the north face of a 7,600-foot-high mountain across the river broke off and sent eighty million tons of rock and earth roaring down, across the river and some several hundred yards up the far slope. Most of Rock Creek Campground vanished under the slide.

Engineers have estimated that the slide at peak velocity was moving at over two hundred miles an hour. As it literally fell into the river, a great gust of compressed air was thrust out from beneath the slide on both sides. The force of this blast hurled people, tents, trailers, and two-ton cars out of the path of the slide and sent them tumbling to safety. Except for this, the death toll would have been much, much higher. As it was, some nineteen persons are missing and their bodies are presumed to be under the slide, and another seven are known dead from the effects of the slide. Two other persons were killed at nearby Cliff Lake Campground when huge boulders rolled down and crushed them in their sleeping bags.

The formation of a lake behind the slide began the moment the slide barred the river. In time that lake would be 247 feet deep, and would be known as Earthquake (Quake) Lake. Such slide dams are unstable and must be stabilized before the enormous pressures of water rupture the dam and wash away everything below it. Such a disaster occurred in May 1927 when a slide across the Gros Ventre River some one hundred miles to the southeast gave way and caused the destruction of the town of Kelly, Wyoming.

The Army Engineers were on the Madison scene almost at once and rushed into the massive task of stabilizing the rock dam. By 10 September they had cut a spillway 250 feet wide and fourteen-feet deep across the top and packed both faces of the dam. They had not finished before water was spilling over the top. But the downstream face of the dam had not been sufficiently stabilized and terrific erosion began. The Engineers went into a crash program to lower the top of the dam another fifty feet and shallow the slope of the downstream face. This was completed on 29 October just as winter snows started drifting down to bring a halt to the work. A blizzard a week later closed the area.

The dam has stood now for nineteen years. The lake, its depth reduced to 180 feet by the cutting of the spillway and subsequent siltation, stretches some four-and-a-half miles upstream. It covers the old highway and a new one had to be built on the slope above the lake. There is a monument on the north edge of the slide commemorating the nineteen persons whose bodies are believed to be under it, and the Forest Service has built an Earthquake Center and parking lot on the top of the slide to accommodate the millions of visitors to the site.

The size of the slide is almost unbelievable. Hoover Dam, 726 feet high, the second highest dam in the United States, contains only one-tenth the material the slide does. Looked at another way, enough rock and dirt slid into the canyon at this point to cover Manhattan Island two feet deep.

Hebgen Dam dropped over nine feet during the quake and its concrete core cracked. But it held, a tremendous tribute to the skill and foresight of its designer. It has been repaired and strengthened and the Montana Power Company believes it can withstand anything except a massive quake directly beneath it.

What about the benefits and losses created by Quake Lake? If there are any present benefits, no one knows of them. As far as losses, other than the lives already mentioned, the lake covered several miles of highway costing millions of dollars, it wiped out four to five miles of what many believe to have been the finest stretch of mountain trout stream in the world. The rainbows caught and kept from the pockets of its raging rapids averaged four pounds and went to over eight, and the stream was utterly beautiful and majestic. Quake Lake is presently ugly, both in shape and appearance. It may hold trout, but fishing and boating are difficult, even dangerous due to the millions of dead trees in the lake, many of which come near or protrude above the surface. It also has covered much of the spawning water once available to the trout. It is a loss, and a severe one. The only apparent gain is that the lake and slide are now a geologic study area.

The third dam of the trinity holding back the waters of the Madison River is Madison Dam a few miles north of the town of Ennis. It is located near the junction of Meadow Creek and the river, and the lake is often called Meadow Lake, but Ennis Lake is the correct name. The dam lies across the head of Beartrap Canyon and it and the lake are the property of the Montana Power Company.

The present dam was built in 1906. The depth of the lake at the dam at the time it was completed was thirty-eight feet—a very shallow lake, and a small one. The lake at the dam face is now twenty-two feet, due to siltation. This is an ominous note, for lakes silt up first at their upper ends, and Ennis Lake has silted to the point that its average depth is only about nine feet. As a matter of fact, no water deeper than twelve feet exists except in the old river channel. Ennis Lake is dying and is in the latter stages of death at that. At present the generating plant at the dam operates on the run of the river, and depends almost not at all on the stored water.

When Ennis Lake was formed, it covered only a small stretch of trout stream and a small grazing area. Its benefits far outweighed its liabilities. The fishing in the lake itself soon became excellent and several resorts sprang up on its shores.

The fishing upstream of the lake improved greatly and for over fifty years this section of the river consistently produced the finest trout of anywhere on the whole river. It still does to a lesser extent—the big brood fish that once

Earthquake Lake, with its slide and scars. Four miles of the best mountain trout stream in the world now lie under this ugly lake.

lived in the lake until spawning time are becoming fewer and fewer, and have almost vanished. The answer is in the shallowness of the lake. As it silted up, the water became warmer and now tops 82° F. in the daytime; this temperature does not cool appreciably at night. By 1980, it is expected the lake's top temperature will exceed 90° F. This will finish it as a trout lake.

The problem of Ennis Lake began the day it was conceived. All lakes, natural or artificial, silt up and eventually become bogs, then marshes, then dry land. None are immune to this dying process. But Ennis Lake was doomed to an early death. It was a very shallow lake when first filled and it lay at the lower end of a large watershed that had been, and was being, systematically overgrazed.

This problem continues in the present day. It has been considerably reduced in the middle Madison Valley and the Ennis Lake watershed, but in the rest of Montana, over half the total land is being severely eroded due largely to overgrazing. At present, three hundred million tons of soil and minerals wash into Montana streams every year. About two-thirds remains there to silt up the streams and reservoirs. The middle Madison watershed has only 19 percent of its area in poor condition, but the improvement came too late to save Ennis Lake, which was extremely vulnerable to begin with because of its shallow panlike bowl.

If the figure of three hundred million tons of soil and minerals given above does not create a picture in your mind, think of it as a pile of soil one mile wide, one hundred eighty miles long, and ten feet deep. Think of that much soil being removed from the land and deposited in the waters every year and it is easy to see how a lake can silt up very rapidly.

Except for the production of power, for which it was designed, and which was its total purpose as far as the Montana Power Company is concerned, Ennis Lake has outlived its usefulness. It offers no recreational benefits at present; too shallow and weedy for boating or swimming, too warm for fishing, at least for trout and grayling, it is now becoming a liability in areas where it once was an asset. The resorts along its shore are dying along with the lake. Now, instead of benefitting the river above, it poses a deadly threat to the river below.

The three lakes on the Madison River offer a unique opportunity to study the benefits and liabilities of lakes both artificial and natural, and lakes young and old. Quake Lake, the natural one of the three, is nineteen years old; Ennis Lake is over seventy years old. One is very deep, the other quite shallow. One has been beneficial in the past; the benefits of the other lie completely in the future.

Quake Lake, as it matures, will sometime in the distant future, offer good fishing, boating, water skiing, and perhaps swimming. This will come some fifty or more years from now when the trees in the lake and around its edge have rotted away. The lake will become more attractive and less dangerous and use and esthetic appreciation will increase.

Ennis Lake, as it continues dying, will pose a greater and greater threat to the fishery of the river below it. This will be taken up again in the chapter on that section of the river.

Hebgen Lake will continue to be beneficial for hundreds of years. Its watershed is and has been in superb condition, and will continue to be unspoiled. So little silt has entered the estuaries of Hebgen in its sixty-odd years that literally none has reached the lake. One can float in a boat or canoe down these estuaries and before the lake proper is reached, the silt bottom will give way to the beautiful clean gravel of the original stream bed.

Even the silt that is there has been beneficial. In the shallow mud flats, millions upon millions of larvae of blackfly, midge, and cranefly exist and on a long summer morning or evening twilight the big trout cruise up out of the lake and begin to feed on them, and on the big nymphs of dragon and damsel-fly that are there to prey on the larvae.

A few years ago I opened two eighteen-inch fish caught over these flats a long cast apart. The brown contained thirty-seven dragonfly nymphs, some as big as the first joint of my thumb. The rainbow held about five hundred midge larvae, none half-an-inch long nor much bigger than thread. Both fish were gorged.

So, if you don't think the mud flats of the Hebgen and its estuaries are that productive, ask yourself this question. Why are all those gulper fishermen so secretive about it?

GOLD, BEEF, AND BRASS

WHEN THE BEAVER TRADE BEGAN TO DIE OFF ABOUT 1834, THERE WERE THOU-
sands of trappers in the northern Rockies, and these men, at least many of
them, were loath to leave the region and what they had come to think of as a
free and easy life. It required little money to sustain them. Tobacco, powder,
and lead were the only absolute necessities they needed to buy; the rest of
life's needs could be obtained from the land.

Several roving bands of hunter-trappers moved up and down the Madison
Valley during the period from 1839 to 1860. They were on sort of a busman's
holiday, wandering wherever the urge took them, hunting and trapping, never
long in one place. Jim Bridger made several trips with these bands, though he
later regretted his joining three of them.

The trappers missed the annual rendezvous, which ceased in 1840, after
sixteen years. This month-long orgy of drunkenness, fighting, and womaniz-
ing had furnished them an outlet, or amusement to which they had become
accustomed. Lacking any other excitement, many of them took to fighting
every band of Indians they met, just for the hell of it.

On several of these forays into the Madison Valley, the trappers encountered bands of Blackfeet making trips to intimidate the Shoshoni and keep
them out of the area. The Blackfeet were armed with old fusees and smooth-
bore muskets. These were adequate to handle the Shoshoni but were almost
useless against the trappers with their powerful and accurate Hawkens. So the
Blackfeet sought to avoid the latter whenever possible. It was seldom possible.
The trappers had the upper hand and knew it, and sought to teach the

"savages" a lesson at every opportunity. It never seemed to concern them that some trappers were almost certain to lose their own life.

This attitude was written about by an Englishman who spent several seasons with the trappers in the 1840s. George Ruxton said of them: ". . . they become callous and destroy human life with as little scruple and as freely as they expose their own. Of laws, human or divine, they neither know nor care to know . . . They have many good qualities but they are those of the animal."

Bridger was involved in three of these useless and needless battles (which he inveighed against) and in one of them took an arrow in the back. This iron arrowhead remained there for some years before it was removed, allegedly by the Oregon medical missionary, Marcus Whitman, who stopped at Bridger's Fort in 1843 while making a trip from Oregon to Washington D.C. to get Congress to settle the "Oregon question" in favor of Oregon.

Bridger was used by the Army's Topographical Corps and the Corps of Engineers as a guide during the forties and fifties. He also acted as guide for some of the trappers from the southern Rockies who had heard of the wonders of Yellowstone and wanted the most reliable man to show them around.

In the fall of 1849, Bridger led a band of about fifty trappers, including Kit Carson, Lou Anderson, and others, into the Green River area where they wintered with the Indians. In the spring they traveled through Yellowstone, marveling at its wonders. It was on this trip that, in showing them the river "heated by friction," Bridger is alleged to have named the Firehole River.

The band went north and then east and joined Father Pierre Jean De Smet in south-central Montana. Bridger furnished that insatiably curious priest with information for a manuscript map on which, for the first time in writing, the name "Firehole River" appears. This would seem to support Topping's assertion that it was Bridger who named the river in the spring of 1850. Bridger met again with De Smet at Fort Laramie the next year and provided additional information that was to make De Smet's map the best of the era, although it contained some errors.

In 1859, Bridger acted as guide for Captain William F. Raynolds of the Corps of Topographical Engineers. Raynolds wanted to explore the Yellowstone area from the headwaters of the Wind River, and refused to accept Bridger's word that it couldn't be done. After failing to get over the mountains, the highest and most rugged in Wyoming, Raynolds then attempted to enter the area from the south, from Jackson's Hole, but was stopped by passes choked with snow.

Raynolds then was forced to circle to the west, across Pierre's Hole (Teton Basin) past Henrys Lake, over the Continental Divide by the low pass that now bears his name, and descend the Madison to Three Forks, where he was bound to observe an eclipse on 4 July 1859.

Much of the Army's exploration during this period was for the purpose of finding suitable east-west and north-south routes for the exploding western expansion. Unfortunately for the emigrants, the onset of the Civil War brought such explorations to a halt before those routes discovered could be well publicized.

The Civil War and its after effects kept the brass out of the Madison Valley for some eighteen years, but this was the very heyday of another group, the gold seekers. Theirs was the first to have a permanent impact on the valley, though little gold was found in the Madison drainage except at Sterling in the lower valley, and this was not discovered until 1867.

Gold was first discovered at Gold Creek in western Montana in 1858, and the first influx of prospectors came from that direction. The first substantial strike was made at Bannack, on the Montana side of the Continental Divide, near the Idaho border in early 1862. Latecomers to that strike spread out in all directions and in May of 1863 a party of six men led by Bill Fairweather made the immensely rich discovery of Alder Gulch. In less than two years the population of a ten-mile radius surrounding Alder Gulch-Virginia City zoomed to 35,000. It was the overflow from this area, just over the Gravelly Range, that became the first permanent settlers in the Madison Valley.

There were two reasons for the prospectors settling in the Madison Valley. One was the violence of 1862–63 wherein robbery and murder became so commonplace in Alder Gulch that honest men feared for their lives. A notorious band of renegades, led by no less person than the elected sheriff, Henry Plummer, held a sway of terror over the mining community that lasted over a year and resulted in an unknown number of murders. When a kindly and inoffensive miner was murdered in late 1863 for $300 in gold, a vigilante group was formed and took swift and completely effective action.

In December 1863 and January 1864, the Vigilantes hanged twenty-one desperadoes, including their sheriff. The word immediately went out, far and wide: stay away from Virginia City and Alder Gulch if you value your neck. In two months the area changed from one of the most lawless to the most law-abiding in the territory.

Those who had been scared out and settled in the Madison Valley were offered almost at once a way to make a living. In the winters of 1862–63, and 1863–64, there developed a trememdous food shortage. Most food for the area was brought in from Odgen, Utah, three hundred miles away, over a rough semblance of a wagon road. When the snows of winter blocked the road for some weeks, the mining communities came near to starving. Beef soared to $20 to $25 a pound and even at that price there was little to be had. In the late fall of 1863, a freighter named Alexander Toponce was on his way from Ogden to the placers of Virginia City with a load of goods. In Brigham City, he spied a dressed hog hanging from a limb. Toponce bought it for $36 and sold it in Virginia City for $600. In the winter of 1864–65, Mormons from Utah were selling flour in Virginia City for $1.25 a pound.

The first Montanan to take advantage of the situation was a one-time butcher, Conrad Kohrs. Kohrs bought some cattle that he found in the Deer Lodge area, drove them to Virginia City, butchered and sold them, and started a veritable empire. But his base of operations centered nearer Last Chance Gulch (Helena) than Alder Gulch, for by then the mines there and at Butte offered a more permanent and stable consumer population. The ranchers in Madison Valley slowly took over the trade of Alder Gulch and its environs.

The whole food-shortage problem at Alder was puzzling. The surrounding Ruby Mountains and the Gravelly Range hosted enormous quantities of big game—antelope, deer, elk, probably moose, and some buffalo. Yet I can find no mention anywhere of market hunting. This is surprising. At the mines in Colorado, of somewhat later date, there is abundant evidence of market hunting. Hunters had no difficulty in supplying five thousand pounds of field-dressed game per hunter per week to the mining communities at ten cents a pound. Five hundred dollars a week was a veritable fortune then, when hunters lived off the land and had only to buy tobacco and ammunition. Some of them got wealthy from their operations. But I can find no similar stories about Montana market hunters of the 1860–65 era.

Ranching gradually took over the Madison Valley, and this has continued to be the major enterprise. Some farming was and is done, but this has been the low end of the agriculture system. The early farming was done for home consumption, but with the building of the stage line from Bozeman to Virginia City and on to Utah, some commercial farming was carried on for a time.

As far as can be ascertained, the first two permanent homesteads in the Madison Valley were those of William Ennis and M. D. Jeffers in 1863 near Meadow Creek. In addition to farming, Ennis helped maintain the freight-road bridge across the river and operated a stage station. Until the late 1880s this station was known as Ennis'; it did not become the town of Ennis until sometime later. Jeffers' place, across the river, is still known by his name.

Because of its favorable location, Ennis' became a hub of activity; three freight roads joined here and two stage routes came through the area, one from Bozeman and one from the northwest—the Helena-Butte-Deer Lodge area.

Gold was discovered at Sterling in the east edge of the Tobacco Root Mountains, ten miles northwest of Ennis in 1867. It was low-grade ore and quickly played out; Sterling became a stage station. Here in 1881 began a tragedy that had its ending in Ennis.

A man named William Douglass had a ranch in the Gallatin Valley on the stage route to Sterling-Ennis-Virginia City. He had a comely young house-keeper named Alice Earp. Douglass, a man of violent temper, fell madly in love with Miss Earp, but she refused to marry him, and caught the stage for Virginia City one day in 1881 to escape his attentions.

Douglass followed on horseback and overtook the stage at the stop in Sterling. Miss Earp was riding beside the driver and when she refused Douglass's importuning, the man's violent temper boiled over and he pulled a gun and shot her.

Douglass was instantly overpowered, and the badly wounded girl was placed inside the stage for a fast run to Virginia City and a doctor. It was a futile effort; Miss Earp collapsed and died at Ennis. The next day, Douglass was tried, sentenced, and was hanged, less than twenty-four hours after he had fired the fatal shot. Such was the temper of justice in the Madison Valley in 1881.

Though prospectors left little mark on the middle and lower valleys of the Madison, one did leave a lasting record of the upper drainage. This was Walter W. De Lacy, who in 1863 led a band of forty "thieves" (prospectors) through the Tetons and into southern Yellowstone, to the head of the Lewis River; then he went over the winding Continental Divide and down the Firehole and Madison.

De Lacy was a well-trained civil engineer and surveyor. Two years after his Yellowstone sojourn he was asked by the new Territorial Government of Montana to furnish it with maps of the southwestern sector. De Lacy's map included the southern portion of Yellowstone and was the first then, and for a long time the only map, placing Shoshone Lake correctly in the Lewis-Snake drainage and not in the Firehole-Madison drainage as was done by De Smet in 1851 and F. M. Hayden twenty years later. De Smet got his information from Bridger and other trappers, hunters, and Indians, all of it second hand. But Hayden was a trained geologist and geographer and had other trained men and excellent instruments at his disposal, and visited the area himself. His blunder is therefore inexcusable.

In 1866, Nelson Story brought a good-sized trail herd from Texas into the Gallatin Valley near Bozeman. Animals from this herd furnished some of the stock for the first permanent herds in the Three Forks area and also the middle Madison Valley (Beartrap to Madison Canyon). These herds prospered exceedingly and were almost untouched by the blizzard of 1886–87 that wiped out over a million head in central and eastern Montana. For a time, the Madison Valley was shipping the largest number of steers to market of any area of the territory and this led to near disaster.

Seeing the wealth pouring from the region of the Madison River, other cattlemen, sheepmen, and homesteaders (called honyockers) poured into the valley, literally overrunning it. The honyockers, a synonym of uncertain origin for nester, squatter, homesteader, sodbuster, scissorbill, and the like, mostly settled in the upper end of the valley near the Madison Range-Henrys Lake Mountains, the section now known as Missouri Flats, so called from the home state of many of them. Ninety-nine percent of them starved out in a few years but they had decimated the land.

Cattlemen and sheepmen took over the abandoned homesteads, rented grazing land for twenty-five cents an acre for three years in the government-owned areas of the surrounding mountains, and started a fifty-year period of overgrazing that nearly ruined the land for a millennium. It was estimated at one period that *three million* animals grazed the watershed of the middle and lower Madison and this continued until vast areas would not support one animal per thousand acres. It takes over a thousand years to replace one inch of topsoil, and erosion caused by overgrazing removed more than that.

This debacle sent the last of the scissorbills fleeing, along with the get-rich-quick stockmen. Those that remained looked around, decided they did not like what they saw, and got together on ways to restore the land. They cut the number of animals grazing the area drastically, put good rotative grazing practices into use, and worked hard to bring back what they had nearly destroyed. No law or government agency or conservation group hassled them into doing what they did. It was their own decision and they have stuck to it for over fifty years.

The activities of the landowners were and are completely self serving—it was their own land and way of life they were trying to save and improve and this, in my opinion, is one of the most powerful motivating forces man is subject to. One might argue that the ranchers should have moved to preserve the land in the first place, before it was seriously damaged. The fact is, man learns only from experience—and sometimes not even from that.

The Soil Conservation Service people at Ennis tell me that the best land-use practices in Montana are to be found in the middle Madison Valley, and the Forest Service and Bureau of Land Management forces agree.

It is far from perfect, however. The Forest Service has permitted more grazing than it should have and says so. The BLM admits that 19 percent of the land it is responsible for in the area is in poor condition due to overgrazing. This compares with 80 percent of its lands in the rest of Montana being in poor to unsatisfactory condition due to overgrazing and 73 percent for the Far West as a whole.

This is largely due, says the agency, to being undermanned to the extent that proper surveys and controls could not be instituted. That much is true, but the fact is that until the mid 1960s the agency's attitude was that they were there to serve the cattle industry and another fact is that it, in many areas, forced larger grazing quotas on the cattlemen than was known to be good for the land. That attitude is changing rapidly under public pressure and, except for some old diehards in the service, will soon be gone.

The Army had little reason to be in the Madison Valley after 1865. The area had become densely settled enough to force the Blackfeet north of the Missouri. Had the area been prime hunting land, the story might have been different. Also, the Army was having its hands full with the Sioux, Northern Cheyenne, Arapaho, Pawnee, and other tribes east of the Rockies. Since the settlers in southwestern Montana were not in need of help, and civilian engineers were plotting roads and trails, and since the Army had not yet got into the dam-building business, they found little reason to return to the valley of the Madison River.

For which, thank God.

THE VALLEY OF THE MIDDLE MADISON

THIS IS PERHAPS THE MOST BEAUTIFUL OF RIVER VALLEYS THAT I HAVE SEEN. It begins at the mouth of Madison Canyon, a half-mile below Quake Lake Slide, and stretches to the head of Beartrap Canyon, some forty-five airline miles north. The valley ranges from four to over fifteen miles wide, flanked on the east by the distinctive peaks of the Madison Range, including the Spanish Peaks at the lower end. On the west the long rolling ridges, rounded domes and high subalpine basins of the Gravelly Range form the divide between the drainage system of the Madison and that of its sister river, the Jefferson.

Though from above it appears broad and flat, from the valley floor itself one can see that it is not. There are hills, mounds of harder material, terraces, and benches from uplift, and deposits of debris from floods in the past.

Mostly, the ground cover is grass, green and rich in spring and golden tan in the fall. The trees are different from those of the Madison Basin. Dwarf willow and aspen are replaced by big willow, red alder, and cottonwood, most of which trace the stream courses of the river and its many tributaries.

The mountains are near at hand, seldom crowding but not far enough away to blur their shapes and details. The slopes of the Gravelly are gentle, with many open meadows and sagebrush flats, while the Madison Range is abrupt—no foothills, and very steep, timber-covered slopes to the timberline. Its peaks are jagged and uneven. When the tops of both ranges are covered by snow in spring and fall, the valley looks like a landscape painting by Thomas Moran.

At the head of Missouri Flats, where the valley begins, the elevation is

121

almost 6,200 feet. At Madison Dam across Beartrap Canyon the elevation is 4,700 feet. In about sixty miles of river run, the drop is 1,500 feet, or twenty-five feet per mile. This is a very steep gradient for so large a river.

However, a river does not run from point to point as do man-made things. It meanders, curves and swings, much in the manner that game trails up a mountainside do; thus the actual gradient of the river appears much less. Still, it is enough to make this one of the most difficult and dangerous trout streams to wade or to float.

The things that cause the river not to plunge directly downhill are the old channels cutting across it, the hills or mounds, terraces, and benches from old upheavals and the waterborne debris, mentioned earlier, which form barriers to the river's course. This debris was deposited by high waters millions of years ago and gives silent testimony to the incredible power of moving water.

The moving power of water increases as the sixth power of its velocity. Double the speed at which a stream runs and you have increased its ability to move objects sixty-four times. If you treble the velocity, you increase the motive power 729 times! A current of two miles an hour will move round rocks as large as a baseball. An eight-mile-an-hour current will move boulders *four feet* in diameter, and the current of the Madison in this area reaches that velocity every spring. Millenia ago, it possibly ran twice that fast in flood stage.

The Valley bears all the signs of the river's earlier history, because at sometime or other the river has run over almost every square yard of it. The floor of the valley is composed almost entirely of rounded river gravel and rubble, over which a fragile soil is thinly deposited.

The valley has been domesticated for only 115 years, yet so intensively has it been grazed that over 90 percent of the native plants have disappeared. Buffalo grass never reached this part of the West but the native bromes, fescues, and bunch grass have been almost entirely replaced by a wan, insipid, domestic variety whose only virtue seems to be an ability to withstand drought. Since the major portion of the valley receives less than eighteen inches total annual moisture, this may be the only non-native grass able to survive.

In general, this is cattle country because it is either too rough or too arid for the plow. It is land, then, that does not interest or cannot support the farmer. In the words of the sometimes wiser-than-we Indian, it is land that is still right side up. Here the grass cover is about the only resource of value save the river itself; the grass is thin and sparse because the soil is thin and moisture scarce, thus the habitations of man are far apart.

Range land has been defined as an area where cattle can graze out the greater part of the year. Such land exists between the Rio Grande on the south to the banks of the Saskatchewan in the north, from the 100th meridian on the east to the waters of the Pacific. In most sections ranches cover vast areas of flat or rolling countryside, but ranches here are somewhat compressed. The country here has a third dimension that farming, seafaring, and even ranching in other parts of the country lack—that of height or elevation.

In the Madison River Valley, the lands along the river are winter range; the summer ranges are in the Gravelly and Madison Ranges. The cattle follow the greening grasses up the slopes in the spring, spend a month or so "on top," then graze on the frost-cured protein-rich golden grasses on their way back down the slopes, reaching the valley as winter reaches the upper peaks. Then and there the herd is separated. The fat steers, yearlings, and barren cows go off to become steaks, chops, and rib roasts, and the fertile cows retire to graze what remains of the summer's grass or to munch on the shoddy hay that is not so much raised as dragged up.

This valley winter range governs the size of herd the rancher can maintain. The profit margin in cattle ranching is so low that only to save himself from bankruptcy will the rancher buy hay to feed a herd through the winter. In order to prevent this happening except in rare severe winters, the ranchers keep their winter breeding herds trimmed to fit the amount of winter range. It is the only way to survive.

A flat riffle section of the middle Madison, showing the bench effect of old uplifts.

The summer range belongs largely to you and me—that is, to the Bureau of Land Management and the Forest Service, the former an agency of the Department of the Interior, the latter of the Department of Agriculture. Between them, these two agencies control over 70 percent of the land here—and in Montana.

The cattlemen lease summer grazing acreage from these agencies at a pittance. An asked-for raise in grazing fees has been met by a powerful cattlemen's lobby and by indecision and inaction in congress. The higher fees are needed to help maintain and control the public land, but since they, if implemented, will be passed directly on to the taxpayer in higher beef prices, congress fiddles.

The cattlemen, already on a short profit string, want beef prices to become lower, not higher, so the people will eat more of their product. The BLM and FS people want higher fees not only to pay increased costs of operating their vast agencies, but to discourage overgrazing by making it more costly per head to graze on public land. This would relieve the land managers of having to set lower quotas for grazing—sure to be violently opposed—making the managers and not congress the villain.

The cattlemen can survive only if consumption of beef stays high. At present, most in the Madison Valley are just surviving and that barely. Yet few consider giving up. Most of the ranches are in the hands of a long-time owner who looks on ranching not merely as a living but as a way of life. His returns are not measured solely in cash—he receives supplementary benefits in self-sufficiency, in independence, in outdoor living in the most beautiful of surroundings. These intangibles hold him to the land more surely than do any thoughts of getting rich.

Some Madison Avenue types try to tell these Madison River types that they can cure their problems by the wonders of modern advertising. But the ranchers know better. The housewife and no one else determines the amount of beef bought and therefore, the going price. A housewife might be lured by advertising to buy a "new and improved" brand of deodorant but beef is what it's always been; no amount of advertising is going to make it look or taste different and the housewife knows this. What will cause her to buy more is a lower price and nothing else.

Despite an ever-present shortage of moisture in the middle Madison Valley, the cattle there fare better than others in some areas where grazing is more lush. It isn't only grass that puts more size and weight on cattle. Minerals in the water and grass have a vital role in doing this. The most important of these minerals are calcium, phophorous, and iodine, and in most areas these have to be provided with mineral-block supplements. These cannot be dispersed to supply necessary minerals as well as nature can do it, and thus are not as efficient in promoting growth and weight. The grass in the Madison Valley is rich in calcium and phosphorous, as is the water; thus iodized salt blocks are about all that are needed to make up nature's shortage.

But the grass is sparse and thin. It takes twenty to twenty-five acres to support a cow and this with supplemental feeding of a ton of hay per animal in winter. It takes about three hundred head of cattle to support a one-family ranch; thus such a rancher must have access to about 6,000 or 7,500 acres of land. About one-third of this amount must be winter range and hay land, most likely owned by the rancher. The rest will be FS or BLM land that adjoins his.

The smaller ranches in the valley will have the minimum land in fee—2,000 to 2,500 acres. But these are not garden plots; each of them will cover three to five square miles, and some of the larger ranches cover forty to fifty square miles, not counting the grazing land leased from government sources. The ranches in the middle Madison are limited to a few on either side of the river; most have reached their present size some years ago in accommodation to the laws of man and nature.

Tourists, especially easterners, often ask why the cattle cannot graze the public land in winter. This land is covered by snow from mid-November to mid-April. Cattle are tropical in origin and in thousands of domesticated generations have not learned to paw through snow to grass as elk and buffalo do. Thus the mountains are useless as grazing land in winter.

Some enterprising ranchers elsewhere have been crossing purebred cattle and buffalo for years, trying to come up with a hybrid that will breed true and carry the favorable characteristics of both creatures in its genes. They have recently succeeded. These hybrids have the endurance, resistance to cold and heat, insects and disease of the buffalo, as well as its hardiness and ability to get down through deep snow to grass. Add to this the thriftiness, rapid growth, and more succulent taste of the purebreds and the result is an animal that appears to have a great future in the northern Rockies and high northern plains. It is almost certain to replace the cattle presently being raised—sometimes with great difficulty—in those areas.

Signs of past overgrazing are still abundant in the Madison Valley. The weeds and forbs that have replaced the grass because of damage to the soil are almost everywhere; the thinness and fragility of the soil make for a long and slow recovery process. The soil is most always only a foot or so deep over the unbiquitous gravel; in some places it is only inches deep. Moisture is scarce and what there is moves quickly through the light soil to the gravel where it is lost forever to the plant life above. One rancher has described the thin soil as being "not much more than a dirty shag carpet."

The above typifies the wry humor of the men who live here, and the succinctness of their speech. The tale is told of one rancher who had in his employ a young man who was a top hand. This young fellow helped out at neighboring cattle gatherings, brandings, and drivings, and became somewhat swell-headed with the praise lavished on him. Returning to the home ranch after a cattle drive, he allowed to the owner that he was worth a sight more money than he was getting.

"Well," said the rancher, "you are some cowboy for a fact. But what do you reckon that I'd have to do if you dropped dead?"

The cowboy thought that over and allowed, "I guess you'd have to replace me."

"That's right, Pete," said the rancher. "Consider yourself dead."

The upper middle Madison in winter, Henrys Lake Mountains in the background.

As mentioned earlier, the ranchers in this valley have made their own efforts to improve the quality of sinkin by decreasing the number of animals grazing the watershed, by use of rotational grazing, and by improvement in ground cover. This latter practice led some of them to attempt to remove the sagebrush on the benches and replace it with grass. This practice is common elsewhere and has had varying degrees of success. But the thin soil and low moisture of the valley has caused erosion problems, since after the sagebrush is gone, it is a long time before anything else replaces it.

Hydrologists agree that the best way to manage *any* watershed is by a *varied* natural vegetation so that surface runoff is minimal and of low energy. Weeds—forbs and herbs—and other plants, such as sagebrush, trap and hold water as well as alfalfa or timber trees, and thus are as valuable on a watershed. Also these are necessary for the survival of some wild game that cannot exist even on the best hay. Typical are the mule deer and sage grouse, neither of which has a digestive system able to cope with domestic alfalfa or other hay. Thus replacing sagebrush on government lands with domestic plants is a process that converts multipurpose land to a single purpose—grazing.

A little-known fact is that the tender new growth of sagebrush is more nutritional than the finest hay, including alfalfa, for animals that can digest it. It contains 16 percent protein, 15 percent fats, and 47 percent carbohydrates, with fiber and ash, and holds other minerals that are in the soil. Among those animals that can digest it are jack rabbit, antelope, mule deer, and sage grouse; it is a necessary nutrient for some of these. Domestic sheep also can digest sagebrush; in fact, it forms a major portion of their diet in certain Western lands, some 130,000,000 acres of which contain sagebrush.

The overgrazing of the 1880 to 1930 period had its worst effects in the Gravelly Range. At one time, it was estimated about 3,000,000 domestic animals grazed the watershed of the middle and lower Madison. About 2,200,000 were sheep and about 800,000 grazed the Gravelly Range, which is still feeling the effects of grass grubbed off to the roots.

Much of the open land in these mountains has a thin and fragile soil that will not support trees, and which responds very slowly after damage. Some erosion due to that earlier damage is still taking place.

Likewise, silt deposited in the river's major tributary in the middle valley, the West Fork, is still causing extensive problems in the river. As silt rolled off the slopes and balds and fire scalds in the pre-1930 era, it built up in bends and slower sections of the West Fork, actually diverting the stream flow greatly, causing it to cut away banks opposite silt beds, thus depositing more silt farther down. Some of this silt eventually reached the Madison and damaged the fishery by smothering the spawning beds.

Now the West Fork is swinging back as a natural stream always does, and is cutting into old beds of silt and volcanic ash deposited fifty to seventy-five years ago. This silt is also finding its way into the main river and again is interfering with spawning.

Logging of the Gravelly Range also took place many years ago, and contributed somewhat to the silt problem. But it was done with horse or oxen-drawn broad-tired wagons that, when loaded, had to move as much across slope as down because of braking problems. It was more convenient, too, for the returning empty wagons to switchback up the slope and thus erosion was not serious due to this logging.

Some logging has been done recently in the West Fork drainage but the Forest Service is much more alert to erosion problems caused by improper logging and maintains no serious erosion is taking place. Certainly, it is less serious than that caused by former overgrazing.

In Montana, about 58 percent of the sediment load in streams is contributed by misused public lands. The watershed practices and studies of the BLM and the FS are so low funded and of such low priority at the present time that BLM estimates it will take sixty years at the present rate to stabilize its watersheds. The Forest Service prediction for stabilizing watersheds on lands it controls is even more staggering—one hundred to two hundred years!

BLM is proposing fewer grazing units be open each year, that some areas be open one year and closed one year in rotation; they plan to adopt this method when money and manpower become available. Also, BLM plans some positive steps, such as contour furrowing and contour plowing of surface hardpan to promote sinkin. They also intend to reseed vast areas with natural vegetation. On paper, the plan looks good. But unless congress allots the money, it's just a plan.

In blunt language, the Forest Service doesn't even have a comprehensive plan. Perhaps it is realistically facing the fact that congress may not ever allot

The middle Madison in the vicinity of the confluence of the West Fork.

the money needed. More likely it will have to be taken to court, as BLM was, and ordered to get up such a plan.

Little mining has been done anywhere in the Madison watershed. There is an abandoned asbestos mine just west and south of Quake Lake Slide. It is located far up on the side of Sheep Mountain and the road leading to it is a low-gradient switchback. This has kept erosion to a minimum. The waste from the mine would have been deadly had any large amount washed into the river but none has.

There is a talc mine operating on the side of Johnny Gulch, some three miles west of the river at McAtee Bridge. I can find no evidence that this mine has caused any problem in, or damage to, the watershed. There are about twenty old gold mines in the area north and west of Ennis, but none are currently operating and none except the Sterling Mine ever produced much. Any damage done by leaching of the tailings at Sterling has long since been overcome by nature.

At present mining is, except for the one operating talc mine, quiescent. Although FS and BLM environmental plans mention several minerals present that could be mined, right now it is not economically practical to mine any of them. The future of mining and potential for damage from mining in the Madison watershed appears remote.

Agriculture, in the form of stock raising, is the largest industry in the valley of the middle Madison, as in fact it is in all Montana. But tourism is the second largest money maker, there and elsewhere in the state. Many of the tourists come to the Madison Valley on their way to Glacier or Yellowstone National Parks, but the largest number remain here because of the river. They are fishermen and their families.

There are about 75,000 man/days of angling on this part of the river between 1 June and 30 September. This averages 1,250 anglers per mile of stream during the season, or about ten anglers per mile of stream each day. About 90 percent are here during the six weeks of the salmon-fly hatch, 1 June to 15 July. Thus the actual concentration of fishermen is many times greater during this period than the rest of the year.

However, we will take up the fishermen a bit later, since I agree with Grover Cleveland, who said about them: "At the onset, the fact should be recognized that the community of fishermen constitute a separate class or subrace among the inhabitants of the earth."

Recreational use in the middle Madison Valley is not restricted to fishing. There is an occasional rodeo to give the local cowhands a chance to demonstrate for the "home folks." Horseback riding is widely practiced throughout the valley and on both flanking mountain ranges. Four-wheel touring is a major recreation activity in the Gravelly Range and has reached levels that is causing both the BLM and FS to consider restrictions. As is usual in these affairs, a few slobs are making it difficult for the law-abiding, environmentally conscious majority.

Boating, as opposed to float fishing, is a growing activity, and is particularly practiced by camera buffs who find far more photographic opportunities along the river than along the highway.

Hunting is perhaps the largest activity after fishing, for the valley is excellent wildlife habitat. The Madison Range offers good but difficult hunting and the Gravelly Range is the best big-game range I have ever seen, not excluding Alaska. The watershed of the middle Madison, including the valley, has moose, elk, antelope, deer, black and grizzly bear, coyote, mountain lion (rare), lynx, and perhaps mountain sheep among the larger animals. Fur bearers in trappable quantities exist; grouse of three or four species are cyclically abundant; and ducks and geese are plentiful for those who pursue them.

In the 1960s the area held an estimated 150,000 big-game animals. It had more deer than any place I've ever seen. It was not uncommon, when driving through the valley in winter, to see several deer herds ranging from fifty to three hundred animals; antelope in the same numbers could also be seen, and the latter were usually visible through the summer into fall.

The deer seen were feeding on the valley floor, and this caused many persons to believe they were feeding on the precious grass. But deer are only incidentally grazers; they are primarily browsers, and what they were actually doing was eating herbs and forbs—the weeds the ranchers would like to get rid of. They also browse widely on the tender tips of many shrubs—sagebrush, bitterbush, buffaloberry, snowberry, service berry, Oregon grape, balsamroot, mountain mahogany, Rocky Mountain, and common juniper. Practically none of the above are utilized by cattle; therefore the deer is not a competitor of range cattle.

Elk do graze and in some areas offer serious competition to cattle. But not to any degree in the middle Madison watershed. Antelope also graze and thus eat some grass that would otherwise be eaten by cattle. Because of this, most ranchers welcome elk and antelope hunters on their lands. I know that I have always been made welcome, and in some cases, the rancher stated I was doing him a favor by cutting down on the number of wild creatures that would otherwise eat grass his cattle needed.

Through 1969, the Gravelly Range was the easiest deer hunting possible to imagine. I never went there a single time without harvesting a deer, and the hunting was never difficult. It was actually possible to take "orders" for age and sex, and fill them.

The last year I hunted there (or at all) my wife told me in no uncertain terms not to bring anything home older than a yearling. This was brought on by the fact the preceding year I had killed a huge buck that I had found badly wounded and had put out of its misery. The meat had been virtually inedible.

Accordingly, I shot a young-of-the-year buck, which grossed less than a hundred pounds. My two companions both killed old, large animals. Our hunt was over by four in the afternoon, we loaded the deer in the back of my pickup and went home.

We passed through the game-checking station at McAtee Bridge across the Madison, and after the warden had checked the animals for tags, he came to the truck window and stuck his head in.

"Who shot Bambi?" he asked.

Horseback riding is a favorite recreation in the Madison watershed. This group will cover fifteen to twenty miles before returning.

The above will probably cause the "Bambi lovers," as outdoorsmen refer to the anti-hunting groups, to take offense. Let them then consider this: that winter over two-thirds of the deer herd in the Gravelly Range was wiped out by starvation, because the herd had overpopulated its winter range. When I was advised of this the next spring, I went back to the area I had hunted in the fall and found the ground literally covered with dead deer or their skeletons. I counted sixty visible from one spot. The total kill numbered over fifty thousand.

I do not hunt anymore because we no longer relish the meat, but I have little use for do-gooders who don't have the slightest knowledge of animal economics or game management. I have seen these people interfere, through the ballot box or by political pressure, with professional game management and always with disastrous results for the animals. The person who thinks starvation is an easy death is a damn fool, and the one who would insist that wild animals be fed so that they may proliferate forever is a bigger fool. However, if man doesn't curb his own overbreeding, and soon, all else will be academic.

The deer herd in the Gravelly Range will recover, but it will be a long, slow process. While it was starving, the herd ate every available food item to the point where at least 60 percent of the graze and browse material was devoured past the point of recovery. The soil in this area is classed as immature mountain soil; this means there is little topsoil, though the earth is minerally rich. The combination of this kind of soil, low annual moisture, and a relatively short growing season make a long recovery period assured.

The antelope and elk did not suffer a die-off, partly because they are grazers, but mainly because they are rovers—they travel and feed over a wide area, sometimes covering as much as one hundred miles in a year. Only a rare deer gets as much as four miles from where it was born.

The hunting is still good by most standards, but since it is not now as easy as it was, pressure is much less; unfortunately, this will cause a quicker return to the condition where the winter range is again overpopulated and there will be another massive die-off. The land can only support so many animals; when they exceed the carrying capacity, starvation is inevitable.

For those illogical ones who think that the hunters, or the cattle, or some other man-caused factor is to blame, let me call attention to the winter of 1974–75 in Yellowstone Park. There are no cattle, no hunters, and little human habitation in the Park's 2 million-plus acres. Massive starvation* of Park wildlife in the spring of 1975 took place just the same. And the same old arguments were trotted out by the hunting and anti-hunting groups. We should have been allowed to harvest the surplus, said the hunters. The animals should have been fed, said the antis. Let nature take its course, said the biologists; it's been doing it for millions of years, without any help. Get rid of all animals and build condominiums, said the developers. Animals don't vote, said the politicians. And so on.

The middle Madison Valley appears to have reached an era where its future is in good hands. The residents who live here year around want to maintain the lovely environment and wonderful recreation opportunities. The ranchers want to improve the grazing land, theirs and the public's. The government people are not under pressure, local or national, to do what's wrong so are free to do what's right. If the do-gooders, and the Army Engineers can be kept out, there is every reason to believe this region will change little over the coming years.

And that will be a small miracle, and a victory for humanity.

*On the order of 10 percent.

FISHERMAN'S RIVER

To anglers from all parts of this country, the middle Madison River is a frustrating, maddening, sometimes haughty, sometimes frightening, but always seductive stream. It is too big, too rough and brawling, too mighty and majestic to become intimate with. Yet the promise of intimacy is always there, just beyond that rock, around that bend, or below that choppy run.

Even Dick McGuire, who has lived and fished and guided on this stretch since the early 1930s will admit that he has never come to know it, although he has often felt on the verge of such knowledge. But, says Dick, "just when I think I have it, she changes on me, and I have to start all over again." This is another example of the many facets of the living river. Not fickleness, but growth and change—and for this river, mostly healthy growth and change.

Dick McGuire probably knows more about this part of the river than any living person, even more than another Dick, Richard Vincent, the Montana Fish and Game Department's field fisheries biologist for the area, who was born here. Their knowledge is of different kinds, although McGuire has more than a modicum of knowledge about the biology of the river. Mainly, though, he knows it as a fisherman; after more than forty years of fishing the river, he is still learning about it.

McGuire told me recently that, with the exception of Quake Lake Slide, no major changes have taken place in the river since he has known it. The slide dried up the river for twelve miles, to the confluence of the West Fork, for twenty-four days after it dammed the river. Fish were stranded in puddles and pools in the uneven bottom, and fish and insect kills were severe. But, said he, the river recovered quickly, and within five to seven years, insects were as plentiful as before and fish also, although somewhat smaller than previously.

There have been numerous small changes, and a steady change in one area. The runs of large rainbow trout out of Ennis Lake upstream have dropped to a trickle. Dick is unsure what has caused this.

Silting due to old overgrazing, the cutting flood of 1970, mentioned earlier, and the earthquake of 1959 has caused spawning mortality to some extent, and has caused the final deterioration of Ennis Lake. Greatly expanded fishing pressure has caused a steady reduction in the size of the fish, he says. And Dick also gave me an answer to a question that has bugged me for years.

The banks of the Madison in this stretch are fragile in many areas. They have caved in badly on long stretches. This has caused locally heavy silting. There has been considerable controversy and even acrimony over what was causing the banks to cave in. Local cattlemen and ranchers blame it on bank-walking fishermen. The fishermen blame it on the cattle, which graze right up to the river banks. Both are wrong, it appears. According to McGuire, it's caused by ice that freezes along the quieter bank waters and to the rocks and roots, and is torn away by fluctuating water levels, taking soil and rocks with it. I've never known Dick to be wrong about matters of this kind, so the ice has it.

McGuire says the size of the fish started to decline about 1950 to 1954 and blames it on fishermen keeping the larger fish while releasing the smaller ones. But Dick Vincent, who has the records to back him, says that is not the reason. There are just as many large fish as ever, says Vincent, but fishing pressure surged from five thousand man days to over 50,000 man/days per year on this stretch in the 1950–54 period. Thus, the large fish were divided between ten times more people. The total catch of large fish, over three pounds, is still the same, within limits of allowable error. So says Vincent. It's a reasonable argument, difficult to refute. And since this part of the river now has some 75,000 man days of angling per year, the pie is cut in smaller pieces yet.

In any event, McGuire probably catches more three-pound-and-up fish than anyone who fishes the river, and he admits that he catches more now than he did twenty to twenty-five years ago. The reason, of course, is that his skill and knowledge have increased—he catches more than his share of these big fish, but he keeps few, preferring to return them to be caught again by others.

Unknown to each other, the two Dicks, Vincent and McGuire, conducted an investigation into a certain aspect of the fishery at exactly the same time, although with different methods. Both arrived at the same conclusions at almost the same time.

In 1968, Dick McGuire helped with the founding of the Southwestern Montana Fly Fishers, of which he is past president and I am permanent secretary. That same year he put together a meeting between our club and members of the Montana Fish and Game Department, including regional fisheries manager Ron Marcoux and field biologist Dick Vincent.

At this meeting, McGuire put forth the premise that the stocking of hatchery catchable trout, which was being done routinely on certain stretches of the

Ron Spainhower with a sizable fish. Trout of this size were never plentiful in the Madison, but there were some and there still are. Circa 1947. Photo courtesy Dutch and Donna Spainhower

river, was harming the fishing. Surprisingly, Vincent agreed. While McGuire based his opinion on catch size-and-numbers rates over a period of years, and Vincent on electro-shocking and actual counts and measurements, both had come up with the same staggering fact—and fact it was.

The upshot of this meeting was that we would take this information before the Fish and Game Commission to see if a study of the situation could be authorized. I was elected spokesman for this effort.

Because we were wary of the politics involved, we did not let it be known that we had previously met with the fisheries biologists. But our fears were wasted; the Commission, chaired by Willis Jones, was as fair and reasonable a group of people as anyone would want. They listened courteously to my presentation, asked a few considered and intelligent questions, conferred for a few minutes, with the Chief fisheries biologist, then granted our desired study with these words from Chairman Jones; "For fifty years our biologists have been telling us that the only way to have better fishing was by stocking hatchery catchables. Now, on the basis of information provided by this interested group, it appears we have been wrong. But before we scrap a program of fifty years duration, I want a thorough study of the matter."

The original study was funded for two years, to be followed by two additional years if there were inconclusions or ambiguities. But there were no ambiguities. This is what happened when the study was conducted:

1. When the stocking of hatchery catchables (seven inches and over) was stopped on one section of the river in 1968, by 1969 the number of *fish of this size had quadrupled.*

2. On a section that had not been so stocked for ten years (control area), no changes in sizes and population were noted.

3. When stocking of catchables was done in a section that had not been so stocked since 1963, population of catchables (seven inches and over) *decreased by 49 percent.*

4. No significant changes in populations or sizes were noted in areas where catchables had never been stocked.

Other information bolstered the above: when stocking of catchables was stopped, not only did the general population triple, but the numbers of trout over seventeen inches did also. When catchables were stocked, the total population *and* the numbers of fish over seventeen inches dropped by nearly half.

The reasons were soon determined for these drastic changes. The numbers of trout and their sizes, in any *stream,* is determined by the holding spaces (hovers, housing, shelter, or whatever you wish to call it)—those areas where a trout can exist in *running water* without working itself to exhaustion. They are strictly limited in all streams and they act as an absolute control on *sizes* and *numbers* of trout. There is no way around them, absolutely no way the *permanent* population of a stream can be increased without increasing holding areas. This is as immutable as the law of gravity and all the wishful thinking in the world will not change it one iota. So, do not waste your time by saying—what if? There is no what if. A fish in a stream either has sufficient protection from the current or it dies. There is no in between. A fish cannot do with a "little bit" of shelter anymore than a female can be a "little bit" pregnant.

Obviously a one-inch fish and a one-pound fish require different size current barriers. And fish are totally aware of this, for it is the basis of their survival. Theirs is first and foremost a rule of territorial imperative—without proper shelter from the current, all else (food, reproduction, growth, and the like) is not only meaningless but impossible. So, in running waters, you will find each fish taking over the best shelter from the current his size, weight, and pugnacity can command. It's the law of the wild.

In 1972, Montana stopped stocking hatchery catchables in all Blue Ribbon streams. The above facts were mainly, but not totally, responsible. It had been found earlier that in most planting situations 70 percent of the hatchery trout died within four weeks and 95 percent died in three months even *if angling was not allowed.* Therefore, hatchery planting was known to be ineffective *unless* a put-and-take situation existed. Since it costs about $1.50 per pound to raise hatchery catchables, the state is saving over $1,000,000 per year by not stocking such trout in streams that have good natural reproduction.

The effort now, on Blue Ribbon streams—of which the Madison is certainly one—is toward habitat improvement, a suggestion that was also made to the Fish and Game Commission by our club in 1968. We were assured that if the catchable program proved detrimental, which it did, that our suggestion of habitat improvement would be instituted when money and manpower became available.

Money and manpower for limited improvement work became available in

1976 and work was started on a section of O'Dell Creek, a tributary that enters the river near Ennis. O'Dell is a smaller, much more manageable stream and the first improvement efforts were here because it would yield results quicker and be easier to evaluate. If the results do show an improvement in the *quality* of the fishing, the work will then be transferred to the Madison—and to other streams—in future years.

It will take scores of years and millions of dollars to improve the trout streams of Montana, and at an estimated cost of one thousand dollars per mile, it will take something in the neighborhood of $100,000 for habitat improvement on the Madison itself. It will also take at least twenty years before the job is done. But with biologists such as Vincent and Ron Marcoux spearheading the work, the future of quality trout fishing on the Madison is looking brighter all the time.

Dick Vincent says that there are two thousand five hundred rainbow trout, five hundred brown trout and eight thousand whitefish of seven or more inches per mile of stream in the Madison from Quake Lake to Varney Bridge (about forty miles of water) and one thousand six hundred brown and one thousand four hundred rainbow trout of this size per mile from Varney to Ennis Lake, with again about eight thousand whitefish per mile of stream. But the Varney–Ennis Lake stretch has much larger numbers of two to five-pound trout than does the river above Varney, due to better holding water.

There are some few brook and cutthrout trout in this stretch of river and on to Quake Lake, but they are rare and accidental. Mottled sculpin, longnose dace, white and longnose suckers comprise the nontrout population. Some grayling are found throughout but are fast disappearing. Grayling, cutthroat, sculpin, dace, and suckers were native to the Madison at the time of Lewis and Clark; the others were introduced at later dates.

Vincent says that fishing pressure on this strecth of the Madison has increased twenty to twenty-five times since 1950, and that at present, anglers are taking about 25 percent of the total stock of trout each year. However, *most* are not kept; the ones that are are mostly those over fourteen inches on up to the top size in this stretch, probably twenty-four inches. This keeping of the larger fish does not result in a smaller strain of trout but it does spread the available sizable fish among over one hundred thousand fishermen, whereas in 1950, the total number of large fish was spread among five thousand or fewer anglers. This spreading has made it appear that the fishing is of lesser quality. Vincent says emphatically that this is not so; the quality of the fishing has not yet reached the point where the mortality rate due to all causes in any age class is greater than the natural replacement rate in that age class. Until that point is reached, angler pressure will have no effect on the overall quality of the fishing. (See the last chapter for a later assessment).

What is affecting the quality of the fishing in the latter part of the season is a pattern that has developed over perhaps the last ten years. About nine-tenths of the total pressure comes in a six-week period, from early June to mid-July. Over 80 percent of the catch is made during the same period, so most of the sizable fish that are kept are kept prior to mid-July. Thus, no matter how you slice it, there are fewer sizable fish for the late-July through November fishermen. While the overall, year-long quality of the fishing may be still as good, it is much less good for the late-season angler than it once was, due to early-season pressure. The quality of the fishing suffers in the latter part of the season, but this has not yet been recognized by the statisticians, who deal in averages. Because of this and their firm dependence on figures and not logic, it is difficult to convince these people that because the overall quality of the fishing has not dropped that quality can be different in one part of the season. They remind me of the story making fun of the reasoning of statisticians, which goes: there was a man sitting in a chair. He had his right foot in a bucket of ice water, his left in a bucket of boiling water. Though his right foot was freezing and his left scalding, on the average he was comfortable. So much for plain statistics. They are a handy tool *but* they must be used in conjunction with common sense or they can be totally misleading and result in inaccurate or inappropriate conclusions.

Thus, the conclusion that the quality of fishing in the Madison has not deteriorated is only partly correct. For the latter part of the season it is not as good as it once was, on a number per capita basis of large fish, due to immense pressure and take-out of large fish early in the season. Nor is the answer so simple as: fish during the early part of the season. The answer, at least in major part, is habitat improvement that will not only provide more larger fish but will make those fish more difficult to catch or kill by making them less vulnerable to *all* predators, not just fishermen.

The temperature of the Madison from Quake Lake to Varney is about five degrees F. warmer on the average (there's that word again) than the section from Varney to Ennis Lake. Spring creeks in the lower section cause part of this vital five-degree drop. The upper section is warmed somewhat by water coming off the *top* of Quake Lake.

There are over fifty tributaries to the Madison between Quake Lake and Varney Bridge, but 90 percent of them are intermittent streams, carrying melting snow in the spring but dry the rest of the year. Of the five or six constant streams, only the West Fork is a significant fishery and its long history of silting makes it a much poorer trout stream than it should be.

Some of the "spring" creeks in the Varney-to-Ennis Lake section, of which there are several, are probably not spring creeks at all. Many irrigation ditches in this area undoubtedly "weep" into the porous substrata and this water pops up elsewhere as a spring creek. This is fairly evident when one considers that the lower part of this section of the river—Varney to Ennis—receives much less moisture than does the area higher up, yet there are far more constantly running streams in the lower section. It has to be the river feeding itself.

This is true on most non-dammed streams furnishing irrigation water. The apparently wasteful irrigation practices are actually beneficial. Water can only be *lost* into plant cells or by evaporation. Excess of water used over what is exactly needed is returned either to the ground water table, keeping it up, or to the river, keeping it up. Reuse of irrigation water occurs in both cases and is a beneficial practice *if* a stream is not drawn below a level required for fish and insects to flourish. *Flourish,* not survive.

It is also probable that some of the spring creeks are merely seepage from the river itself, because of the porous nature of the river banks and bottom. It may be that O'Dell Creek is of this nature. One reason for believing it may be is the fact that it rises only a mile or so from the river at Varney Bridge, below a long slant in the river that puts a section directly upstream of the heads of O'Dell Creek. The creek runs almost perfectly parallel to the river for its entire length, appearing to be more of a cutoff from the river than a separate stream. Unfortunately, I have not chemically tested the two streams near the headwaters of O'Dell and thus am unable to say if they are identical. I've done this on scores of other streams in this area, but O'Dell Creek is a little farther than I normally range in my water testing. So, my conjecture that O'Dell is part of the Madison by virtue of seepage is just that, but the geography and geology of the area make it reasonable.

O'Dell is an excellent fisherman's stream. It hosts few large trout but a very good number of fourteen- to sixteen-inchers. It is a small stream, not difficult to wade; a good fly caster can reach any spot in it with ease. It is a most pleasant stream for the fly fisher, and quite rewarding. It enters the Madison about two miles below the Ennis highway bridge.

The insect populations of the Madison and O'Dell are similar, if not identical. It would take at least a five-year study to determine either way. Both are blessed with a plenitude of types and individual numbers.

One biologist told me that the river itself contains over one thousand different species, but fishermen imitate less than a dozen. He pointed out that one thing that makes the Madison such a great trout stream is the many kinds of insects in it, as well as numbers. Trout fry and fingerlings can eat only a few species of insects and cannot survive if these are not present in the streams in which they live. Small, almost microscopic insects and crustaceans are absolutely necessary to the diet of fry, as are the less active, very immature forms of some larger insects. These, while necessary to the survival of fry and fingerlings, are of no use to the fisherman; he cannot possibly use or imitate them.

Among those that are of use and can be imitated are Ephemeroptera (mayflies), Plecoptera (stoneflies), Trichoptera (caddis flies), Zygoptera (damselflies), Hemiptera (water bugs), Coleoptera (riffle beetles), and perhaps some members of Lepidoptera (aquatic moths).

Unfortunately, except for one creature, the biologist didn't know the genus and species of the most prevalent forms. The one he did know, *Pteronarcys californica*, the giant stonefly, is known to everyone who fishes the river as the "salmon fly."

My knowledge of the insect forms in this section of the river is fragmentary, yet I know of no one who is better informed. I wish I did. I know that there are one or two species of *Epeorus*, perhaps *longimanus*, or *albertae*; some *Ephemerella*, species unknown; several *Trichoptera*, generically, *Brachycentrus*, *Rhyacophila*; and one species of *Leucotrichia*; plus a very large species of

Hesperophylax, which species I don't know. There are midge and blackfly among the *Diptera,* and several species of cranefly as well. Dragon and damselfly nymphs are confined to slower, smooth-bottomed areas, around creek mouths, or the channels below islands that block the flow. The same is true with beetles, bugs and their larvae, and the larvae of aquatic moths.

I'm not acquainted with more than a dozen of the above creatures in this stretch of river, yet I believe I know more of them than even Dick McGuire, Bud and Greg Lilly, Jim Danskin, or even Dick Vincent. Most of these people and most of the fishermen are not interested in doing the time consuming research it would take to acquire even the skimpy and fragmentary knowledge that I have. My excuse for not knowing more is that I have been involved in such research on the upper river and other streams closer to home for fifteen years and I still have much to learn about them.

There is no information that I'm aware of which outlines which fish eat which insects in this or any section of the Madison. Thus, information on competition for food among the various fish species is absent. The dace, sculpin, and suckers are thought not to be competitors of the trout, because they are largely vegetarian, although they will eat about anything that comes into their maws.

Whitefish are thought to be in direct competition with trout for both food and shelter. Both are members of the *Salmonidae* and their needs are thought to be virtually identical. On the basis of forty years experience with them as a fisherman with an investigating mind, I can find nothing in the habits, food, and habitat of the one that is not matched in the other. Whitefish are less aggressive than trout and thus are dominated by them in a contest for shelter.

It is unfortunate that the whitefish is not more highly regarded. It is an excellent fly fish, as discriminating and as difficult as any trout; it runs to excellent sizes, seventeen to twenty-one inches; it acquits itself well if not spectacularly on the end of the line; and it is far superior to any trout on the plate. Further, I have eaten smoked salmon, sturgeon, barracuda, mullet, goldeye, sailfish, carp, trout of five species, paddlefish, mackerel, eel, haddock, shad, and some others, and I find smoked whitefish the equal of any of them and better than most. I would welcome an education program on the part of my state's Fish and Game Department to educate the public on the value of this fine fish.

Unfortunately, the whitefish's appearance is against it. It is humpbacked, coarsely scaled, and has a submedian mouth. Many confuse it with the sucker. But this is no sucker. It has exactly the same skeleton as a trout or salmon, with exceedingly minor differences. Its flesh is firm and pure white, and exceptionally flaky. My favorite fishes for eating are red snapper and pompano among salt-water fishes and channel catfish and grayling among freshwater types. The whitefish is the equal of any of these. I seldom keep any fish, except those I need for my ongoing investigations, and again, except for whitefish, I seldom eat fish. Smoked and poached in milk and butter, they are better than the finest finnan haddie; fried, or baked, they are tops among fishes. They should be skinned for frying, scaled for baking, and neither for smoking.

Should you come upon this prince of fishes, treat him as he deserves—as a proper game and an excellent fly fish, the equal of any on the plate, and without peer when properly smoked.

Since whitefish outnumber trout almost three to one in this section of the Madison, keeping the former and releasing the latter will allow you to eat your cake and have it, too. I heartily recommend this course to you. It is most worthy of your consideration.

I have dealt earlier with some matters that later consideration leads me to believe should be dealt with in greater detail. One of these is the impact of stocking hatchery catchables in a good, naturally producing trout stream. If I've left the implication that Dick McGuire, I, or our fly-fishing club was the prime mover in reversing this undesirable situation, I was wrong. The man almost entirely responsible was Dick Vincent. We were a tool, a mouthpiece, a method of getting the information before the proper authorities and in showing *public* interest. This, because governmental organizations are what they are, was necessary lest a charge of empire building or worse be raised against Vincent. But our part should not be minimized. Had we not agreed, due to the investigations of McGuire, the thing would have been delayed, maybe for years.

Habitat improvement was a goal of Vincent also, but I think he was surprised that we not only had considered it but had strong ideas about it, what it should and should not be.

I may not have been clear as to the effects of stocking hatchery catchables. When you dump X thousands of living units into any area not totally a desert or wilderness, you create an immediate shortage of shelter *and* you create an intolerable sociological pressure on those biological units already there. It does not matter whether we are talking of fish, rats, monkeys, or humans. The result is precisely the same: chaos. All *normal* living patterns are destroyed. In a running stream this is the equivalent of forcing families, including children, to leave a set of fixed quarters and to exist on a freeway. Even the oldest and most experienced will make mistakes and some of these will die because of what some unthinking or inconsiderate organism has decreed as progress. And the young practically never survive. Or, to put it differently, few young will survive. By doing what you have done you have set in motion a rate of mortality many times the normal rate.

In big cities, what I've just outlined results in an increased crime rate, an increased suicide rate, an increased divorce rate, and a lowered birth rate.

In trout streams it results in an enormously enlarged mortality rate. You cannot live "in the streets" in a trout stream. At least, a trout can't.

Earlier I mentioned the rainbows running to spawn out of Ennis Lake and that this run had declined in recent years, for reasons apparently unknown.

One reason may be that as the lake grew warmer, it became too warm for large, spawning-size rainbows, which were forced to remain in the river year around and thus were more exposed to predators, including fishermen. Small fish have a more favorable surface-to-volume (skin surface to body volume) ratio than do larger fish and are thus able to endure substantially higher water temperatures for a longer period of time than can larger fish.

Another possible reason is the predominance of brown trout in the lower end of the river at Ennis Lake. Brown trout are the most territorially aggressive of all *Salmonidae* and will take over the living space of other trout larger than they, and this increases the mortality rate of the less dominant species, which is forced out of its hold to live "on the freeway."

I have recently been informed by Dick Vincent that the O'Dell Creek habitat studies have been suspended due to a series of problems and the press of other work. One of the problems has been the effect of the warming of Ennis Lake on the lower Madison fishery, including a major fish kill. This will be taken up later.

As it stands now, the section of the middle Madison is still a very fine trout stream, and it appears that the only threat to it is from the fishermen themselves. But there are ways of controlling them and so we may look forward to this stream remaining as good as it is now, and it may get better.

If it does get better it will be because of the efforts of such as the members of our Southwestern Montana Fly Fishers, and fellows like Dick Vincent.

Dick told me just the other night that the Madison is "his" river, that he was born and raised on it and he does not intend to let anything happen to it. Since he just may be the finest fisheries biologist this country has, that kind of reassurance is like money in the bank. For about 95,000 fishermen countrywide, it's the best possible news.

THE LOWER RIVER VALLEY

THOUGH MEN, BOTH WHITE AND RED, CAME TO THE MADISON RIVER FIRST BY WAY of its lower valley, the red men only came to visit, and the first whites also. Settling by whites started a few years later than did settling of the middle valley, but once started went much faster. The reason was that the land, while also suitable for grazing, had far deeper and richer soil than the middle valley; and especially along the river, various crops did very well, helped in some cases by irrigation.

There is some little record of what those first farmers raised: wheat, grains of other types, hay, legumes, and of course family gardens. These are still the primary crops, but they are raised in different amounts than earlier—wheat now is the major crop in the area. Cattle, some sheep and pigs, and horses are raised but *most* ranches here do not have access to public summer range and thus individual herds are small.

Below Beartrap Canyon is more of a flood plain than a valley. Encompassed in it are the Gallatin River on the east and the Jefferson on the west. The three valleys are practically one and this is indicated by the name, Trident, for a village near Three Forks, where the three join the Missouri River Valley.

It is a pleasant area, verdant and lush in summer, golden and peaceful in the fall, at harvest time. It has a milder climate than anywhere farther up river; the winters are seldom severe, and while summers are occasionally hot, the humidity is low and there are pleasant breezes. It is a typically low (under five thousand feet) western valley and climate, less extreme than the Midwest, somewhat drier also. Annual average total precipitation varies from fourteen inches in the Beartrap area to twelve inches at Three Forks. This is much below what is needed to sustain most crops. Though 60 percent of it falls during the growing season, irrigation is most always required.

The valley, or flood plain, is framed by faraway mountains. On the east the beautiful Bridgers, the northern tip of the Gallatin Range, and the Spanish Peaks can be seen. On the south the Beartraps are a rounded, irregular ridge. To the west, the Tobacco Root and Silver Bow ranges move north to meet the Big and Little Belts to complete the encirclement. There are numbers of passes through these mountains, some rather high, and except for the Beartraps, all these ranges approach ten thousand feet. One will look far before finding a lovelier pastoral valley, or a better watered one, with three major rivers and scores of lesser creeks.

The area became a crossroads for travel almost as soon as whites settled in the lower valley. At that time a wagon road from Deer Lodge-Butte-Helena already had reached the Three Forks area. Almost at once, this was joined by the Bozeman Trail, and freight roads from the above communities and Bozeman went up the valley to Ennis and over to Virginia City and Alder Gulch. Roads from there went to Bannack and Dillon, and south to southern Idaho and Utah.

An enterprising man named Gilman Sawtell had settled on Henrys Lake in Idaho in the early 1860s. Homesteading the area now known as Staley's Springs, Sawtell at once began to expand into many fields of endeavor. He built quarters for travelers, raised food for sale, and netted fish from the lake for the same purpose. He built a wagon road from the lake over Raynolds Pass, and down the Madison to Ennis to join the existing roads. Over this route Sawtell hauled vegetables, grain, produce, and fish to the miners at Virginia City-Alder Gulch. Sawtell's road also connected to the wagon road to Ft. Hall on the Snake (Henrys Fork), and thus to Salt Lake City.

Later, Sawtell expanded his road system, with help, over Targhee Pass and into the Madison Basin, where it was continued on up the Madison and Firehole rivers to Old Faithful. Thus Sawtell not only opened up connections with the lower Madison Valley but with its uppermost regions also. In recognition of his services, the southernmost peak of the Centennial Mountains, flanking Henrys Lake on the west, and forming the boundary between Montana and Idaho, is named Sawtell Peak. It has an FAA air-traffic control radar system on its top and a good road leaves highway 191 not far from Mack's Inn and goes to the top of Sawtell Peak. The view from the top is breathtaking. One can see parts of three states, a dozen mountain ranges, lakes, rivers, valleys, and canyons galore. Anyone in the area who doesn't visit Sawtell Peak is missing a great experience.

Sawtell's road had a great impact on the lower valley because it was, at the time, the easiest route from a major population center (Salt Lake City) to eastern Montana, the Dakotas, and the upper Midwest. People poured in from both directions; between 1862 and 1875 over one hundred thousand came into or across the lower valley. Most were going someplace else—the placers of Virginia City or Last Chance Gulch, the farms and ranches of Deer Lodge, or back to the East; but their very numbers caused the Blackfeet to withdraw in shock across the Missouri, and never again pose a threat to southwestern Montana.

The ease of transportation caused the area to prosper; Bozeman and Three Forks became important supply centers. Good roads meant that not only could the farmers and cattlemen sell their products at a good price to the mining communities, but they could also import goods from east or west at a decent rate. It was this ease of transportation, this network of good roads, that caused the lower valley to be settled so quickly and so permanently. The population peaked within a few years because all the available land was settled, and this area has been one of the most stable in the entire state. It has changed almost not at all in over a hundred years. The dirt roads are now blacktop and concrete, the Bozeman Trail is Interstate 90, the freight and stage roads are U.S. 287, and the area has electricity. The ferry at Three Forks has long since ceased operation, and the Northern Pacific (now Burlington Northern) Railroad has taken over freight hauling. But these are minor changes. There has been modernization, but that's about all. The area has always been a beautiful, pastoral farming-ranching area. It still is. A resident there in 1878 would have no trouble finding his way around today.

Though this area was overgrazed somewhat between 1886 and 1910, it never reached crisis levels, largely because public land was not much involved, and the fact that great quantities of supplemental cattle feed have always grown here. But there are problems.

This *is* a flood plain; it has been so for thousands of years. And a flood plain means floods. There is some flooding every spring, serious flooding every four or five, and catastrophic flooding about every twenty-five springs. The farmers and ranchers have always known this, yet each time it happens, they act shocked. In the past they have resorted to individual ditching and diking to reduce the problem. But a recent collateral decision that the Madison is a navigable river has caused this practice to become illegal. It can be done with permission from the Army Corps of Engineers, but such permission now requires an environmental impact statement, so involved and costly that the landowners refuse to do it. So, like most modern Americans, the farmers and ranchers are crying for the government to do something. By something, they mean build levees to keep floods off their land, using taxpayers' money for the sole purpose of protecting their investment.

The landowners in fact have aggravated their own problem. If they had left a broad band of trees, shrubs, underbrush, and ground cover on the banks of the river and all its tributaries, they would have reduced flood damage to practically nothing. The land would still overflow but the cutting power of the stream would have been almost completely nullified. Instead, in order to obtain more arable acreage, the farmers have cleared all growth right up to the edge of the normal flow. They not only have bought themselves an ogre, they have actually lost more land, due to erosion, than they have gained. And it will get much worse before it gets better.

Joel Shouse, the local director of The Blue Ribbons of the Big Sky Country

Areawide Planning Organization recently gave a presentation of some of the area's problems for a group of us here at West Yellowstone. Included was a blood chilling before-and-after slide show. The before pictures showed a looping, oxbowed slow-water creek on a flood-plain farm. This type of stream is absolutely typical of flood-plain streams.

The banks of this sinuous stream were densely covered with dwarf willow, probably the best stream-bank stabilizing plant of any. In one particular oxbow, the willows covered an area of one-and-a-quarter acres. The farmer had decided that this acreage was wasted. He bulldozed the willows off, roots and all.

The after picture showed the grim results. The loop had been straightened, the banks ravaged, and not only did the farmer lose that one-and-a-quarter acre but an additional several acres as well where the stream ate a great reverse loop out into his unguarded wheat land. This kind of shortsighted program has been going on in the lower Madison Valley for over a hundred years, in spite of the advice of the Soil Conservation Service and the county farm agents. However, there is some evidence that all but the most hard-headed farmers are coming to realize that more is not always better.

The buffalo are long gone from this area, and most of the elk and antelope. There are deer in the foothills that now and then come out into the flood plain in winter, but big game is rare in this valley.

Pheasants have been introduced and have prospered, grouse of two species may be found, ducks and geese like flood-plain streams and are here, some staying the winter. But hunting is mostly an adjunct to farming in the lower valley.

Fishing has largely been a food-gathering process. In the upper and middle sections of the river, nonresidents comprise 90 percent of the fishermen but along the lower river, residents form 90 percent of the anglers.

Though the fish populace below the Beartrap Canyon has been different from that above the canyon, in the last twenty years the ratio of different species has changed faster than in the preceding thousand years. Ennis Lake has caused these last rapid changes.

When man, white or red, came into the lower Madison Valley, the fish native to the lower river were cutthroat trout, grayling, mountain sucker, longnose dace, mountain whitefish, longnose sucker, sculpin, stone-cat, and burbot (ling). Introduced fishes are white sucker, carp, yellow perch, and flathead chub among nongame fishes. Brook, brown, and rainbow trout are introduced game fishes.

The changes in fish populations have been caused by the warming of the water from Ennis Lake, where the summer daytime high temperatures often top 82° F. The lake is so shallow that surface and bottom temperatures are virtually the same. Above Ennis Lake, the high river temperature seldom exceeds 70° F.; mostly it is below 65°, which is about ideal for trout growth and reproduction. Temperatures in the river from Madison Dam to the confluence of the Missouri have been topping 80° the past few years; trout still live in the river but growth and reproduction have been dramatically slowed. There are about two thousand trout per mile of stream of seven inches and over; but there are fifteen thousand whitefish per mile of this size, and untold thousands of carp, sucker, burbot, and chub.

Dick Vincent says electroshocking of this stretch at present shows few trout over two pounds. There *may* be larger trout in the Beartrap Canyon stretch, which, because of its dangerously fast flow, cannot be safely and successfully electroshocked. However, catch reports are not encouraging. Few larger trout are reported from this area, which was once noted for large trout.

However, other effects from Ennis Lake are affecting the lower river. High winds, which stir up the shallow lake, send heavy loads of silt down the Beartrap channel and onto the bed of the lower river where lesser current speeds allow it to settle out and cover insect and fish spawning areas. Also, excessive amounts of algae break loose during windstorms and this has a suffocating effect on the lower river. In summer 1976 a massive fish-kill took place in Beartrap Canyon. Since this canyon is the best aerated section of the lower river, oxygen depletion by algae degeneration does not seem a factor. Temperatures at the time were no higher than usual. No other implementing factors were found during an extensive study *after* the kill. What caused it? No one knows.

Madison Dam and Ennis Lake will be a continuing problem to the lower river. The problem can only get worse. At present rates, the *thermal* pollution of the lower river from Ennis Lake will exceed the capacity of trout to adjust in ten years.

Why can't the problem be removed? That's easy. Economics. Madison Dam was built over seventy years ago—it's long ago paid for, but, as a run-of-the-river generation system (not dependent on a head or pool from the lake) it produces between 60 and 70 million kilowatts per year of electricity—about $500,000 of clear profit a year for Montana Power. Why, then, should they want to do anything that would destroy that source? The answer is, they wouldn't. Nor can they be readily blamed.

Montana Power says it will go along with anything the Fish and Game Department wants to do as long as it neither costs the company money nor any loss of power generation. Though this seems a hard-nosed attitude, it is a reasonable one. Montana Power did not build the original dam, nor is it responsible for the silting that caused the present problem.

As related earlier, Ennis Lake was doomed to an early death due to severe overgrazing and to its shallow bowl. At present rates, it will silt-up completely except for the river channel in perhaps fifteen to twenty-five years. But while it is doing this, it will destroy the lower river as a trout stream due to thermal pollution. Can anything be done, in time, to save this section of the river?

The Montana Power Company will acquiesce to any solution that doesn't cost it money or generating capacity. Based on this position, the Montana Fish and Game Department, Blue Ribbons, the U.S. Fish and Wildlife Service, BLM, the Bureau of Reclamation, Trout Unlimited, and county commissions, planning boards and conservation districts for Madison County formed a committee along with Montana Power to consider possible solutions. So far, they have considered these alternatives:

1. Removal of the dam.
2. Reducing the level of the lake.
3. Heighten the dam to make the lake deeper.
4. Constructing dikes to keep the river water in the channel.
5. Underwater piping of water from the river directly to the dam, thus bypassing the lake.
6. Deepen the lake by dredging.

Of these proposals, Montana Power is unalterably opposed to choices 1 and 2. Number 3 would be extremely expensive and would provide only short-term benefits, as would number 6. This leaves numbers 4 and 5 as possible avenues to pursue. Both would be expensive, though less so than options 3 and 6, and these two, 4 and 5 which, in effect, would eliminate the lake or at least its effects on the lower river, would be long term. Option 5 would probably be permanent, since river water would be carried directly to the flume and thence to the 120-foot drop to the generators, eliminating any silting. Option 4 would last until the channel at the dam face silted up to the opening of the flume. After that, no one knows what would happen.

At present the committee is still studying the matter. It is aware that the situation is critical. At present, Ennis Lake is acting as a giant (six-square-mile) solar collector (it takes twenty days for water to cross the lake to the flume and the sun has this long to warm it). The water temperature directly reflects the ambient air temperature, with a delay of seven to ten days, as water both warms and cools by contact with the air, but at a slower rate. This means that a week or ten days of 90-degree weather would push the lake up to that temperature and probably result in a massive fish-kill on the lower river. All trout and whitefish would die, as might the forage fish. This is a possibility that faces the committee if some affirmative action is not taken. It is unlikely that the committee can act in time.

In the past few years, knowledgeable local anglers have ceased to fish the lower Madison in summer. The river has been taken over by sun-bathing tube floaters and coarse-fishing bait-fishermen. No one begrudges these activities but they reflect the grim fact that the lower river is literally finished as a trout fishery. It can be restored *if* cooler water can be drawn in some manner from Ennis Lake. It is doubtful if it can be saved.

EXPANSION FROM EAST AND WEST

IN LATE 1863, AN ENTERPRISING AND FORWARD-LOOKING MAN NAMED JOHN Bozeman began to look for a better way of getting food and materials into the Alder Gulch-Virginia City mining areas. At that time everything was coming into southwestern Montana from or through Ogden, Utah. There was no road closer and no rail connection as close. Many of the goods arriving at Ogden came around the Horn on sailing ships to the Pacific Coast, then over rough and dangerous wagon roads more than 1,100 miles, then over an even rougher road to southwestern Montana. Bozeman thought there might be a better way.

The western terminus of the Union Pacific railroad was at Omaha, Nebraska, a bridge having just been built across the Missouri River from Council Bluffs, Iowa, in preparation for expanding the line to the West Coast. The Civil War temporarily halted this expansion but Bozeman knew that it would soon continue. Accordingly, he worked out a route from Julesburg, Colorado, where a good freight road from Omaha ended, and where roads and cattle trails from Kansas, Oklahoma, and Texas had junctions, to Bozeman, and Virginia City. He asked for, and got, U.S. Army posts to guard dangerous sections of the trail. This led directly to the Red Cloud War.

The Indians of Wyoming and Colorado had earlier, in 1854, granted the use of the Oregon Trail across southern Wyoming and had seen that treaty, which was for passage only, repeatedly violated by whites building forts and homesteads, occupying the area and getting Army protection from the Indians whose land they were stealing. The Indians had never been able to have the treaty upheld, the congress and the Army simply ignored them, and they saw in the Bozeman Trail an even worse division of their lands.

However, the Indians did not resort to war until the opening of Fort Phil Kearny, just south of present Sheridan, Wyoming. After repeated efforts to have the illegal fort removed by peaceful means, the Indians isolated it, laid siege to it, and in December 1866, destroyed a major portion of the garrison in the so-called Fetterman Massacre. Because the fort could not be successfully supplied and reinforced, it was removed, as were Forts C. F. Smith and Reno, and a new treaty signed in 1868. Red Cloud and his band, who had forced the removal of these forts, scrupulously adhered to the new treaty; as usual the whites did not.

The Fetterman affair calls to mind the bitter wryness of a famous Indian, Jim Thorpe, who commented on it to reporters while at Carlisle Indian School.

Said Thorpe, "When one thousand whites kill one hundred Indians it's a great victory, but when two hundred Indians kill fifty whites it's a massacre."

Prior to the closing of the Bloody Bozeman, as the trail became known, an event of considerable significance for Montana and the Madison River took place.

In 1866, Nelson Story brought up a large herd of cattle into Montana, along the Bozeman Trail. This was to be the nucleus of most herds in the area through the 1880s. Most of these cattle remained in the Gallatin Valley between Bozeman and Three Forks, but enough found their way up the Madison to above Ennis to establish permanent herds in that region, and to begin over half a century of overgrazing.

The Bozeman Trail, though officially closed in 1868, was reopened in the late 1870s after the Sioux had been suppressed. It formed the best and most direct route from the South and Midwest, running from the terminus at Julesburg along the route of the Union Pacific to Cheyenne, Laramie, then north, crossing the Powder River at Kaycee, Wyoming, following this river to the Yellowstone, then along the Yellowstone upstream to present Livingston, Montana, over Bozeman Pass to Bozeman, on to Three Forks, up the Madison Valley to Ennis and over to Virginia City. At that time, because it traveled nearly its entire length along broad, gently sloping river valleys fairly easy for wagons to negotiate, it was the most important trail into all of Montana and between 1864 and 1886 an estimated 50,000 people and 5,500,000 cattle used the trail. Not until railroads penetrated from the East into Montana did the Bozeman Trail lose its importance.

During the years of official closure, 1868 to 1879, it was still used but without official sanction and without Army protection. Emigrants passing along the trail at this time were required to belong to a group that had at least fifty wagons, forty well-armed men, and an experienced leader. These determined people often had to fight their way almost continuously from Ft. Laramie to or across the Yellowstone, and the trail became littered with dead animals, discarded goods, and the graves of emigrants. Still they came in steadily increasing numbers, and their influx, coupled with a similar situation in the Dakotas caused the Sioux to become more and more aggressive. The situation culminated in the Army mounting a massive campaign, of which, the Custer debacle was a part.

The campaigns of Generals Terry and Crook and Colonel John Gibbon eventually forced the Indians out of the area, thus putting an end to the "Indian troubles," which were not caused by the Indians but by hordes of greedy whites surging into the region looking for gold and free land.

The Northern Pacific Railroad, formed in 1864 but not put into operation until much later, pushed a route from Minnesota on the east and Tacoma, Washington, in the West, which joined at Gold Creek, Montana in 1883. A branch line was built to a terminus at Gardiner, Montana, in 1903. These routes brought flocks of gold and land-grabbing whites. It was survey teams in the Wyoming-Montana border region during the period 1869 to 1879 that kept fanning the fires of resentment among the Indians and kept the pot of trouble boiling.

Despite the difficulties and the risks, large numbers of whites kept coming into Montana in a series of surging pulses. Had all of them remained, Montana would have a much larger population. But for each ten thousand that came, approximately seven thousand left, disappointed at not finding gold, broken by farming in a too-arid area, or fed up with harsh winters and living conditions.

At the same time the eastern expansion was going on, white pressure in eastern Oregon and western Idaho was sending both whites and Indians into western Montana. The Indians were the peaceful Shoshoni and the Nez Percé. Our dealings with the latter tribe form the most shameful passage in the history of any nation.

In 1876 the whites in the Wallowa Valley area decided that the Nez Percé treaty lands were too good for "ignorant savages" and moved in to take them over. It was a fatal misjudgment. Instead of reacting with war and savagery, the Nez Percé simply rounded up the whites, without killing one, and ushered them off Indian lands. This neutralized the Army; without "provocation" it could not act.

But the whites were masters of chicanery, deceit, and conspiracy. The white farmers, the government's Indian agents, and the Army got a few Nez Percé drunk and had them sign over the treaty lands to the whites. This affair had the same legality that a half-dozen minor stockholders signing over IBM would have. But the Indian agents and the Army solemnly declared that the treaty lands now belonged to the whites and ordered the Indians off.

The proud and honorable Nez Percé declined to go, and in a series of battles, handed the Army a licking. The Army furiously ordered up massive reinforcements and seeing the futility of a small tribe resisting a large, powerful and unseeing nation, the Nez Percé began its long retreat, unequalled for noble restraint on the part of one force, and shameful excess on the part of the other.

When the Nez Percé got to Montana, they made the first of two terrible mistakes. They assumed that because they represented no threat to the citizens of that state and harmed nothing and no one, they would be allowed peaceful passage. How wrong they were.

In their passage down the Bitteroot Valley, they paid for everything they got, kept away from populated areas, and caused no trouble of any kind. Yet when the local populace found out that the Army was pursuing the Indians men grabbed their guns and set out to exterminate them like vermin.

At their camp on the Big Hole River, the Nez Percé slept well, never dreaming they would be set upon shortly by butchers. But they were, and Colonel John Gibbon and his Army force were among them.

The Indians were ambushed on a cool, foggy August morning. The attacking force opened fire while most of the Nez Percé were still asleep and the ravening whites killed everything that came in front of their guns—braves, women, children, even babes in arms. Fifty-three women and children were slaughtered, far more than the number of men killed. No white person writing at any time about this butchery has ever called it a massacre.

The Nez Percé fought their way out, taking their households and goods and left enough dead whites behind to have a sobering effect on the rest. They moved south and set up camp at Camas Meadows in Idaho, where they were ambushed again, on 20 August 1877.

Once more the Nez Percé fought their way clear and moved eastward past Henrys Lake, over Targhee Pass, through the Madison Basin, and on up the Madison River. They went up Firehole Canyon to the Fountain Flats area, encountered some tourists, and here the long-suffering "savages" reverted to "nature." They began shooting some whites without provocation.

Among those they shot was George F. Cowan of Radersburg, Montana, and another member of the party, a man named Oldham, who eventually died.* Cowan was shot in the head, abdomen and leg, but crawled, in a couple of days, some ten miles from beyond the Nez Percé Creek (named for this affair) over horrendous terrain, to Madison Junction where he was found by General O. O. Howard's Army force. He was transported by wagon to Virginia City, more than seventy miles over the worst of roads. On one occasion the wagon went over a bank and turned over. Then, when he was finally put to bed in Virginia City, one side collapsed, ejecting Cowan onto the floor, whereupon this tough old goat is said to have exclaimed: "Why don't they bring on the artillery; they've tried everything else!"

The Nez Percé left the area of Fountain Flats, going up Nez Percé Creek, over Mary Mountain into Hayden Valley. Here they encountered another group of tourists and some shooting and killing took place. The reports of this vary according to who is giving the account, but it seems a mutual distrust triggered the affair. Reports of marauding Blackfeet in the area (true) may have had a catalyzing effect.

The Nez Percé took some hostages, and one white as a guide, and wove their way out of the Park by a devious route. At the time, in spite of the skills of the Nez Percé, they were being cut off and surrounded.

*There are conflicting accounts of Oldham's death, perhaps because the party contained more than one man named Oldham.

The transcontinental telegraph had been completed in 1861. It was this that put the famed—but money-losing—Pony Express out of business. When the Nez Percé were retreating through Montana, Idaho, and Yellowstone Park, branch lines already existed to Virginia City, Bozeman, and along the Yellowstone in eastern Montana. General Howard was in touch with Army forces both north and east of the Indians route of march. Still, so cleverly did the Indians maneuver, constantly feinting one direction while moving another, that they might well have escaped the trap. But just short of the Canadian border they stopped—horses worn out, wounded, in desperate condition, short of food, tired, but still in good spirits. They had made their second mistake. They thought they were in Canada and safe.

Their capture and ultimate fate is widely known, as is the fact that the government reneged on the promises made them by Nelson Miles and Howard, and took them to a reservation far from their own land. This, one more crime in a long history of crimes in our dealing with the Indians, is better known than most, because many journalists were impressed by the noble Joseph and the restraint with which, for the most part, the Nez Percé had conducted themselves while surrounded and constantly attacked by whites trying by every method to exterminate them.

The "Indian troubles" never bothered Montana overmuch. The main battle at the Little Bighorn was an accident of timing—the Sioux caught a major enemy force in a mistake of dispersal and made them pay but Montana was not fought over by the Indians as were other areas.

The Blackfeet, the largest and most aggressive tribe in the territory, chose to fight the other Indian tribes—Crow, Assiniboin, Cree, Kootenai, Kalispel (Pend d'Oreille), and Flathead—and not to molest and irritate the white settlements. Perhaps they saw the handwriting on the wall. By the time of the Nez Percé affair, the end of the nomadic Indian in the West was being written, not by the U.S. Army, but by another army—that of the buffalo-hide hunters, who between 1871 and 1883 slaughtered an estimated 40,000,000 buffalo on the Great Plains and put an end forever to a way of life for the Plains Indians.

In May 1871 Major Richard Irving Dodge (Ft. Dodge, Dodge City) was still able to describe a ride through a huge buffalo herd along the Arkansas River in southern Kansas. The mass of animals was over twenty-five miles across and was composed of individual herds or groups of fifty to two hundred animals, closely packed but distinct from other groups. Dodge estimated the total at about two million animals. Within five years, no herds of any size existed in most of Kansas, Colorado, and Nebraska, nor in Texas or Oklahoma. In five more years the buffalo of Wyoming and the Dakotas were gone.

Between 1880 and 1883, a solid cordon of hide-hunting camps stretched across Montana from the northernmost bend of the Missouri to the Idaho border, and a firing line of hide hunters was so closely aligned that no buffalo could escape either north or south. By 1883 they were gone, the last of these shaggy beasts, forever, from the open plains. Only about one hundred twenty-five were left in the ravines and remote canyons of Yellowstone Park, and a few hundred survived in Canada. About 3,500,000 buffalo per year had been slaughtered for twelve years, their hides taken, their bodies left to rot on the ground. Some historians have estimated that 48 billion pounds of edible meat was wasted in this twelve-year period. What the U.S. Army had started, the containment of the Indian, was finished by the slaughter of the buffalo.

The way to the Madison Valley had never been barred by Indians on the south or west, and until the 1870s, most of the influx of people into the area was from this direction. However, few of the immigrants who came had originally started out for the Madison Valley. Most were headed for the gold mines at Alder Gulch-Virginia City or those at Butte-Last Chance Gulch (Helena).

When they failed to strike it rich, as most of them did, it became necessary to desert the mining towns and their rarified prices to look elsewhere for a way to make a living. Apparently the land in the middle Madison Valley looked like good farming land and between 1863 and 1886 a steady stream of feckless miners, their hopes of riches dead and gone, moved in and squatted in the area. They found even less here than they had in the mines. They would stay a year or two or three, then depart, leaving behind little except disturbed land to show that they had been here.

As some homesteaders left, others came to replace them, to try in other areas what others had failed in. To their sorrow they found that the bottom lands of the Madison River in no way resembled those of the Midwest and East from whence most had come.

Eventually they quit coming and in a few years there was no sign of their brief stay. The homes they built were fragile, built in a hurry, never to last, and they tumbled down almost as fast as they went up. Now and then, in the deep grass away from the river you will stumble onto the ruins of a shack or cabin. A few curled and sun-dried boards, some tumbled piles of stones, or perhaps a pair of rusty hinges clinging to a weathered, splintered jamb are all that remain of what once were hopes and dreams.

The great blizzard of 1886–87 put an end to most squatting in the valley. This historic disaster swept across northern, central, and eastern Montana and wiped out 90 percent of the cattle in those areas. How many died is not exactly known but it ranged into the millions.

The Madison and Gallatin valleys were untouched by the blizzard and the cattle in these two areas became extremely valuable, as food and as the basis for other herds. The ranchers expanded, spread out over nearly all the available grazing area, thus shutting out future homesteaders. The future of the Madison Valley may have been decided by a blizzard that didn't touch it.

MY PART
OF THE RIVER

One cannot own a river or even a part of it, except in one's heart. But if affection, pride, knowledge, and experience for and about a river counts for anything, then that part of the Madison River in Yellowstone Park belongs to me. It also belongs to 220 million other Americans, but few know and love it as I do.

It can be said that I was first brought to fish it by the writings of others. I had visited the stream in 1938, as a tourist, but had no time on that trip to fish it. Ten years later, I did. In the interim, I had read Howard Back's lovely and charming *The Waters of Yellowstone with Rod and Fly,* which painted a picture of the streams and the fishing that no angler could resist. I had also read Ray Bergman's *Trout* and his *With Fly, Plug, and Bait,* both of which extolled the fishing, with much emphasis on the Firehole and the Madison Rivers.

My part of the Madison is that part in Yellowstone Park. There is over twenty miles of river between Madison Junction and the Park boundary just upstream of Baker's Hole. It is a very varied stretch of river and a very rich one, running over one hundred and twenty parts per million of calcium bicarbonates. Thus it is a chalk stream—as far as is known, the largest in the world. From Madison Junction to where it exits the Park, the average gradient is ten feet per mile. But one cannot find a single mile of the river where this is true. Nor are there any other "averages" one can trust about this river. Each short stretch is different from any other. One may find two stretches that appear similar but close examination will show that they are not.

The section just below the junction of the Firehole and Gibbon is lovely water but terribly overfished by the mob of campers who flood the Madison Junction campground from 15 June to 1 September. The campers' interest in the stream wanes sharply a quarter-mile below the campground and vanishes a half-mile from it. Here also, the river has had time to mingle thoroughly the waters of its two sources, get the kinks out of its system, and become what a famous Irish angler called "that darlin' river."

Here the river is typically meadow stream in appearance. But one must always be aware, in this part of our country, that what looks like a meadow stream may be a mountain stream running through a stretch of meadows. The differences are of current speed and bottom type. Mountain streams have gravel-rubble and rubble-boulder bottoms, and currents of three miles per hour or more. Meadow streams have smoother bottoms and slower currents.

This stretch of the river might be called a composite stream. It has the fine bottom material of meadow streams but the current speed of a mountain stream. This disparity causes some problems in fishing it.

The surface appears smooth, almost glass, and fishing the dry fly would seem not to be at all difficult. It is. The bottom, though of fine material, is ridged and humped, full of mounds and dropoffs. Then there are weed beds, almost, or even to, the surface and these, while helping slow the current, work with the uneven bottom to make it diabolical. Even the most experienced dry-fly fishers have a difficult time getting a drag-free float and the novice finds it impossible. This is one reason you see so few anglers more than a half-mile below the campground, even though the river is beside the road for another half-mile.

The insects are mostly small, and of only a few species. For reasons of adaptation to different bottom materials, the different species will be found only in areas suitable to each. Some such stretches are only a hundred feet long and this produces a phenomenon that baffles visiting anglers, no matter how knowledgeable.

The insects will commence to hatch but no fish, or at most, only a few small trout, will begin to feed. The insects will usually be Pale Morning Dun (*Ephemerella lacustris*) or a variety of *Baetis* in the mayfly group and Little Grey Caddis (*Brachycentrus*) in the caddis family. These are not difficult to match; the commercial flies, Pale Morning Dun or Grey-Winged Olive will match *lacustris* well enough; Blue Upright, Blue Dun, or Blue-Winged Olive will do for the *Baetis* hatch; and Grey Colorado King is difficult to beat for the caddis hatch. Still, few fish will be taken.

The reason is that it takes a prolonged hatch with saturation of flies coming for a good period of time—fifteen to twenty minutes—before the larger trout will commence to feed. The hatches in this area *in daytime* are seldom long-lasting or prolific enough to bring up the larger trout. On occasion, in July or even late June, a caddis hatch will commence at dusk and last on into the night. If one is there when it happens, and has a size sixteen or eighteen Grey Colorado King on a 5X leader, good to even fabulous fishing can be had. But one must be aware of the closing hour, which is at 10:00 P.M. Mountain Daylight Time and at this lattitude (44° 38N.) it can still be daylight at that hour.

I have had some success using an emergent nymph in the above situations, fishing it with dry-fly tackle and in exactly the same manner. In fact, the only trout of over a pound that I have ever taken at these times has been on the emergent nymph. I use my Natant Nylon Nymph for all such hatches, varying the size and the color, light or dark, to suit. But commercial versions can be had locally and these work well enough. The Grey Nymph in size sixteen does well, as do the Hendrickson, Blue Dun wet, or Al Troth's Hare's Ear Nymph.

One will, on *very* rare occasions, come upon a very sparse hatch of *Siphlonurus occidentalis,* the Grey Drake. This will bring up a few of the larger fish in spite of there being only a few insects on the water at a time. But these are large flies, size eight or ten, and the Grey Nymph in those sizes and the regular Grey Drake wet or dry patterns will do the job.

Both dragon and damselfly nymphs are found throughout this area. These are *always* found on the bottom; they will range in size from size four, 2XL for the *Libellula* dragon nymphs at maturity (July), down to size ten or twelve for a somewhat immature *Argia* damselfly nymph.

Local patterns of the above are scarce, but a commercial Beaverpelt or Fledermouse in size six will work for the dragonfly nymph and a dark-brown mayfly nymph or, sometimes, a Brown Hackle wet will do for the damsel nymph.

A friend of mine, Bob Holmes, a truly fine fly fisherman, solved the damsel nymph problem another way some years ago. He had tied some Muddlers much darker and sparser than usual and has had very good luck fishing these in the proper manner. That is, crawled along the bottom, with now and then a short twitch. On one lowering summer day, with thunder showers in the making, Bob took eight trout of two pounds up along here on his bastard Muddler fished in the above manner.

The Big Bend section, where the river swings away from the highway and over along the base of Three Brothers Mountain and the Madison Plateau, is more familiar water to easterners and midwesterners. It is a giant elbow pool, nearly five hundred yards long, and over five feet deep in places. The bottom is mostly smooth, the banks grassy and undercut, and on the far side there are some dead down trees in the water.

Pools, as Paul Needham once said, are excellent resting places for large trout but they are also good sulking and hiding places. Thus, fishing them, and especially this one, is a very chancy business. I have never seen anyone take a fish here on a dry fly nor have I ever taken one. But the dragon or damsel nymphs worked along the bottom with thorough coverage will produce the odd fish, usually a very good one of three pounds up. It is slow, painstaking work and a Hi-D line will facilitate matters.

The meadow section from the confluence of the Firehole and Gibbon to where the river comes away from the plateau and back to the highway, comprises a mile and a half of really excellent water, full of trout and whitefish; it is first class, somewhat easier, except for the Big Bend section, after mid-July.

The hoppers come then, filling the meadows with their rattling crackles, and on those prevalent windy days, filling the water as well. At these times, the fish lose much of their caution. They come from their hiding places, from under the weeds and out of their deep lies to shoulder along the bank, to lie in wait for the bonanza of large hoppers. Put on a Dave's Hopper, or another low-lying hopper pattern, on not too fine a leader, and have at them. One fishes from the bank, moving up a step between casts, dropping the hopper a foot from the bank on a short line—twenty or twenty-five feet is plenty, fisherman to fly. It is exciting and rewarding fishing, and if the wind is really gusting, one can get into a really large fish. Do not be too quick to pick up your fly from the water on these days. I have seen big browns come ten feet for the hopper pattern on really windy days, their mouths agape in their eagerness to get the fly. If you can hold your fire and not pull the trigger too soon when this happens, you're a better man than I, McGee.

Where the meadow pinches in and the lodgepoles commence, there is a short stretch of water that is very productive. The river narrows and the current picks up speed. This, or some other condition, causes the fine bottom material to become furrowed and channeled. The deepest channel is in the middle, just out from the little island on the highway side. When the fish are here, one must go down for them; they will not come up to your fly.

On both sides, there are shallow stretches. On the highway side there are strong currents, and a good insect composition. But tourists and fishermen alike are constantly running down the high bank to the water, and the fish are excessively spooky when they are in these shallows. On the far side there is a benchlike shallow, about eighteen inches deep. This is a backwater off the main current and there are logs and tree limbs in it. This, or some other factor, makes it a preferred feeding area, and if one goes softly and quietly about his business, he may have a banner day.

For a long time I was convinced that one had to have just the right nymph or wet fly to fish these shallows. The Grey Nymph or Grey Drake wet fly were best, plus perhaps a Light Assam Dragon nymph or a Fair Damsel (*Argia*) were the only correct medicine, I felt. Then one day I found out that I was wrong.

I had come down to fish this stretch only to find another angler just getting into position at the upper end of the shallows on the far side. Since this fellow appeared to know what he was about, I felt I might learn something by watching him. In this I was correct.

The angler was fishing a sunken fly on a floating line, the right medicine if he had the right fly. He used easy searching casts with a minimum of false casting, and retrieved each cast with a slow hand twist. In about an hour and a half, he took five trout, running from over one to above three pounds. When he had released the last one, he put the fly in the keeper and waded over to my side.

From the fact that he went directly to the only place in this area where one could wade across, I knew that he was well acquainted with this piece of water, something I had already concluded from his expertise in fishing it.

As we talked, I congratulated him on a masterly job of fishing and he said he had been fishing that particular water for over twenty years. Meanwhile, I was unobtrusively trying to get a look at the fly he had used with such good results.

Fishermen have a sixth sense about these things, and finally, with a smile, the man held out his rod so that I could see the fly. It gave me a shock.

It was about a size six, 2XL, tied on the order of a wooly worm, *but* it had black chenille front and back, and a broad band of white chenille in the center. The hackle, wound wooly-worm fashion, was *white*! It was a most unlikely looking fly to have done such execution as I had just seen.

We chatted a while longer and the fellow mentioned that the year before he had taken a trout of six to seven pounds from this area on the same fly, and his picture with the fish had appeared in Bud Lilly's catalog. When I got back to the Trout Shop that evening, I checked with Bud and Greg, who verified the man's story. His name, Bud said, was Blaine Gasser, and he had introduced his strange fly, which he called Wooly Bugger, into the West Yellowstone area from the region south of Pocatello, where it was a favorite on Portneuf River. I've been thinking about that fly for several years, and one day, when I get my nerve up, I'm going to try it.

No extensive studies that may have been done by biologists or entomologists on this part of the river are known to me. There is one study of the weeds (aquatic) in the stretch just covered, and another, very limited study, of insects in a single riffle in that part of the Madison in the Park. The latter was done as part of a Ph.D. dissertation, and may be found in the library of Montana State University, Bozeman, Montana (*The benthos and drift fauna of a riffle in the Madison River, Yellowstone National Park.* 1966, J. R. Heaton, Ph.D. dissertation). Since insects vary considerably on even short stretches of this part of the river, the above study is of severely limited use to the angler.

My own studies have been mainly for the purpose of allowing me to tie better imitations of the insects and to fish them in a lifelike manner, in the right place. Thus I have seldom needed to carry identification beyond genus. In the case of the two most prevalent insects in the area, *Baetis* (mayfly) and *Brachycentrus* (caddis), this has been entirely satisfactory. I know from experience that there are at least three species of each of these available to the fish, yet to the unaided eye, the only thing that distinguishes one species from another within the genus is size. The habits, habitat, and color of all the *Baetis* nymphs are for all practical purposes the same; this is also true of the various species of *Brachycentrus*. Since no practical advantage would accrue from further identification, I have not bothered to pursue the matter beyond my stated needs.

This upper meadow stretch is easy of access; only at Big Bend is the river more than one hundred yards from the road. The scenery is restful and pleasant. The Canada geese nest here, many families of them, and the elk calve in the wooded triangle formed by the Firehole and the Madison proper. During the middle of the day when the campers and their children are off sightseeing, this area appears as it must have when first discovered.

It was in this meadow that the Langford, Washburn, Doane exploration party camped on 20 September 1870 and it was later alleged by some members of the party that the idea of making Yellowstone a national park was discussed. However, there is no mention of this in any of the members' extant journals and historians concede that the idea actually came later. But it came and reached fruition in less than two years, for which we should be eternally grateful.

Below the meadows the river bed tilts sharply, there is a quarter-mile-long rocky riffle, which actually approaches a rapid. Here the gradient is much more than the average. Except in the fall, when the browns are running, this is an unpropitious area, except for a spring hole on the far side about one hundred feet below the commencement of the riffle.

This spot is perhaps fifty feet across and four or five feet deep near the edge of the main stream current. It is an excellent holding spot for a big bully fish and such have indeed been taken there, including browns of near nine pounds. One must wade across, fighting the racing current and the smooth round—but not slick—rubble and boulders of the bottom.

It is difficult to fish this spot from any angle. If you cast your fly into the backwater, with your line in the main current, it will quickly be snatched away. If you cast the fly into the main current with your fly in the stiller water, an immediate bad drag occurs. But if you have both fly and line in the backwater, they just lie there, giving a big trout far too long a look at the counterfeit fly.

What one *can* do is cast from near the far, wooded bank, across the backwater and hand retrieve at a speed suited to the natural of the fly you're using. Or you can try to deliver the fly *and* the line to the current shear—the seam where the two contrary currents mingle. It takes great skill to do this once out of five casts. But it's the best hope for hanging the current resident, and the size of the fish makes it worth the effort.

In the fall, the long rocky riffle will contain an occasional fish but there is no way of telling where such trout might lie. You could fish the whole riffle and not get a touch, and at most, you'd get one fish. So most anglers give this stretch a pass; in fact, I have never seen anyone fish it.

The meadow stretch at the end of the riffle is good dry-fly water. The river divides around islands here and there, providing more undercut banks for holding areas and causing the stream to be narrow enough so that one can cast across them easily. These meadows are narrow, the lodgepoles crowd in on both sides, and one gets a feeling of isolation. It may be that this causes the novice to shun the area; nearly all anglers seen along this water are experienced.

A long, curving pitch leads from the section above to a medium deep gliding run. This run is about three hundred yards long; then it becomes wider and smoother as it enters the upper end of famed Nine Mile Hole. This lead-in run, the upper end of which slides along the base of a steep talus slope, is an unusual piece of water.

During most of the year, it will be barren of good fish, although a hatch will bring up hundreds of tiddlers to attack the hatching insects. But some peculiarity of this stretch causes running spawners to choose it as a resting place, even though the current is fairly stiff and there are few rocks large enough to break the racing flow and provide holding spots. Nine Mile Hole, into which it runs, would seem a far better place but running spawners shun the place. A friend suggests that this is because all the good spots in Nine Mile

Hole are occupied by fish larger than the running spawners—fish able to defend their lies against intrusion. It's an intriguing theory.

This is the run where Ernie Schwiebert and Gene Anderegg did such great execution. They hit it at just the right time. A day earlier or later and there may have been no sizable fish in the entire run. I've seen it barren many times—in fact, most of the time.

I've seen Nine Mile Hole when it appeared barren, too, but I knew that the trouble lay with me on those days, for this is an exceptionally endowed piece of water for trout welfare. In the words of the Hollywood press corps, it has everything.

It begins at an upper curve and runs straight for almost a quarter-mile to a lower curve. At first glance, it looks all of a piece, but to so consider it is a fatal mistake.

At the upper end one sees the first of the giant boulders that are found only here on the entire river. These have been broken off the canyon wall, which towers over the north bank of the river, by earthquakes in centuries past. One can still see where some of them once were, and one can also still see the snags and stumps of trees broken off when the boulders broke loose and came bounding down to lodge in the river in later, more recent times.

These rocks breast the current, and over the years some have collected all sorts of debris. Logs and roots lodge on the upstream face of the rocks, and limbs, weeds, moss, and smaller flotsam builds up until another, more violent flood carries away most or all of this mat.

Silt has collected against the upstream edge of some of them, forming bars and even small islands, while on the downstream side the swirling eddies have spun out deep mysterious holes. On the other hand, some of them have had the bottom excavated on the upper side and the silt deposited on the lower. It all depends on the exact angle and speed of the current, and also on what, if any, debris guards the upper edge.

The big boulders and the piles of waterborne debris cause the current to run in many directions. In some places it will be moving at right angles to the axis of the stream bed. Some such pieces of current are only fifteen feet long but they must be dealt with because your nymph must drift naturally without drag for any of the sizable fish here to be interested. One cannot dawdle or dream on this long deep run or you might as well be playing tiddlywinks.

One may find it impossible to get any kind of decent drift in the swirling eddies behind the larger rocks. The answer here is to treat this as pocket water. Approach closely, cast the fly into the eddy on a very short line, hold the rod high to keep slack off the water, and do not pick up the fly as long as it remains in the area.

Sid Terrell, who has fished this Nine Mile Hole for over fifty years, says with emphasis that persistence is the key to taking fish from it even if you are doing everything right. A few or a dozen casts into the same area are not enough. You must throw the fly into the same spot twenty or thirty times or until a fish hits. Sid presumes, of course, that you know the right fly and the right method of fishing it and I am living proof that this just ain't so. I've been skunked here often, even when I was sure I had the right fly and the right method.

There are some few *Pteronarcys* nymphs along here and also scattered *Ephemerella grandis* (Western Green Drake) nymphs. This makes a size six or eight black nymph the best choice. Locally, favorites are the Montana Nymph or the Martinez Black but a black wooly worm is also quite effective.

Down through the middle of this stretch, there is a deep channel about two-thirds of the way across. The current shoots down this channel at a good speed. On both sides, silt beds have built up, but the bottom of this channel is clean gravel, and one wants the black nymph to bounce along these rocks in a manner simulating a nymph swept away by the current. A sink-tip line is preferred, and a leader no more than seven-and-one-half feet, to 3X. Keep the fly riding again and again, deep in the channel, ticking the bottom. Work the water thoroughly and you should succeed.

On the far side a small creek enters. This has pushed a delta of silt out into the quiet waters alongside the channel. At times a terrific hatch will come on here, bringing the trout out of the channel and onto the flats to take the floating flies. But this represents a problem. A cast across the currents of the channel is a waste of time because the channel current will put an oxbow in your line so quickly that you will seem to have a drag before the fly hits the water.

The channel is too deep to wade and there are only a couple of places in the entire section where one can wade across. By the time you find the right place to cross, the hatch, which is always of short duration, will be coming to a close. Is there a solution?

Yes, locate your crossing spot *before* you commence to fish. Then when the hatch comes you can be on the other side and in position in a couple of minutes.

But what about the line? We were fishing a sink-tip, remember? Well, I always carry several kinds of lines on extra reel spools in the back of my vest. While I'm wading out from the channel, I'll reel my fly right up to the rod tip, remove it, and reel up the remaining leader. Then off comes that reel spool, I snap in a different spool with my floating line *and* leader while I'm walking to my wade-across spot. Once on the far bank it takes only a minute to string up and tie on a dry fly.

What fly? Ah, there's the rub. It can be Pale Morning Dun—if the season is right. If it's fall—late August through September—it may be White-Winged Black (*Tricorythodes*). But not always. It might be Golden Olive Dun (*Ephemerella infrequens*) or it might be one of three caddis types, which would call for the Grey Colorado King in size sixteen or eighteen, the Brown Colorado King in the same sizes, or perhaps Troth's Elk Hair Caddis in size eighteen. You'll have to see which fly is coming off the water—and you'll have to make sure that the trout are taking the dry fly and not the emergent nymph.

All this is up to you—no one can do it for you and there is no one who can tell you within some weeks just what flies will be hatching when. But isn't this one of the things that are so fascinating in the fly fisherman's day? You can seldom predict exactly what's going to happen out there on the stream any time you are on it. The only thing you can be relatively sure of is that something *will* happen for which you are not prepared. This is Cotton's Law.

Some very nice trout are taken from Nine Mile Hole on streamers each year. Some of the fellows have taken to using them after repeated skunkings on other patterns, and after seeing other anglers take nice fish on streamers from this difficult water. I don't use streamers anymore because I caught more tons of trout and salmon on streamers the two years I spent in Alaska than I care to think about. But they are a legitimate way to take good fish if one can put up with the mindless casting and retrieving that I find frankly boring.

The best streamer for Nine Mile is the Spruce. I prefer it tied with golden badger rather than white badger hackles because the dace it represents has a golden olive tint in these waters. Years ago, this golden Spruce was known as Dark Spruce, but if you ask for a Dark Spruce streamer around here you will get a fly with the Spruce body but with streamers of brownish orange dyed grizzly. Who perpetrated this outrage, I don't know. Since I tie my own flies, it makes no difference to me. For the visiting angler it is one more local idiosyncracy to beware of.

The best size is two, 2XL, but they are used up to 3/0 and tied bulky in the bargain. Our local streamer experts prefer a large streamer rather than a dainty one, and their consistent success proves them right. The Brown and Gray Marabou Muddlers, so successful in other parts of this river, do not work nearly so well here. I don't know why.

Below the little island on the highway side at the lower end of Nine Mile Hole is a quarter-mile stretch of really excellent dry-fly water. The upper end is easy of access but the lower end merges into the swampy area pushing up above Seven Mile Bridge, and one should not pursue the trout too far into this troublesome and dangerous area.

Seven Mile Run, below, or rather starting just under, the bridge, is choice dry-fly water. The mass of water weeds filling this stretch make fishing any other method, except the emergent nymph, frustrating. However, there are times when fishing the emergent nymph just prior to the hatch can be the best of all methods.

The activity will commence, usually, under the bridge near the right bank (banks of a stream are defined looking downstream). For some minutes, no flies will be in evidence. In June or early July, the hatch might be the Western Green Drake, and a Martinez Black, or my Ida May nymph in size ten drifted along in, or just under, the surface film will produce some lovely fish, mostly browns, mostly from fourteen to seventeen inches.

But you must be alert to changing conditions. The trout will start to refuse your fly even with feeding activity increasing. Look closely at the water and you will probably see the duns, with dark-green bodies and slate wings, drifting along like tiny sailboats. That is the time to change over to the dry fly.

There are several commercial Green Drake flies available locally, but none are really satisfactory. All are a touch too green in the body, and the wings mostly too bluish. A brownish—not yellowish—green is what's wanted and the wings should shade more to oxford grey than dun blue. Does that confuse you? Colors *are* difficult because no two people see them quite the same. Just remember that the fly is darker than it looks on the water, and much more so than it looks in the air. Try to get one in your hand.

The fish do not appear overly selective when this hatch is on. They will readily take the chartreuse commercial flies and will even take the palmer-tied dry fly called Madsen, named after Earl Madsen, a Michigan guide. This fly is tied with an emerald-green body with brown hackle palmer-tied over it. At the front there are two turns of grizzly hackle, and the tip of the hackle is tied upright as a single sailwing. This is one of the best flies to use anytime on this stretch. It and the Hair Wing Variant (House and Lot) are the only two flies I use here when "prospecting"—that is, fishing the water instead of the rise. Both are high-riding, highly visible flies and the trout take them well.

There are weeds to or nearly to the surface all along this mile and a half stretch. You'll have better luck fishing over the channels between beds than directly over the beds themselves. Do not go below 3X on the leader even when fishing the tiny size eighteen Colorado King or Blue-Winged Olive dries in the fall. Any fish that takes your fly is instantly going to head for weeds. How to handle such fish is always a problem. Do you hold hard or give slack?

G. E. M. Skues, in *Minor Tactics of the Chalk Stream* (and the Madison here is a chalk stream) says, "The checked fish goes to weed," and also, "The unchecked fish flounders on the surface." I wish I could be so positive about how to handle fish in weeds. About the only positive statement I can make about trout in weedy waters is, "The trout will always do what you don't want him to." But even if you lose them all, and some flies too, it will be fun for there are many good trout here whose antics upon taking your fly and going to weed will set your heart a-pounding. At least, they do mine.

You may remember that I mentioned in another chapter that I sent two young French lads to this area. They reported seeing several fish over three pounds, hooking some, landing some—but only those under two pounds. Pierre said that it was an enjoyable experience, in spite of much frustration, but one that shouldn't be repeated too often, as too much frustration is bad for the liver. I agree.

There are many dead trees down in the water along the right bank and these provide havens for really fine trout; but, added to the weeds, they also make frustration the order of the day.

Between a quarter and a half-mile below the bridge, the river makes a sweeping turn left. The tree-covered right bank gives way to a steep sagebrush covered slope. Dave Whitlock calls this bank "Grasshopper Bank" because from mid-July on until late September the grass and sagebrush hosts a multitude of hoppers and a big hopper pattern dropped along the bank with a juicy splash will cause quite a commotion among the trout that lie here just waiting for such a fat morsel.

Your chances of landing the larger trout here are much better during hopper season because you are using, or you should be, 1X leaders. I've known some fellows who fish big size six, 3XL hoppers on 4X and 5X, but these fellows have very lofty ideas—and not many big trout from these waters.

This section of Grasshopper Bank, so named by Dave Whitlock, is better fished from shore. One is too exposed out in the stream.

The hinging action of such a large fly on a hair-fine leader will weaken it in just a few casts to where a dead pull of four ounces will break it. Try it sometime.

The otters love this piece of water and these clowns of the woods and waters will often be with you. At times they will paddle leisurely through and among the rising fish that you are trying to catch, scaring the hell out of the trout and infuriating the angler. They seem, at these times, like those tourists who run down the bank to see what it is that you're doing. But one gets the feeling that, while the tourist is just ignorant and means no harm, the otter knows exactly what he is doing and he means to bug you. At least he will stay around until he has put every fish down, then with a flirt, a flip of the tail and a splash, the otter will depart, leaving the angler with the sound of a fiendish chuckle in his head.

Since I live here, I find the antics of the otter most amusing but I can see how the vacationing fly fisherman, who probably will not see another hatch and rise in a week, might be driven wild by them. Still, they are excellent evidence of a healthy stream; you will not find them on impure or unproductive waters.

There will be Canada geese and trumpeter swans most any day in summer and fall, and probably elk along the upper slopes of Grasshopper Bank. And if one chooses to fish along that bank, he will probably not even notice the constant stream of cars mindlessly hissing along the highway on the far side. But be careful where you wade across; there are some very deep channels along here: because of the clear water, they do not look nearly so deep. This is the only slow-water area of the entire river where I use a wading staff, not to brace me against a strong current, but to probe the depths ahead. I recommend this to you, especially in June and late fall. It can save you a dunking, and you will find it extremely tough wading out on this yielding bottom with your waders full.

Below the curve at the head of Grasshopper Bank, the river splits around a good-sized island. The channel on the highway side pushes hard against the highway bank. Because this was causing erosion, the Park people rip-rapped it. The hundred-yard-long deep run here is thus known as Rip Rap Run. There are always a couple of fish of two to three pounds in the deepest part of the channel, where the bottom is clean gravel instead of sand-silt.

These trout will not come up to the fly because of current speed, which is sharpened here due to the squeezing effect of the island. A black nymph or Wooly Worm in size six or eight, 2 or 3XL, is the best medicine, day in, day out. A sinking or sink-tip line is a must.

Geese nest on the island, and should you feel the urge to go look them up, please don't. I know one man who did and was attacked by the gander, which flogged him severely, knocking his glasses off into the water, where they were lost. Then this fellow, near-sighted, as am I, had to fumble-foot his way across the treacherous bottom of the channel, getting dunked twice in the process.

Beasts and fowl in Yellowstone Park are better for being observed at a distance. Better for them and for you. Buffalo have killed persons who have approached them too closely, and elk and bear have injured many. I repeat: this is a wilderness in spite of the highway's running through it, and the animals are wild and sometimes dangerous. Yellowstone Park is *not* a zoo.

If you think I'm taking this too seriously, think again. Each year I get letters from at least a dozen people who want to come out, spend "half-a-day seeing the Park and photographing the animals." Yellowstone Park comprises 3,400 square miles, making it larger than Delaware, Rhode Island, and the District of Columbia *combined.* There are an estimated twenty thousand elk, one thousand buffalo, six hundred mountain sheep, three hundred moose, one thousand antelope, an equal number of deer, and an estimated two hundred and fifty bears* in the Park and these are *wild* animals and often unpredictable. I urge you to leave them strictly alone and admire them from a safe vantage point. Remember, this is their home and you are a visitor.

There is perhaps a half-mile of water downstream of Rip Rap Run that used to be excellent. But the lower end of this reach is barred across by a damlike stretch of upraised bedrock bottom that causes an abrupt slowing of the

---

*These figures are subject to change, by season and year.

current and has silted up this lower section to the point where much of it is too shallow to be very productive of larger trout. However, there is a good insect population and on a misty morning in July or August, one can have fine dry-fly fishing for trout of eight to twelve inches. The insects are small, sizes sixteen to eighteen and a Blue Dun or a Colorado King in those sizes will answer most times.

From the breakover downstream, it is almost three miles to Cable Car Run; this stretch is an almost continuous shallow riffle of eighteen inches or so, shallower here, deeper there. There are perhaps half a dozen deeper spots in the entire length, none of which are more than one hundred feet long or twenty-five feet wide. These spots will nearly always hold one or two fish of a pound up but they are not easy to locate.

The rest of Long Riffle is barren of larger fish except in the fall when a running spawner may stop somewhere along its length. Trying to locate one of these fish represents about the same chance as selecting, without prearrangement, the exact restaurant in a large city where someone you know will be dining.

One sees many fishermen either fishing the river here or rigging up along the highway where the river is out of sight, which it is for most of Long Riffle. Most I have talked to are fishing this water because it reminds them of stretches of their home rivers in California, Colorado, and New York. Upon being told the fish run only eight to twelve inches, they nod and say, "Yes, that's about what we thought—it's the same at home."

In 1973, Art Flick paid a visit to this area and I undertook to show him around. Art had been here a couple years earlier with Dave Whitlock and had exceptional fishing—along the far bank of upper Long Riffle. Bob Holmes and I tried to dissuade him from fishing what he said was the right place, pointing out that he would catch only small fish. Art insisted and fished for about two hours. He is one of the very finest dry-fly men I've ever watched, but he was not able to take any fish larger than ten inches and agreed that he must have been mistaken about the spot. Later, I learned from Dave that Grasshopper Bank, about two miles upstream, was where he and Art had fished. I cite this instance to show that even the most skillful of anglers, and Art merits that description, still have to know something, and often quite a bit, about a stream in order to catch the larger fish. This is where a guide earns his money.

Long Riffle ends about where the Montana-Wyoming border crosses this section of the Park. It perturbs me that these state lines show on maps because Yellowstone Park has never been a part of any state; both Montana and Wyoming were *Federal* territories when Yellowstone became this nation's—and the world's—first national park. Thus, the Wyoming state sales tax charged in Yellowstone Park is an illegal tax. In some other national parks, the state was established before the park; therefore the park is a part of the state and state laws apply. Not Yellowstone. It has always been Federal property, and except for this illegal tax law, it is entirely governed by Federal law; crimes committed in it are handled by the FBI, U.S. Marshals, or National

Park Service rangers, not by local or state police of any description. The sales taxes collected go to the state of Wyoming, none to the Federal Treasury or apply to any of the costs of operating Yellowstone Park. It is flagrant taxation without representation.

Perhaps the above should have been taken up at some other point in this narrative. However, since the so-called state boundary crosses here, at the upper end of Cable Car Run, it seemed a reasonable time to point out this anomalistic law, which was rammed through congress during World War II when no one was watching. Thus, while there is a Federal law allowing Wyoming a tax in a Federal reservation, it is an unconstitutional law. Ralph Nader, where are you?

Cable Car Run is about a half-mile long; its lower end is also the beginning of Hole Number One. The water of Cable Car Run is deeper than Long Riffle because the river is pinched between high banks. The bottom is rubble-boulder and there are some deeper channels and potholes that hold good fish, although the general run is largely barren.

The predominant insect here, and for the next three miles, is *Pteronarcys californica,* the giant stonefly (salmon fly). Its presence is almost surely why larger trout run up from deeper water below, to feed here with less competition. There are always some resident fish of good size but you will have your best days when fish from below are here on the feed.

Hole Number One is different from the rest of the "holes," and even the general run of the stream. Part of the bottom of Hole One is bedrock. Whether this has broken off the large slabs one sees on the far bank or is actual bedrock, I don't know. But bedrock does not offer as many holding spots as does rubble-boulder bottoms, and Hole One contains fewer fish than does any other of the numbered—or unnumbered—runs along here.

But it will occasionally produce a very large trout, of six or more pounds. I know from personal examination that such fish are *not* present most of the time. What factor or factors bring them to this run at certain times is a complete puzzle.

Over the thirty years that I've fished it, the channel has slowly moved from the far edge of the stream to near the middle. Boulders once in the upper end have been rolled along down the bedrock section and now most of the good lies for larger fish are in the lower middle of the run. No change in fishing methods is required; the deeply sunken, dead-drifted stonefly nymph is still the best fly and method; but less time should be given to the upper one-quarter of the run. Concentrate your efforts on the lower three-quarters. Also, this is a living river and the channel and holding areas will be located still farther down years from now.

Another riffle runs the half-mile between Holes One and Two. There are always some catchable fish in this riffle but only rarely will a good one be taken from the potholes in the bottom. There is insufficient depth or cover for good fish to feel secure.

Hole Number Two is end-of-road. No vehicles are allowed beyond here. It is a popular piece of water, and I have seen as many as a dozen vehicles parked here, with a number of people standing in line waiting their turn.

It is located on a bench that extends for three-eighths of a mile to Hole Number Three, where the river again pitches sharply downward. The water pouring down from the long steep slant above Hole Two has gouged out a deeper, bowl-shaped area in the bottom, producing a very mixed-up current.

Along the far, steep bank, a backwater has caused the deposition of silt over the years. There is a shallow bench, covered profusely with flowing water weeds (*Potamegeton*) and at the edge of the silt bed, there is a sudden dropoff to four or five feet. The weeds trail over the edge, making this a fine holding spot. I've seen numbers of trout over two pounds in it, and there is a five-pounder or two in it most anytime.

At the edge of this silt ledge, the current runs upriver. This band of contrary water is over the deepest section of the river bed. It is about two feet wide, and can only be fished with control from the silt bed itself. Any attempt to fish it from its own right side will find your fly tangled in the overhanging weeds. To reach it from the left bank one must cast sixty feet across a raging current. Any attempt at a natural drift under those conditions is hopeless.

There are numerous tiny mayfly nymphs living in the silt and weeds and at times these flies hatch in unbelievable numbers. One is a species of *Tricorythodes,* the White-Winged Black, which hatches, molts, mates, and dies in a half-hour period. But when this is going on, the entire surface of Hole Two will be alive with fish gobbling the tiny spent spinners. *Tricorythodes* hatches here in August and September and a good imitation can produce fantastic fishing for a few minutes *if* one is rigged properly at the start of the hatch. This fishing requires a rather long rod, dry-fly line and leader of nine feet to 6X. The fly is size twenty-two to twenty-four with long *white* tails, black fur body, and wings of white deer hair or polypropylene.

I cannot see this fly more than ten feet past my rod tip even in smooth water. In the raging currents of the main channel of Hole Two, I can't see it at all. Fishing a 6X leader in rough water for large trout is in the same class as promising your infant son he will be heavyweight champ if he eats his spinach; it's far beyond even wishful thinking.

There is a later hatch of tiny mayflies all along this section of the river. I've never seen the hatch, but the spinners fly upstream by the millions, ten to twenty feet above the water. They are about size twenty-two, of a golden color with clear wings and on a bright sunny day they look like millions of golden sparks. I've not been able to identify them but strongly believe that they are a species of *Centroptilum* because this genus is found hatching in October on many Montana spring creeks. But I cannot be sure until I've done more work and study. Whatever they may be, they cause pandemonium in late afternoon when the dying spinners literally cover the water.

The nymphs dwell in *shallow* silt along the bank edges, in the backflow along or below some islands and in the main stream where the bottom is of gravel with a mixture of silt. This is preferred habitat of nearly all of the *Centroptilum* genus, and reinforces my belief that I'm correct in my assumption.

The major insect in Hole Two, and all through here, is *Pteronarcys californica.* These huge nymphs cover the bottom in midstream when they are quiescent, hiding beneath the stones that give them their common name, stonefly. They become active at least twice each twenty-four hours, and come from under their rocks to feed on algae, which forms 98 percent of their diet. They are the boldest and widest rangers of any nymph and this, with their great numbers and large size, make them the preferred food of the trout.

The nymphs are stirred to rove and feed *in summer* each time the water temperature comes in the range of 58° to 62° F. This occurs twice daily—once as the water warms in the morning and again as it drops in late afternoon or evening. Since the Madison has become very warm due to the warming of the Firehole, many of these feeding periods take place during the hours of darkness and the fisherman is unable to take advantage of them because no fishing is allowed in Yellowstone Park between 10:00 P.M. and 5:00 A.M. Mountain Daylight Time.

When the temperature is not favorable, the nymphs remain hidden in crevices between rocks, and the fish are usually inactive at these times.

In spring and fall, when the waters are colder, the magic temperature seems to be 52°, and the insects will move and the fish feed on them when that temperature is reached.

In late May or early June, when the water reaches 60° and holds there for at least forty-eight hours, these nymphs will commence to hatch into the adult "salmon fly." Once the process of hatching has started, it will continue even though a cold rain or snow chills the stream. It will take longer for all the flies to hatch when this happens, but they will continue until all mature nymphs are hatched. In the lower river, below Quake Lake, the hatch starts at the lower elevations below Ennis Lake and moves upstream two to four miles a day. But in this part of the Madison the right temperature is reached at about the same time from Baker's Hole to Madison Junction, and the hatch seldom lasts more than a day.

If you have been checking the temperatures for several days before they reach 60°, you will have some excellent fishing using the nymph imitation, because when these insects approach hatching time, they commence to crawl from the center of the stream to the edge and the fish feed on them vigorously during this trip. Once they reach rocks along the stream bank, they hide under them until the rising water temperature triggers the hormones within their bodies and causes their incipient wings to start to swell. They then clamber out on the bank, changing from a water-dwelling to an air-breathing insect, climb upon a twig, reed, or blade of grass, split their shuck, draw themselves free of it, dry their wings, then fly to a nearby shrub or bush to wait for the mating time. They have not *yet* become available to the fish as a mature, floating insect.

They do when the flight in search of mates commences, and the time of day this happens is directly related to the hatching time; it is a few hours later. I have seen them emerge on the Yellowstone, the upper Colorado above 10,000 feet, the Feather below Lake Almanor, and other very cold streams at sundown, which means the flight to find mates took place at or after dusk. Richard Muttkowski, when observing this flight on the Yellowstone, termed it *crepuscular,* apparently believing that it took place at dusk on all streams. It doesn't.

The stonefly is a very poor flyer. It flies with its body in an upright position, its four wings flogging the air furiously. When crossing back and forth over the stream, many do not make it and the trout are waiting for them—and your big dry imitation.

However, the big rise to them occurs when the females fly upstream to lay their eggs after mating. This takes place here and on the lower river between daylight and 10:00 A.M. most days; however, if it is cool the flight will be between noon and four o'clock. Many fall into the water and the rest plop down onto the surface to lay their eggs and never rise again. These egg-laden females, one-and-a-half to two or more inches long, are the richest of trout food and when this egg-laying commences, the trout feed in a veritable frenzy until they are glutted.

The flies mate on trees, grass, or shrubs, and the males generally die there; the ground will often be carpeted with their exhausted bodies. It is the females that provide the bulk of food for the trout after the hatch.

These are the most important insect to the fish for most of the next seventy miles of river. Therefore, the fisherman who approaches his craft intelligently will want to know all possible about them.

If you catch the day of the upstream flight here on the Madison in the Park and you have a fair imitation of the natural in size six, 3XL, or four, 3XL, you will find the trout feeding heavily and unsuspiciously and some will be the largest in the river. Local patterns are the Sofa Pillow, Bird's Stone Fly, Bucktail Caddis, and one with a clipped deer-hair head called Salmon Hopper because it works either as a big stonefly or a grasshopper. I prefer Bird's Stone Fly because it lies low in the water as the natural does.

The season of the dry stonefly is short here in this section of the Madison, but the nymphs are in the water three or four years before hatching and thus there are three year-classes available to the trout year around. So the knowledgeable angler fishes the nymph all season. It is best fished with a long rod, HI-D line of six, seven, or eight, a short leader, (four to six feet) to .010–.012 inches and an upstream cast. This rig and method is intended to simulate a nymph swept along the bottom after being dislodged. These nymphs do not swim and even if they could no nymph alive can swim in currents of this speed.

Another species of large stonefly is appearing here and in other streams of the area. This is *Acroneuria californica,* about three-quarters the size of *Pteronarcys* at all stages of growth. The nymph is flattened where *Pteronarcys* is nearly round, and is mottled brown and yellow. *Pteronarcys* is slate grey, chocolate brown or black, depending on the color of the stones under which it lives. The adults of the two genera are almost indistinguishable.

Acroneuria is carnivorous and preys on immature stages of other insects. So far it hasn't reached such numbers in any stream I know as to imperil the mayfly and caddis forms in those streams. I have reason to believe that it has always been present in area streams but has been multiplying to the extent of becoming more visible only for ten or twelve years. What factors caused its increase in numbers is unknown at present.

Pteronarcys is the nymph imitated locally by the commercial patterns, Bitch Creek Special, Rubber Legs (Girdle Bug), Troth's Terrible Stone, Montana Nymph, Mossback, and of course by the Black Wooly Worm. The only commercial patterns to imitate *Acroneuria* are Bird's Stone Nymph and those tied by Randall Kaufmann of Portland, Oregon, called Stone Nymph. Bud Lilly handles my patterns of *Pteronarcys* and *Acroneuria*, which I call Montana Stone and Yellow Stone, respectively. Bud has them tied commercially since I no longer tie flies for the trade. So there is no reason, in this area, to be without a passable imitation of these nymphs.

The various "holes" along this section are separated from each other by riffles, although the inexperienced find it difficult to tell hole (run) from riffle. One sure way to do so is to wade down the center of the stream. When you go in over your crotch, you're in one of our local "holes."

In all these deeper stretches, the deeper channels have large boulders in them that cause a choppy surface. This combination of broken surface, depth, and current barriers makes excellent holding areas for large fish; thus the channels are the places to fish, from one side or the other. Frequently, one will find from experience that a channel is much easier fished from one side than from the other. But in a living river, which side this is changes over the years.

Hole Number Three, three-eighths of a mile downstream from Hole Two, used to be far easier to fish from the right bank. But in the thirty years I've fished it, the channel has steadily moved across stream and now it can be fished equally well from either bank. This is also true of other deeper stretches throughout this area.

One *must* be aware of the fact that three things must be present anywhere along here in order for there to be sizable fish: depth, large boulders, and a choppy surface. The latter, due to current speed and the boulder-rubble bottom, is always there—the entire river, except for isolated backwaters, is choppy. So one looks for depth—over thirty inches—and boulders larger than average.

Sometimes these are large enough to cause white water at the surface; most times they are not. But any rock large enough to provide a barrier for a good fish will always produce what Dan Bailey calls "standing waves"—a hump on the surface, a short dipping glide of a foot or two then a sharp peaked wave *that always breaks in the same place.* Upstream some three to eight feet of that standing wave will be your rock—and your trout.

Although Hole Number Three is the last of the locally named—or numbered—holes, there are actually ten of these deeper channels before one gets to the quieter deep water of the Beaver Meadows. They have no names below Hole Three because in the days when identifying names were being given, it was never necessary for anyone to fish farther down than Hole Three in order to catch all the fish he could carry.

About a half-mile downstream from the lower end of Hole Three is the next deep spot. This actually is a *hole,* a deep one of about five feet and not more than twenty-five feet across. It was formed by a barrier of harder material that barred the stream and forced it to turn at right angles to the left before proceeding on.

In time, the inexorable power of the river cut past this barrier on both sides, leaving an island that used to be quite large but is now only a few feet across. The piling up of the waters against the barrier over the years caused the whirling current to carve out a deep, bowl-shaped hole in the stream bottom, which is still there. The old stream bed is now a backwater slough cutting off to the left, and what has become known as Drop-off Hole is located in the river at the mouth of this backwater.

For some years this hole was occupied by a big bully rainbow of six to eight pounds, which may have been hooked and lost by more people than any other trout. I had this fish on five times and lost it. Bob Jacklin hooked and lost it. Art Flick hooked it briefly. Bob Holmes had it on once or twice. Several other people I know had brief encounters with it. No one ever caught it.

How can a fish continue to escape the hooks of experienced anglers? The problem was caused by the contour and current of Drop-off Hole. At the upstream edge of the drop-off, the water raced swiftly over a bottom of rubble; it was about eighteen inches deep, then, abruptly, it was five feet deep. This caused a rolling turbulence in which it was impossible to keep control of your fly. The fish either took instantly, at the edge of the drop-off, or not at all. Consequently, it was always lightly hooked, and its swiftness, power, and ripping tactics soon caused the hook to pull out.

That big rainbow was never caught, but it is gone. Less than one-tenth of 1 percent of stream trout live to be seven years old and it was more than that long ago that I first hooked it. But it will be long remembered by many anglers as the one that always got away.

There is a large island downstream of Drop-off Hole. The river's left fork is a shallow riffle on the left side, but is deep on the island side; the river makes a left turn here, and the current of this fork pushes hard against the island. The right fork goes past the island, is intercepted by a cutoff from farther upstream, slams into a high gravelly bank, and turns sharply left. This channel is a fast deep run and it is getting to be a better fish-holding spot each year. Be sure to give that right bank channel a good searching before moving on.

Two hundred yards farther, after the river rejoins itself, is a high bank with a small inlet at the upper end of the bank. There is a deep pocket here, surrounded by sedge and salt grass waist-high. The river turns right along the base of the bluff and the deep choppy flow hosts good, good trout. It was here that I hooked the strongest brown trout of its size that I've ever encountered.

I was teaching a friend of a friend the deeply sunken stonefly-nymph method that I pioneered more than fifteen years ago along this stretch of the Madison. He was fishing from the right side, having waded out about half way. I was standing on the high bluff just opposite, watching closely and trying to coach what had turned out to be a very recalcitrant pupil.

He was allowing too much slack, and never felt any of the four good trout that took his fly. I advised him of each hit and patiently explained how he could better control the slack. After the fourth fish, he answered my advice with a petulant snarl to the effect that I was lying to him and that there were no fish in this run.

If I could have reached him, I would have throttled him. Instead, I took the big nymph from the keeper ring and slammed it out into the deepest part of the run. There was an immediate sledgehammer hit and the fish without pause or hesitation turned downstream and ran like a gut-shot wolf.

I was using a forty-five-foot shooting head, fifty feet of shooting line, and fifty yards of backing. The fish was into the backing before I got over the shock of the strike. I bolted along the bluff, dodging and hurdling sagebrush like a halfback in a broken field. Still the fish gained and when I reached the fisherman's path along the bank at the downstream end of the bluff, I had less than two yards of backing left, and I didn't gain an inch in the two-hundred-yard sprint to the head of the Greeny Deep.

Here the fish took refuge in the deep water below the weedy dropoff that gives the place its name. I recovered my line, and my breath, and we fought it out. I beached the fish just as the other fellow arrived. It was only twenty inches long and three pounds, but it was a deep-shouldered, small-headed, perfectly conditioned fish and no fish had ever given me such a tussle.

The Greeny Deep slides out of its upstream straight into a lower curve that is also the head of Willow Run, a long, medium-deep run that is almost as good as a dry-fly stretch as it is for the big nymphs—very unusual for this piece of the river.

Willow Run marks the beginning of Madison Basin proper. The stream becomes convoluted, turning and twisting against a series of barriers of harder material that are only visible because of the curves of the stream. The pockets of willows become more numerous, grass begins to replace sagebrush, and there is a widening of the heretofore narrow river valley.

There is a whole series of short, fast, deep runs along here, none much more than fifty feet long and all formed in a similar way. There will be a pinching in and a damming appearance of the upper end over and through which the water pours, digging out a deeper section. These are almost always curving and the deep spot will be in the elbow of the bend, on the outside. As the water comes away from the curve, there is a short straight stretch, a shallowing glide or tail, then the damming and pinching effect that signals the end of this run and, almost instantly, the beginning of the next.

The high gravelly banks and benches pull away, the ground flattens and becomes boggy. The grass is tall. The willows in thick clumps and the holes, tunnels, ditches and other signs of beaver become numerous. We are entering the area of the Beaver Meadows, a four-mile stretch of largely deep gliding runs that look like pools, connected by short faster stretches. (When I speak of mileages in this chapter I am talking of *stream* mileage, not airline distance.) The stream bottom changes from rubble-boulder to gravel and quickly to sand-silt. The insects change from the big stonefly to small or tiny caddis and mayfly. The fish become fewer but larger.

Usually, only two methods are used by those who fish the Beaver Meadows. The dry-fly men use big cricket or hopper imitations and drop them along the bank or even into the grass and then shake them loose. Personally, I've had more success with the cricket, but most favor the hopper, possibly because a good cricket imitation is not available commercially.

The nymph men use big flat-bodied fur nymphs: Beaverpelt, Fledermouse (properly Fledermaus), Pussycat, Thunderbug, and even a large Trueblood's Otter Shrimp. All these should be in sizes eight, 3XL, to size four, 2XL. All are twitched slowly along the bottom and all are meant to be dragonfly nymph imitations. All work in direct proportion to the skill, knowledge, experience, and *patience* of the angler.

The first large trout I saw from this area was an eight-pound brown taken on a size eight, 2XL, Fledermaus in 1948. All the big trout that I know of that have been caught here since were taken on the above listed nymphs except one which was taken on a Brown Wooly Worm. There have been a number between four and five pounds taken on hoppers and crickets, but those larger than six pounds have all fallen to the underwater fly.

This is an area to treat with care. Even if one avoids the many pitfalls laid by the beaver, one still has to be alert for moose, mating elk in season, and grizzly bears. No one has ever been injured by one of these while fishing the Beaver Meadows but several anglers have been frightened into gibbering ineptitude by coming suddenly upon one or the other around a clump of willows. I once saw an angler running full out in waders up the face of one of the steep gravelly banks that I couldn't have climbed with an alpenstock and climbing shoes. Turned out he had parted the willows along the bank to peer at the stream only to come nose to muzzle with a bull moose. What was puzzling about this encounter, as the panting fishermen explained it to me—it had taken place on the *other* side of the river.

These glides, or pools, as everyone chooses to call them, are a regular chain for almost four miles, each connected to the next by a fast little run of only a few yards length. There are also islands, some quite large, channels or cutoffs that wander out into marshy areas and disappear, or sometimes appear out of a beaver pond and make their way to the stream.

These smaller "streams" are profitably fished in the evening with small match-the-hatch dries but no one ever does it more than once, including me. The place is a nightmare to get out of after dark and show me a hatch-matching evening fly fisher who can be dragged off the stream before pitch dark. But once is enough. I've known such persons not to get out of the Beaver Meadows until daylight the next morning and one can never escape the area after dark in less than three or four hours.

Unless you hustle right along, it takes more than a full day to fish from the head of Beaver Meadows to Baker's Hole. I set out with a friend to do this once because my friend wanted a crack at a trophy brown. My wife dropped us off at Hole Two at ten in the morning and said she'd pick us up that evening at six sharp at Baker's Hole. About three o'clock, a look at the landscape showed me that we'd only covered about a mile-and-a-half. We'd have to

Beaver dams create these grass-willow swamps, which are home to both moose and beaver. These moose are standing knee deep in browsed-down willows.

move on more swiftly. But by four-thirty, we still had a long way to go, so reluctantly we put our flies in our keepers and headed out.

It was a warm, muggy August day, with threatening thunderstorms that cracked and roared on all sides in the mountains but circling the basin as thermal convection storms always do.

Our route out had to be along the river until we got below the old city dump, where for ten years the town of West Yellowstone had dumped its garbage. This had attracted bears of all kinds. As many as eighteen grizzlies had been counted at the dump at one time, including Old Snaggletooth, a patriarch estimated to weigh nine hundred pounds; it was later jacklighted and killed by a poacher.

This dump has since been closed and replaced by a sanitary landfill three miles north, but at the time it was a place everyone fishing the river gave wide berth. We finally struggled clear of the marsh and willows below it, and climbed the bench to the lodgepole flat, drenched with sweat, steaming in our waders, mosquitoes feasting on our backs and shoulders. I still shudder when I think of that day, and in later times I never tried to fish the entire stretch in a single day, although there are still those who do.

By planning ahead, one can fish the area in three ways without too much exertion. Plan one: park at Hole Two and walk directly to the Beaver Meadows and a mile into them. Turn around and fish back to the head of the meadows, then take the old dirt road back to Hole Two. Plan two: park across the highway from the airport turnoff two miles north of West Yellowstone on highway 191 to Bozeman, and walk straight east to the river. Fish up or down a half-mile and back to where you hit the river, then walk out west to the highway. Plan three: park near the river at Baker's Hole, walk to the Park boundary, about two hundred yards, fish up a half-mile or so, cross over and fish back.

Each of the three plans will get you into different stretches of the river. Plan one gets you to the upper end, plan two to the middle, and plan three to the lower end. Plan three gives you more fishing and less walking and therefore is most used. By altering your approach angle on different trips, plan two gives you more water to fish, and, in my opinion, larger trout to fish for. The big fellows have plenty of hiding places and are not bothered overmuch on this center section and this suits them just fine.

And so we arrive at the end of my part of the river. I do not care to compete with the tourists and their kids around Baker's Hole and below to the highway, and below the highway the river becomes less interesting so I do not fish it.

It is always difficult to explain why one prefers one river, or a section of it, to another. I *believe* that I like this section more than others because it is so varied. In its twenty-mile length we have fast, medium, and slow water; we have pools, runs, and riffles; and we have bottoms of silt, sand-silt, gravel, gravel-rubble, and rubble-boulder. We have mountain stream and meadow stream and stretches that are a composite of both. We have banks covered with dense forest, sagebrush, grass and sagebrush, grass, and willows. The stream is narrow in some places, broad in some. It has channels and cutoffs and islands. It has high banks and low banks and, in spring, areas of no-banks.

Except for rapids and cascades, it has every kind of trout-fishing water that there is. And it has trout, browns and rainbows, an occasional cutthroat or grayling, and of course, whitefish. It is a splendid river for fish and to fish. It is rich in calcium, that great building block of underwater life; it is saturated with oxygen and equable in temperature. It is pure and prime and beautiful, unsullied by man and blessed by nature.

There are many more fishermen now than there were thirty years ago when I first came to fish and to love this river. Yet though one may see fifteen or more gathered at Hole Number Two, I have never seen a single day when there was an *average* of an angler per mile. The river's varied attractions are the reason for this. It is fished hardly at all in June—the anglers are pursuing the "salmon fly" hatch and the fish on the lower river. In July and August, the dry-fly fishers will gather on the upper smooth sections but I've never seen a dozen on any drive from the west gate to Madison Junction and I've made that drive hundreds of times.

I make a point here that I do not count as anglers the tourists and their children who fish the half-mile of river at the Madison Junction campground. They do little harm, except to trod down the grass along the bank. I've never heard of one of them catching a fish and believe that the fish had become conditioned to avoiding the area during camping season. Fish do that, you know.

This is a wild river, the highway nearby notwithstanding. I've fished rivers in remote parts of Alaska, and none were any more natural than this part of the Madison. And it is a charming and pleasant place to fish, made more so by its ease of access, which in a hundred years has left it unspoiled.

Those are some reasons. I know and you know that I've probably left out some, perhaps some important ones, maybe even the major reason that I love this river above all others. On the other hand, I doubt if I know myself why it is so important to me. I only know that it is.

THE FISHERMEN -AND THE MIDDLE RIVER

MANY PEOPLE FIND THE FLY FISHERMAN A HILARIOUS SPECTACLE. THERE HE stands, draped in more equipment than a telephone lineman, trying to outwit a creature with a brain little bigger than a breadcrumb and often getting licked in the process. So says Paul O'Neil in "In Praise of Trout—and Also Me." It is true. Non-anglers find fly fishermen not only strange but incomprehensible.

They will spend thousands of dollars on equipment and travel hundreds of miles to get to a place where they can spend more money and struggle more miles to a wilderness where they will be attacked by millions of mosquitoes and blackflies. They will risk their lives wading raging torrents over a bottom of boulders that resemble nothing so much as greased cannon balls. They will stand for hours up to their armpits in icy waters, wallow through endless bogs, labor over mountains, through impenetrable forests, put up with bad food, lumpy beds, intolerable weather and the idiosyncracies of others just like them. Then they return home sunburned, fly-bitten, bearded and smelly, scarred and scorched, and bore everyone for weeks telling them what a great time they had. And they will do this in order to catch fish that are sometimes not as large as those they have used for bait for other fish.

There seems to be no end to the lengths to which they will go in torturing themselves in their pursuit of what they term pleasure. Nor is there anything new in this. The very first writing on sport fishing mentions briefly the trials and tribulations of the angler, while at the same time defending it as the pleasantest of sports.

In the 1700s an Irish fisherman wrote that it was as hard a trial as one could imagine to stay up all night in a cold, damp cabin drinking new whisky so that when daylight came he could struggle twenty miles in the rain on foot through a bog to reach a salmon stream. Why did he do it? Because that's where the fish were.

What seems even odder than the fact that the fisherman will put up with unspeakable tortures to do what he does is that he will not only come home and tell about it, he will put it in print for the whole world to read. Henry Guy Carleton wrote about a fishing trip in the 1880s as follows: "The blackfly is not as large as a bull-dog, but he can bite with both ends. There is not a single blackfly in the Adirondacks. All the blackflies there are born married and have large families.

"The blackfly earns his living by raising lumps like the egg of a speckled hen on the forehead and behind the ears of a man, who will simultaneously wish that he could die and be out of his misery. One hundred and seventy blackflies can feed on each square inch of a man's ears, but the simple-hearted natives of Maine, the Adirondacks, and Canada do not mind them until they settle down nine deep.

"The lumps raised by a blackfly will grow seven days, and then burst into a rich dark red bloom, which is much admired by the angler when he sees himself in a looking-glass trying to shave."

Carleton also wrote that a friend who took a two-week trip into blackfly country enjoyed every minute of it, but rather than go again he would go to prison for nine years. But, alas, he was no angler.

In the Madison Valley and Yellowstone Park, blackflies are known as buffalo gnats because, someone said, they had a buffalo for breakfast every day to hold them over until the anglers arrived. But blackflies are only one of angling's multitude of joys, all of which the fisherman willingly inflicts upon himself.

In 1843, before the days of waders or wading boots, William Scrope, in *Days and Nights of Salmon Fishing in the Tweed,* gave the angler some friendly advice. It is inadvisable to wade in water deeper than the fifth button on your waistcoat, (about two inches above the waist) if you're of tender constitution and the weather is frosty. If it is February when it freezes very hard, get to the bank now and then and pull down your stockings. If the legs are black, or even purple, it might be well to give up wading, but if they are merely rubicund you need not worry.

Anglers haven't changed much. My friend Jack Heartz, in the forties, waded wet in the Eel in northern California in January. Three days later he was dead of pneumonia.

Then there was the angler I saw once on the Madison. I was down at the section between McAtee and Varney bridges. It was mid-June, the salmon-fly hatch was on, and I was trying to find a clue that would allow me to locate the "head of the hatch," that section where the trout were not feeding on the crawling nymphs and were not yet glutted on the floating adults.

It had been raining all day—a cold, miserable, steady rain. A dozen or so

Salmon-fly time at McAtee Bridge. The swallows gorge ravenously during this period and so do the fish—sometimes.

boatloads of anglers and guides had floated by me as I worked, huddled in their rain jackets and looking unhappy. About two o'clock the rain changed to a wet snow and it was then that I saw him. He and his guide came out of the wall of snow and headed for the gravel bar where I stood.

The guide was dressed normally for June in this area, wool pants and shirt and a rain jacket. The angler was not dressed, normally or otherwise. When the boat grated on the gravel, he leaped out and raced into the thick willows, while the guide began assembling the ingredients for a fire.

"What happened?" I asked, helping pile up the driftwood for a roaring blaze, which I thought would feel most welcome.

"He was standing up in the bow, so he could see and cast better," said the guide. "We hit a submerged rock and he took a header. We took off his clothes and wrung 'em out; that's why we landed here, to build a fire to dry 'em off."

I wanted to ask the guide why he hadn't at least given the man his shirt, but thought it might be too personal. But he understood what I was thinking.

"Tried to give the damn fool my shirt and undershorts but he wouldn't take 'em. Said it was his own fault for standing up in the boat and that he'd suffer for it. He sure has."

The angler came out of the willows holding a clump of branches over and around his shoulders, to catch some of the snow coming down. He huddled up to the fire, shivering pitiably.

"I - I - I've b- b- been t-trying t-to c-c-catch this hatch f-for ten y-years," he stuttered, 'I-I-I'm not about t-to g-give up n-now."

I recognized the symptoms of hypothermia, and drew the guide aside.

"You'd better get him to a hospital quick," I told him in an undertone. "Your man is on the verge of low-temperature shock and if he goes into it, he won't last an hour."

Luckily, they were only fifteen minutes by boat from their car and fifteen minutes more from the hospital at Ennis.

This is the only angler I've ever known of to have hypothermia. In the thirty years I've fished the Madison, I've fallen in and gotten soaked dozens of times in all kinds of weather; I've known scores of anglers who have done so, and heard of hundreds of others falling in; but none suffered hypothermia. Yet during the same period, dozens, even scores of hunters in the area have suffered it, and two have died from it.

It's not a matter of colder weather. Hypothermia kills at temperatures of 50° F. when the subject is wet or it is raining with a light breeze. These are the things more apt to happen to fishermen. Still, they survive with apparently few ill effects.

The late Arnold Gingrich speaks of being swept away in the Esopus when the air temperature was 22° and the water only 43°. He fished the rest of the morning in wet clothes, and far from suffering hypothermia he never even caught cold. Nor did he ever, from any mishap while fishing, he said.

Hypothermia is a killer. People who do not survive it are said to have died from exposure. What kills is the dropping of the body temperature, causing low-temperature shock. The symptoms are uncontrolled shivering, slurred speech, stuttering, lethargy, and a complete ignorance of what is happening to one. When you are wet and cold, and any of these symptoms appear, stop what you're doing *at once*; get dry and warm by whatever measures it takes. If you notice the above symptoms in any member of your party, apply strenuous efforts to getting that person warm and dry, because almost never does the person affected realize that he is in deadly danger.

The salmon-fly season on this section of the river is from early June to mid-July most years. June is also our rainy month, eighteen days of rain is normal, and in 1964 when my wife and I were building our home in the mountains west of West Yellowstone, it rained twenty-six consecutive days and nights in June. And anywhere along the Madison, rain can turn to snow anytime.

So if you are among the thousands who come to the middle Madison for the salmon-fly hatch, bring warm clothing, bring a change, and bring a good rain jacket. Don't let the weather and the threat of hypothermia spoil your trip. The flies and the fish will probably arrange to do that.

The weather on the middle river in June is not always bad; in fact, the rain tends to come in periods of shower activity, followed by bright, warm sunshine. Whatever the weather, the flies hatch, the fish feed, and the fishermen swarm to the river.

Over 80,000 anglers come during the six-week period of the hatch and June and early July is carnival time on the middle Madison. In normal times the

The aspect of threatening weather is always with one during salmon-fly time on the Madison.

constant parade of boats would put the fish down completely during daylight hours. But during the height of the salmon-fly hatch it is doubtful if the fish could be put down with dynamite.

The bank runners storm up and down the banks trying to locate the "head of the hatch," a half-mile-long area where the floating adults are being taken. Since, when salmon flies hatch, and have mated, they fly upstream, the "head of the hatch" has no relation to where the flies are actually hatching, and there *can* be a stretch of ten miles or more where the bushes, shrubs, trees, grass, and even the air are filled with adult flies. Somewhere in that ten-mile stretch will be the head of the hatch.

There are long stretches of bank where there are no public access areas, so often the bank runner will be forced to enter six or eight miles from where the head of the hatch *might* be and trot up or down until he finds it. And trot they do, in full regalia, waders, heavy-laden vests, rod at the couch, panting, sweating, stumbling over rocks, falling in muskrat holes, fighting the willows—and smiling like dentifrice ads. There are no amenities at this time when Greek meets Greek along the banks, and there is only one greeting, delivered in loud tones—"*Where is it?*"

The nymph of the "salmon" fly, Pteronarcys californica, *and my imitation, Montana Stone Nymph.*

"It," of course, is the head of the hatch, and no one is interested in anything else. If you don't have the information, or do not know what is meant by the greeting, you'd better get off the river and quit cluttering up the raceway. You could get run over.

The situation is worse on the highway. Cars stream in both directions, according to the occupant's hunches, or where they've been. Rods sprout from windows like procupine quills, and when two rod-bearing cars approach each other, there is a screech of brakes, the squall of tires, heads blossom alongside the rods and there is a concerted shout—*"Where is it?"* Local people drive warily, or at night, or not at all during salmon-fly time.

Sometimes two cars will stop and the occupants will dismount to discuss where it isn't so that they will not waste time going there. This causes a chain reaction and cars will be parked for a half-mile along the shoulders, the occupants trotting up and down the ditches, passing information on the fly as they meet: "It isn't at Varney." "It's not yet to Hutchins." "It's above McAtee." "It's not at Snoball." And so it goes.

Once, returning from below Varney with some friends, we saw a light plane that had smacked a telephone pole and was crumpled in the ditch. We never heard what caused the accident but we knew. The pilot had flown so low over such a parked-car conclave to shout *"Where is it?"* that he had clipped the pole. There couldn't be another reason.

Although most of the anglers who come to fish the Madison at this time are from the western states, every state in the union is represented and over the years, many foreign countries. I've entertained anglers from England, France, Canada, New Zealand, Switzerland, and the Caribbean who have been drawn here by stories about this massive fly hatch and the frantic feeding of the trout.

The hatch, or rather, emergence, is nearly always massive. The adult flies hatch by the tens of millions and they are large. A local saying is that it only takes nine of them to make a dozen. They range from one-and-a-half to two inches long; many of the egg-laden females will weigh a quarter-ounce, making them larger and meatier than cocktail shrimp. And they become available to the fish in unbelievable numbers. I've opened fish that had adult flies hanging out their mouths *and* their vents. I caught a twenty-inch rainbow once that had fourteen adult flies in its mouth alone; there simply wasn't room for them farther down the chute.

Yet the fishing, or rather the catching, is often much less impressive. Part of the problem is the difficulty of locating the "head of the hatch." Part also, a very large part, is that many trout have gorged themselves on the mature nymphs and seldom or never come to the surface for the adults. But there is another reason.

Normally there would be scores instead of these few salmon flies clinging to the willows. But high winds scattered the 1978 hatch over wide areas.

The Madison in June and early July is at the peak of its power. You take no liberties with it. It is, quite simply, dangerous to wade or float *if* you cannot see exactly what you are doing. Yet much of the time the female flies come to the water to lay their eggs, and thus become available to the fish, between an hour before daylight, or in the first hour from dusk until full dark. Simply put, if the fish are feeding before daylight or after dark, they will find few fishermen on the scene. One may fish twenty-four hours a day during the season, but one who values his life will not fish the middle Madison in the dark during June and July.

Those who fish the river, in salmon fly, or any other time of the season, comprise a full spectrum of the American people—physically, mentally, politically, economically, and, unfortunately, morally. These latter are those who consider that no one has the right to regulate how they may fish or how many they may catch. On two occasions in the last ten years, persons have been apprehended with *more* than 1,000 trout in their freezers. What anyone could do with over a thousand trout eludes me; but what eludes me even more is the reasoning of these people. Both told the judge that fish were put on earth by God for man's use and no man had the right to limit another's use. On that basis, land was also put here for man's use. Does that mean they (the perpetrators) believe they have the right to take all the land they want?

Millionaires come here to fish, and I've been instructor on fishing waters and methods to some of these. I feel sorry for them, at least the ones I've dealt with, because all of them put the catching of trout on a competitive basis—them against the trout. I've often wondered if they approach lovemaking on the same basis or with the same attitude.

Paupers come also. These are the fishing bums who have given up literally everything else in order to be able to fish for trout. Many are well-educated, some are brilliant. I feel sorry for them, too, because I feel sorry for anyone who feels that any one thing in life is more important than all the rest. What happens to people when they can no longer compete for money or fish for trout? It may give some insight into my own attitude, though, when I note that I have several friends among the paupers, none among the millionaires.

But the mass of the fishermen who come are those who are and have been the backbone of this or any other free nation—the great middle class. And this brings to mind an anecdote, appropriate here not only because of the subject matter but because it involves a great American, a lawyer, government official, economic adviser to presidents, winner of the Distinguished Service Medal and the Legion of Honor, devout fly fisherman—and the first student Dan Bailey and Lee Wulff taught fly tying in the 1930s.

As one of his governmental duties, Jack (John Jay) McCloy* was detailed to shepherd around a British diplomat during World War II. One of their visits took them to a bond rally, attended by many thousands. The Britisher, a very stiff-lipped upper-class champion, white tie for dinner sort, was impressed by the tremendous amount of bonds sold ($11 million worth).

---

*McCloy has fished the Madison since the 1930s.

Auto camping along the Madison in Yellowstone, 1925. That year, nearly 40,000 people visited Yellowstone Park. National Park Service Photo

"To what station would you assign most of these people?" the Britisher asked when the total sales had been announced.

McCloy had gotten a little fed up with this fellow's patronizing attitude and sought to deflate him. "To Grand Central Station," he replied.

The Britisher puzzled over that a while, then his brow cleared. "Oh, I see. Of course. The great middle class." McCloy has denied the whole thing, but fishermen are such liars.

The millionaires send their families out in May, even as they used to do on the Willowemoc, the Brodheads, and the Beaverkill at the turn of the century. Then they jet out to join them for the salmon-fly hatch. The paupers come a little later, when it warms up, in vehicles that long ago should have been condemned, either for driving or for living, because, like the gypsies, these fellows travel and live in the same slum dwelling.

The rest come in everything that has ever been put on wheels. Some few years ago, I saw, along the Madison, an A-frame *trailer!* Neither God nor man has ever invented anything less effective or useful than that; I can only assume that the owner was one of those who would rather be different than conscious, or that the effects of living in ski resorts and salmon-fishing lodges so designed had convinced this poor soul that it was the only shape.

In salmon-fly time, people do not get away from it all—they bring it with them. One of the more conventional rigs one sees along the Madison at this time.

However, on second thought, that may not be the worst. I've seen log cabins on pickup campers; sections of culvert pipe serving the same purpose; tractor cabs converted to this use, and you name it. One disciple of Bucky Fuller shows up every year with a collapsed mass of nylon in the back of his pickup. When he reaches a camping spot on the Madison, he uses a car-battery-powered compressor to blow this up into a nylon igloo, complete with airlock, in which he lives—when he's there—for the salmon-fly season. What he does or where he goes in between, I know not. Probably an MIT or Cal Poly student.

Lest you think that I'm making fun of my fellow fishermen, perish the thought. The first few years I came here, I slept in a luggage trailer, later in a tent. It was several years before I was able to afford to rent a travel trailer and assume some semblance of respectability. But I would have come if I had to travel and sleep in a pumpkin.

The boats that these fishermen use are as weird as their travel and living arrangements. One can see every sort of floating idea ever thought up and often, most often, they are homemade. At one time or another, I've seen go by me while I was fishing, rubber rafts of every size and description, car-top boats likewise, canoes, catamarans, kayaks, rowboats, and dismasted sailboats. I've seen two Air Force jet drop-tanks lashed together with a platform atop, and once I saw a bearded buffoon riding four truck inner-tubes with a square of plywood on top on which he perched.

Most of the boaters are fishermen; the river is divided into float-fishing and non-float-fishing sections. The object is two-fold; to rotate the angling pressure and to give the fisherman a choice. If you are wade-fishing the float-fishing section, you may grit your teeth as boatload after boatload of anglers go by, putting down the fish, but you understand. These are not beer-drinking joy riders such as clutter up Missouri's Current River or Michigan's AuSable. Still, they do affect the fishing and there is a continuous smoldering animosity between waders and floaters.

Mentioning the Current River, on which I was raised, brings to mind that the French *couriers des bois* who named it *La Riviere Courante* (Running River) later saw the name Anglicized and mis-called Current River. But the Madison was already named by Lewis and Clark before the French trappers came, so their naming it La Riviere Courante had no effect, and not one person in ten thousand has ever heard it so called. But the name fits.

Though the exploration of Lewis and Clark benefitted us in many ways, it seems to me it robbed us of place names applied by the French and Indians that are nearly always more descriptive and beautiful. I have in mind such names as Spotted Horse, Red Lodge, Lame Deer, Medicine Hat, Lodge Grass for towns, and such rivers as the Medicine Bow, Picketwire (Purgatoire) Sweetwater, Seeds Ke dee (Green) Greybull, Red Rock, Beaverhead, and the Roche Jaune (Yellowstone). However, I suspect that I am alone in my feeling, and that few of today's fishermen really care by what names their rivers are called.

The Madison fishers are not nearly so varied in tackle and methods as they are in living and travel arrangements. About 80 percent are fly fishers, the rest are prone to use some sort of spin-gear, even those who fish such bait as live stoneflies, their nymphs, or live sculpins. Some use all three methods—flies, spinners, and bait, according to time of year and their particular hunches.

The salmon-fly hatches bring by far the largest numbers, yet I believe that the best fishing is not then, that what makes it seem so is sheer numbers of fishermen and the total catch, which seems high even though the individual catch is not.

One can have excellent dry-fly fishing after mid-July by concentrating on places of quieter deeper water such as exists around some creek mouths. Very large trout are occasionally taken on small dries along the mouths of Squaw, Aspen, Moose, Wall, Wolf, Bobcat, Dry Hollow, Indian, Cherry, Haypress, Spring, Papoose, and Moore creeks, all of which can be covered in a day if you don't dawdle.

Incidentally, the middle Madison looks so much of a piece (it has been called a fifty-mile-long fast riffle) that about the only way its various sections can be differentiated is by the creeks that enter it. Sometimes a section will be mentioned by the names of the creeks at its upper and lower ends, such as the Squaw-Wolf Creek section, which is also called Snoball because that creek enters the river between Squaw and Wolf creeks.

This is important information, because if you are being directed on where to fish, your informant will most likely do it by using one or more of the creeks as a frame of reference. Though some of the old timers may use such terms as Shaw Ranch or Shelton's or other ranches, most fishermen think of the creeks first. But knowing the name of the creek is no help if you don't know where the creek enters the river or how to get there.

This is where USGS quadrangle maps come in. Most local tackle shops sell them or you can order them direct from the U.S. Geological Survey. These maps have a scale of one inch equals one mile, and each quadrangle covers fifteen miles; so five or six will cover the middle Madison Valley. Are they important? I would rather be without my fly vest than my supply of quadrangle maps. They are invaluable for stream study, planning fishing trips, or just to dream over when the winter snow is up to the window sills.

If you are a fly fisherman, you may find that tackle which is suitable for other streams in other areas is not so for the middle Madison. This is a big, brawling, wide river; many stretches are not wadable if you are not an exceptional wader. So long rods and heavy lines are the norm. Most anglers find a rod of eight feet for a number seven line as light as is consistently useful. We've had a number of excellent anglers show up with their six-foot, two-ounce sticks and find trying to fish the river in all conditions as difficult as trying to feed bran mush to a gorilla with a plastic spoon.

In deciding on a leader tippet size, the factor of current speed and fish size had better enter into your calculations or you may go home fishless—and flyless. My friend and editor, Nick Lyons, is a more than common sensible man—though like all fly fishermen, he dodders on certain points and places in our craft. It took his friend, Thom Green, some time—and a number of lost fish—to convince him that a leader that was perfectly okay in the Beaverkill or Willowemoc was a waste of time on the Madison. Before you lose that trophy brown is the time to switch to a leader matched to the current speed and the size of the fish you expect to catch and not to someone's idea of what's sporting.

The major nymph on the entire middle river is *Pteronarcys californica*, the nymph of the "salmon fly," and when there is no significant surface activity, this nymph dead-drifted along the bottom is the best producer. Dry versions, of course, are the proper medicine for the hatch and to save you referring back, the local patterns of choice are the Sofa Pillow, Bird's Stone Fly, and the Salmon Hopper. Others used are the Bucktail Caddis and orange-bodied bucktail-winged flies. All should be size six, 3XL, to size four, 3XL.

For "shotgun" flies, used along of the edge of the current when there is little surface activity and you're trying to pound 'em up, the Grey and Royal Wulffs, a large Goofus Bug, or the Bivisibles in size ten are local choices. Grasshopper patterns in hopper time, and a selection of small dries and streamers should see you through.

The mayfly and caddis hatches are not of great importance but they do happen and one should be prepared. The Adams, Blue Dun, and a Grey Colorado King in fourteen and sixteen are among the best bets for match-the-hatch conditions.

The fish are more plentiful and larger, the farther down you go. The section from Varney Bridge to Ennis Lake produces more fish and bigger fish than does the section above McAtee Bridge. It is best fished by traveling by boat, and dismounting to fish choice spots. This is nearly all surrounded by private land and access is limited so the boating angler has more chance to reach the good spots without trespass. The river here is considered navigable, and the angler has the right to the water and the stream bed.

This is a difficult river to learn and a guide is a big help in learning it. It is not as easy to fish as it looks, but then no river is. Even though one doesn't wish to fish from a boat, as I don't, it is better to travel by boat, stopping to fish the better spots by wading. This is allowed even on stretches closed to float fishing.

Long stretches of the river have no sizable fish because there are no holding spots of sufficient depth and cover for such fish. These are the riffle areas where the water is almost uniformly of a depth, and too shallow to provide security for larger trout. There are more of these uniformly shallow stretches in the upper end of the middle river, toward Quake Lake, but you will find them all the way to Ennis Lake.

Nymph fishing has not been explored much on this section. Guides, especially the younger ones, are coming to realize the importance of the method and if their client is amenable, will provide instruction. However, most fly fishermen who come here are devout dry-fly fishers.

My experience is that the nymph is a more reliable lure for larger trout, and that the dry fly will produce more trout twelve inches and under. Though I've taken browns of near five pounds on nymphs, most such fish are caught on streamers, lures, and bait. Streamers produce more trout in the three to five-pound class; fish larger than this are usually taken on live sculpins.

As of right now, because of information just recently available, and which will be covered in the last chapter, the section from the highway bridge below Quake Lake to the mouth of Wolf Creek is not the place to fish if you are after the larger—two pound up—fish.

The best area for fish in the five-pound class is the section below Varney Bridge known as the Channels, where the river breaks up around islands, forming narrower, deeper streams. There are many of these. Some are better than others and which ones these are is the province of the local guide. West Yellowstone and Ennis both have numbers of first-class guides who can and will help one become acquainted with the river here. It is a much more varied stream here than anyplace else on the middle river, and it cannot be learned in a day.

If I might, I would suggest that each angler determine, by experience, which section of the river appeals to him or furnishes the kind of fishing experience he is after. Work this out beforehand with your guide and you will find that somewhere along the river is a spot especially suited to you and your method of fishing.

Take your time and use your head. This is a mighty river; it cannot be swallowed at a gulp. Take it in easy sips, get acquainted with all its facets and you will find that it will well reward those who let the river show the way.

THE RIVER NOW -AND IN THE FUTURE

WE HAVE BEEN FORTUNATE IN MANY WAYS REGARDING THE MADISON RIVER. ITS valleys did not contain enough minerals to support a viable mining industry, nor enough fuels to cause that rape of the land which has taken place in the East and Wyoming, and which is currently threatening eastern Montana.

The soil was neither rich enough nor extensive enough for agribusiness to be interested. There were not enough Indians in the area to encourage either missionaries or the Army to interfere. It was and is too isolated for great numbers of people to settle here and cause pollution and political corruption, which has happened in other parts of the state.

About all the hydroelectric development that feasibly can be done has been done. Irrigation, which can cause catastrophic problems in areas of poor drainage by causing salts to be brought to the surface, ruining the land, has not done so because the permeability of the subsoil has so far prevented it. And further irrigation does not seem practical, assuring no future disruption of stream flows.

The Montana Power Company has options for the licensing of two further dams in the Madison Valley, one on Squaw Creek or the river at Squaw Creek, and one just below Quake Lake in an area known in the planning document as Lyon. I have been unable to find the name Lyon on any map but the planning document locates the area about four miles north of Quake Lake, in the vicinity of the Cliff Lake Road bridge. In any event, both Montana Power and the Federal Power Commission note rather sadly that it does not appear that a dam at either location is economically feasible, now or in the future.

The land in the watershed is being managed now better than it ever has since the white man came. It is still suffering in some areas from the overgrazing of the 1880 to 1930 period, but recovery is proceeding slowly, due to shallow soil and low moisture, but proceding. One way of measuring progress is by the growth of long-time or native plants.

In areas of the world such as the Middle East and Africa where overgrazing is endemic, scientists some years ago noted an amazing adaptive process among native plants. As overgrazing progressed, these plants, continually grubbed down, matured and produced seed at a smaller and smaller size until plants that once stood three feet tall were mature and bearing seed at two or three inches. Only native plants were capable of this; domesticated varieties had apparently lost this ability.

These scientists were able to gauge the progress of recovery in areas where grazing was stopped, because each year the once-shrunken plants grew a little taller until, after fifty years, they reached their former height. The scientists then judged the land to be fully recovered.

This process is going on in the Madison watershed, and in some areas these remaining native plants have reached three-quarters their normal height. However, in most places they are only about half as tall as normal—so it will be at least forty years before that point in the land's recovery is reached.

Logging, which has always contributed less to erosion than overgrazing, is being done with more care, and perhaps less is being done. But the practice of clear-cutting, which is much practiced, is damaging these immature mountain soils because regeneration is very slow, or in some cases, nonexistent.

While gains have been made in the private sector, and the BLM and the Forest Service are leaning toward progress in ecological protection, the BLM is still too grazing oriented, and the FS is still pursuing a single-minded policy of timber production. Until there is a complete change of personnel in those agencies, progress will be slow.

At present, the dangers to the river from man, in order of importance, are overgrazing (still), logging, future mining for minerals known to be present but not economically feasible to harvest now, overfishing, overboating, and possible increases in irrigation activities.

From nature, the warming of the waters by Quake and Ennis lakes, earthquakes, drought, overbrowsing by game animals, flooding, and forest fires are present dangers. In this last area, there has been a complete change in thinking in the last five years.

Prior to a few years ago, forest fires were thought to be all bad and mighty efforts and educational programs were financed to stop them. It is now known that that was a mistake. It was a mistake founded on the Forest Service's monomania with timber production.

A mature or virgin forest may be beautiful, and offer excellent watershed protection but these are its only virtues. Such a forest does not offer the best timber production—a progressively growing forest does. Evergreen trees bind up many minerals from the soil, and keep them from the water. Cutting the timber removes these minerals forever, but a forest fire returns them to the soil and water. A virgin or mature forest supports little wildlife—a few birds, porcupines and pine squirrels. There is no food for other creatures.

Hot forest fires occur in such forests because the debris and detritus has built up to dangerous levels. Such hot fires not only destroy every living plant in its path but burn up many nutrients in the soil, turning it to powder, making it extraordinarily susceptible to erosion. When rains come, following such fires, they wash the silt of the burned and exposed soil away and into the streams, clogging the gravel, damaging spawn. Snow and rain, with nothing to hold back the moving waters, drains off as soon as it falls or melts, making short fierce floods in spring and drought in summer and fall. It will be years before any plant can take root in an area where a hot forest fire has burned. There is a small area of such a burn in Yellowstone Park. It happened over fifty years ago and today, except for a few burned snags, nothing stands or grows there.

The practice now, and in the last few years, is to let naturally started fires burn, under scrutiny, and sometimes control, but not to make any effort to stop their burning. This has not only saved millions of dollars in fighting fires, it has benefitted the plants and the animals. A slow, controlled burn does not kill all the trees; it burns them down in spots, kills some scattered throughout, leaves some areas untouched.

Sunlight can now get to the soil, which has been enriched by the return of bound-up minerals. A varied natural vegetation replaces one of only trees, animals move in, and the great change of renewal that is nature's lasting heritage begins. It was thus for millions of years until man disrupted the schedule.

In England and Europe, controlled *deliberate* burning has been done to create conditions for multiple use, for centuries. We have, until just recently, stubbornly resisted following this beneficial practice.

This, and many other changes have taken place during the three years that I have been researching and writing this book. In that time the attitude of the people and of government agencies have changed for the better. The agencies, under public pressure, are beginning to operate as they should. And the people, especially those in the Maidson watershed, have come to understand that more is not always better, and that what benefits all also benefits the few, and not the reverse.

In a series of meetings in West Yellowstone and Ennis, conducted by the Blue Ribbons organization, county commissioners, and the Fish and Game Department in the past two years, people have given overwhelming support for policies that protect the environment and that recognize recreation as a major economic factor. The actual support has been estimated at 98 percent for the policies and only 2 percent against. This is a major victory and an amazing change of attitude.

The policies they favored were for more careful practices in logging and road building; restoring areas damaged by these activities in the past; giving tax credits to farmers and ranchers who encouraged buffer zones along streams on their land; and accepting regulations on recreational activity for the good of all.

One great change was in the regulations affecting fishing on the river, a major recreational and economic area. Such regulations had been resisted in the past and the studies of fishery biologist Dick Vincent had seemed to support the position that more restrictive regulations were not needed, as mentioned at length in another chapter. As late as January 1977, Dick and Ron Marcoux, the area fishery manager, had met with groups at Ennis and West Yellowstone to reaffirm that position.

However, Vincent admitted their position was not as firm as it had been because summer mortality rates on the area of the river known as Snoball had skyrocketed, for no apparent reason. We were asked to support closing this section to angling for the 1977 season. Vincent said he did not believe that angling pressure was the reason for the excessive mortality rates, but it could be eliminated as a factor if, after a season's closure, there was little or no change in the mortality rates.

But that is not what happened. The studies conducted in 1975 and 1976 had shown summer mortality rates of 75 percent each summer, a stunning figure, which had produced the request for the closure. The area was closed to angling for the 1977 season and the summer mortality rate dropped to 15 percent! Angling pressure *was* destroying the fishery and at an amazing and terrifying rate.

The results of this closure and study brought Vincent and Marcoux back to West Yellowstone and Ennis in December 1977 to ask for support before the Fish and Game Commission for stringent regulations. They got overwhelming support, so much so that the Commission went even further in imposing restrictions upon catch and methods.

The fishing regulations on the middle river for 1979 are as follows.

1. Quake Lake to McAtee Bridge.
   a. No-kill section
   b. No float fishing allowed
   c. Use of flies and lures only for taking fish.
2. McAtee Bridge to Ennis Lake.
   a. Three fish limit, only one of which may be eighteen inches or longer.
   b. Float fishing allowed
   c. Flies, lures and bait, excluding sculpins, allowed for taking fish.

Only three years ago, the Southwestern Montana Fly Fishers had conducted a survey on similar restrictions and had received only a 51 to 47 percent favorable response. In three years the public attitude had undergone a complete change. What brought it on?

Apparently a concerted though uncoordinated educational effort by our

This Special Research Area yielded results that led to catch-and-release fishing with flies and lures only. In a single year (1978) this section (Quake Lake to McAtee Bridge) made a tremendous comeback. In five years it will be great.

club, the F & G people, and local conservation organizations had caused the change. A large part of it was undoubtedly due to the fact that Marcoux and Vincent had been conducting a regular and continuing series of public meetings, in which they had explained what they were doing, what future plans were, and what information had been so far developed. They had asked for public input and had answered all questions courteously and fully. This had caused a very favorable response because the people felt that, finally, here was a government agency that would tell them what it had been doing and why and would listen to questions and accept advice. Everyone had had a say and even those in direct disagreement had been listened to and their point of view discussed. Beyond any question it had caused a feeling of satisfaction about the agency and there is no doubt that Dick and Ron's calm, reasoned explanations had converted a great many people.

The Commission, in setting the new regulations, had made it clear that if the biologists and the public, after a period of time, thought the regulations not restrictive enough, and could present affirmative information and a similar undivided front, that it would favorably consider further restrictions. The attitude that seems to prevail throughout is that the fishery should not be subject to the whims of a few greedy people but should be protected and enhanced as a quality fishery for all. Also, the people most directly concerned, those in the Madison watershed, have come to realize what a terrific economic asset recreational fishing is to the community and that people who spend millions of dollars to come and stay here will not come to fish for small fish or in order to keep large numbers.

The increased awareness has led to an assessment of the area's assets and an intention to manage them for the long, rather than the short, term. This, combined with improvements in the recent past, gives a favorable outlook to the future. The watershed has improved over a few years ago, and this will continue. The attempts to prevent overgrazing have resulted in the shipping of most animals as calves and lambs, thus reducing the number of adult animals grazing the available land.

The population is stable, a slow growth is taking place to handle the increase in recreational activity by larger numbers of people. The two towns in the watershed, West Yellowstone and Ennis, have upgraded their sewage systems and both are rated A-1 in disposal and effluent quality. Some biologists have discovered coliform bacteria in the Madison and have accused the towns. But the State Health Department refutes the charge, and points out that *all* mammals produce coliform bacteria and the thousands of head of cattle and big game are the probable culprits.

The various county agencies are working to control any damage to the environment by their agencies and are slowly repairing past areas of damage. Efforts are being made to work with Montana Power to maintain and improve water quality, and Madison and Gallatin counties both have watchdog water-quality boards. The powers of the Fish and Game department have been expanded; it now has laws to stop such destructive practices as stream alterations by individuals or organizations, even municipalities. And all the people

How some Montana fishermen feel about developers. It hasn't come to shooting yet, but it's heating up.

are made constantly aware of the precious things that still exist here that have vanished in many other places because of apathy and greed.

The future, then, is looking better all the time. Meanwhile, the present is still very good. The scenery and the river are still beautiful; the river is still pure if not pristine. The otters appear to be increasing, not only in the Park but along many of the tributaries.

The dipper (formerly ouzel) plies its trade along the stretch between Hebgen and Quake lakes, as well as on the Grayling, Duck, South Fork, and tributaries farther down. This unique bird is found only along clear, cold streams that host large insect populations. Its habits, such as nesting behind waterfalls and wading completely submerged along the bottom to pick up insects, has caused many anglers not to trust their eyes.

A few years ago my brother Ken was visiting here and one day went fishing on the South Fork. He had an excellent day but his attitude that evening didn't reflect it. The following day he went to the Grayling, again with good results, but once again, he acted strangely. Finally after supper, he approached me in confidence.

"Big brother," he said, "do you have a chunky grey bird with a short tail around here that goes into the water?"

"Sure," I said, realizing what had been on his mind. "It's called a dipper or ouzel and it will fly right into the water and walk along the bottom, picking up insects. There are several on the streams leading into Hebgen Lake."

His face lit up. "Well, by dern!" he exclaimed, "I saw that happen yesterday on the South Fork and again today on the Grayling. But I'd never heard of such a thing and I thought maybe I was seeing things."

The river is still lovely, to float and to fish. The habitations of man are still relatively far apart, except at West Yellowstone and at Ennis—and, it suddenly occurs to me—at Jeffers, across the river from Ennis.

I never see this village or hear its name without wondering if M. D. Jeffers, who founded it, and who was English, was any relation to Richard Jeffers, a naturalist of the 1800s whose ideas were so advanced and different that writers called him Looney Dick.

Jeffers loved rivers—in fact, all nature. And he wrote this about one of them: "The brown Barle river. . .enjoys his life, and splashes in the sunshine like boys bathing—like them he is sunburnt and brown. He throws the wanton spray over the ferns that bow and bend as the cool breeze his current brings sways them in the shade. He laughs and talks, and sings louder than the wind in his woods."

Anthropomorphic nonsense, wrote one barren critic; a river is not a man. Nonsense indeed, but on the part of the critic who had not the vision to see the comparison.

There are perhaps more people today who feel as Jeffers did, and one of them was the late Roderick Haig-Brown who wrote about rivers as well as anyone ever has.

The following, from his *A River Never Sleeps,* has been much quoted, perhaps because there was no way of saying it better: "I still don't know why I fish or why other men fish, except that we like it and it makes us think and feel. But I do know that if it were not for the strong, quick life of rivers, for their sparkle in the sunshine, for the cold grayness of them under rain and the feel of them about my legs as I set my feet hard down on rocks or sand or gravel, I should fish less often. A river is never quite silent; it can never, of its nature, be quite still; it is never quite the same from one day to the next. It has its own life and its own beauty, and the creatures it nourishes are alive and beautiful also. Perhaps fishing is, for me, only an excuse to be near rivers. If so, I'm glad I thought of it."

Haig-Brown's thesis is that one can never solve the mysteries of a river; you come to know them and that is enough. Coming to know the Madison River has occupied a number of years of my life and every one of them has been more pleasant because of this. I hope to spend many more years coming to know it better.

I do not live on the Madison River, but a few, very few, miles from it. I'm often asked why, when I settled here, I didn't build my home on the river. Perhaps one reason was that I had not yet come to know it. And perhaps I was looking still for my ideal home.

I have long thought that the ideal place to live would be on a low bluff above a narrow beach facing the sea, with a silted tidal flat and the ocean beyond, the estuary of a trout stream near at hand, and the mountains rising hard in the back. But no such place exists. In Alaska, where the mountains and trout streams cooperate, there is no beach and the tidal flat is as narrow as a bookie's hatband, or where it is wide, it is miles wide, an impenetrable, unlovely mass of muck and glop.

So, I go to the sea in winter, to live near the beach, to cast flies off it for what manner of creatures I know not, to dig clams on the tidal flat and dangle horsemeat for crabs from a boat a bit offshore. But I return in spring to the mountains, to the headwaters of the streams I love, to be refreshed and renewed and to begin all over again.

Man born of woman is of short life and small expectations. He fleeth as a shadow and is cut down. But if he remembers that rivers are eternal and returns to them often, his life will be longer and full of peace and learning, and the years will treat him kindly as they have me.

MADISON RECIPES

THESE ARE INCLUDED FOR THOSE WHO LIKE TO TRY SUCH THINGS. THESE ARE NOT offered as authentic because there was no such thing. The Indians used whatever was available; if certain ingredients were not, they were simply left out. On the other hand, when all ingredients were plentiful larger portions of them would be added to the basics.

It should be remembered that Indians *did not* smoke fish or meat originally as a preservative method. Drying was the primary method of preserving meat or fish. But in summer, since flies would infest the meat with their eggs if allowed, a smudge built under the drying racks discouraged the flies. That was all.

I spent a considerable amount of time with Eskimos in Alaska and noticed that fish and meat dried in the fall, after frost, was never smoked. The primitives of any country were not inclined to unnecessary labors (consider me a primitive).

The recipes for pinole were brought into this area by trappers from the Southwest where it is a basic storage food item, as pemmican was here and farther north. The recipe for smoked fish came from Candian Cree Indians who were with the French trapping brigades of the Hudson's Bay Company.

PEMMICAN
10 parts dried meat
3 parts melted suet
2 parts roasted marrow
3 parts dried fruit

This was the preferred mix, due to its high food value and excellent taste. The meat was pounded coarsely with a wooden pestle, the suet and marrow heated, the berries (usually) mixed with the meat and the heated suet-marrow mix poured over the whole. The mixture was kneaded and pressed to get the air out, packed into animal bladders or stomach membranes, and stored. It would keep indefinitely. It could be eaten as is, heated with or without water, and some trappers made a flour gravy with it, on the order of creamed chipped beef. It was never salted before cooking.

Pinole: This originally was parched corn, coarsely ground and stored in leather bags. It is an excellent emergency food, I have eaten it often. It is never salted until eaten.

PINOLE PLUS
10 parts parched corn
2 parts raw sugar
3 parts dried fruit

Here again, this is a preferred mix. There was no standard mix. The parched corn is coarsely ground, the raw sugar (pinoche) and fruit mixed in. This must be stored in moisture-proof containers. It is a fine food eaten as is or heated with a little water as a gruel. It provides quick and lasting energy. Raw (unrefined) sugar is available at many stores.

Dried Fish: This is simply fish, cleaned, split and dried, either in the sun or over a low, smokeless fire. It will dry in open sun in three days if the air temperature is at least 70° F. and there is a breeze. The exposed flesh must be flinty hard. This also must be kept in moisture-proof containers. It can be boiled, poached, soaked for a day in water and baked, and may be steamed, flaked and mixed with a cream sauce, seasoned to taste. No salt is used in the curing process.

Smoked Fish: Fish are cleaned, split, and hung in a cool smoke for ten hours for one pound fish, twenty-four hours for two-pounders. The smoke temperature *at the fish* should not exceed 110° F., nor drop below 90°. Wood used for smoking in this area was green aspen, cottonwood, service berry, or other deciduous tree or shrub.

The modern method is the same except that the fish are soaked in a strong brine (to float a potato) for eight hours, dried and smoked as above. Both kinds may be eaten as is, or prepared as dried fish, above. Some persons like to flake and pulverize the fish and mix in enough olive oil for a heavy paste and spread on toast or crackers. Eskimos use seal oil.

Echarqui (Jerky): The meat is prepared by cutting it into long strips or sheets no more than one-quarter inch thick, and dried in the sun or over a low smokeless fire until flinty hard. It will keep indefinitely if not presalted. It can be eaten as is, boiled, soaked for a few hours and fried, chipped in a cream sauce, or mixed with anything else, such as parched corn (excellent) or boiled with vegetables. Modern taste prefers the meat soaked in brine overnight before drying. This will not keep as well as the unsalted version unless kept absolutely dry.

Smoking: While the Indians hung their meat or fish over poles out in the open, if one prefers the smoked taste, a smudge or smoke-fire under such conditions will produce only a faint smoke taste.

The preferred modern way is to use an electric smoker made for the purpose but a good smoker can be made cheaply. Dig a pit two feet deep and two-and-a-half square. Dig a trench from one edge four feet long and deep enough to hold two joints of common six-inch stovepipe with two inches of dirt on top. Both ends of the pipe must be open.

A large cardboard carton with wires strung through it will hold the meat or fish. It is turned upside down over the open pipe end. The top must be closed.

The fire in the pit may be started with paper and kindling—never petroleum products. After it is going well and there are some coals, put on the green wood for smoking. Preferred woods are aspen, poplar, cottonwood, birch, hickory, apple, or almost any deciduous tree or shrub.

Use a piece of scrap metal or a tub to cover the fire and adjust to provide a draft. Temperature in the cardboard box should never exceed 110° F. It takes 450° F. to ignite cardboard.

A SELECTED BIBLIOGRAPHY

The books listed are only some of those that I read in researching and writing this one. They are included here for those who wish to pursue certain avenues of exploration further. Some have only a bare minimum of information concerning the Madison River or its environs but are delightful reading in themselves.

Back, Howard. *The Waters of Yellowstone with Rod and Fly*. New York: Dodd, Mead and Co., 1938

Barnett, Lincoln, Editor. *The World We Live In*. New York: Simon and Schuster, 1955

Bartlett, Richard A. *Nature's Yellowstone*. Albuquerque: University of New Mexico Press, 1974

Bauer, Clyde Max. *Yellowstone Its Underworld*. Albuquerque: The University of New Mexico Press, 1948

Beal, Merrill D. *Intermountain Railroads: Standard and Narrow Gauge*. Caldwell: The Caxton Printers, 1962

Beal, Merrill D. *The Story of Man in Yellowstone*. Caldwell: The Caxton Printers, Ltd., 1949

Bennett, Russell H. *The Compleat Rancher*. New York: Rinehart and Co., 1946

Bergman, Ray. *Trout*. New York: Alfred A. Knopf, 1938

Bergman, Ray. *With Fly, Plug and Bait*. New York: William Morrow and Company, 1947

Blankinship, Joseph W. *Native Economic Plants of Montana*. Bulletin No. 56. Bozeman, Mt., Agricultural Experiment Station, 1905 (Also found in: *A Century of Botanical Exploration in Montana; Collectors Herbaria in Bibliography*.)

BROOKS, CHARLES E. *Larger Trout for the Western Fly Fisherman.* Cranbury: A. S. Barnes and Co., 1970

BROOKS, CHARLES E. *The Trout and the Stream.* New York: Crown Publishers, Inc., 1974.

BROWN, MARK H. *The Plainsmen of the Yellowstone.* New York: G. P. Putnam's Sons, 1961

BURLINGAME, MERRILL G. and K. ROSS TOOLE. *A History of Montana.* N.Y.: 3 Vols. Lewis Historical Publishing Co., 1957

CHITTENDEN, HIRAM M. *Yellowstone National Park.* Palo Alto: The Leland M. Stanford University Press, 1949

CHRISTOPHERSON, EDMUND. *The Night the Mountain Fell.* Missoula: Earthquake Book, 1960. Subtitle: *The Story of the Montana-Yellowstone Earthquake.*

DAVIS, JEAN. *Shallow Diggin's.* Caldwell: The Caxton Printers, Ltd., 1962.

DELACY, WALTER W. *A Trip Up the South Fork of the Snake River in 1863.* Contributions to the Historical Society of Montana. Vol. 1, 1876

FERRIS, WARREN A. *Life in the Rocky Mountains (1830–1835).* Denver: The Old West Publishing Co., 1940

GARCIA, ANDREW. *Tough Trip Through Paradise 1878–1879.* Boston: Houghton-Mifflin Co., 1967 Edited by Bennett H. Stein.

GARD, WAYNE. *The Great Buffalo Hunt.* New York: Alfred A. Knopf, 1959

GOETZMAN, WILLIAM H. *Exploration and Empire.* New York: Alfred A. Knopf, 1966

HAFEN, LEROY R. Editor. *The Mountain Men and the Fur Trade of the Far West.* Glendale: The Arthur H. Clark Co., 10 Vols., 1965–1972

HAFEN, LEROY R. Editor. *Ruxton of the Rockies.* Norman: The University of Oklahoma Press, 1950

HAINES, AUBREY L. Editor. *The Valley of the Upper Yellowstone.* Norman: University of Oklahoma Press, 1965

HAINES, AUBREY L. *The Yellowstone Story.* Mammoth: The Yellowstone Library and Museum Association with Colorado Associated University Press. 2 Vols., 1976, 1977

HAINES, AUBREY L. *Yellowstone National Park; Its Exploration and Establishment.* Washington, D.C.: The U.S. Department of the Interior, National Park Service, 1974

HALL, E. RAYMOND, and KEITH R. KELSON. *The Mammals of North America.* New York: Ronald Press Co., 1959

HANSON, CHARLES E. JR. *The Plains Rifle.* New York: Bramhall House 1960

HOWARD, JOSEPH KINSEY. *Montana, High, Wide, and Handsome.* New Haven: Yale University Press, 1959.

IRVING, WASHINGTON. *The Adventures of Captain Bonneville.* Edited and Annotated by Edgeley W. Todd. Norman: The University of Oklahoma Press, 1961

KENNEDY, MICHAEL S., Editor. *Cowboys and Cattlemen.* New York: Hastings House, 1964

LAVENDER, DAVID. *The Rockies.* New York: Harper and Row, 1968

MARQIS, THOMAS B. *Thomas H. Le Forge, a White Crow Indian.* New York: The Century Co., 1928

MATTES, MERRILL J. *Colter's Hell and Jackson's Hole.* Yellowstone Library and Museum Assn. 1962

MUTTKOWSKI, RICHARD A. *The Ecology of Trout Steams in Yellowstone National Park.* Ithaca: The Roosevelt Wildlife Annals, Vol. II, No. 2, Oct. 1929

MYERS, JOHN MYERS. *The Saga of Hugh Glass.* Boston: Little, Brown and Company, 1963

NASATIR, ABRAHAM PHINEAS. *Before Lewis and Clark.* St Louis: Historical Documents Foundation, 1952

OGLESBY, RICHARD EDWARD. *Manuel Lisa and the Opening of the Missouri Fur Trade.*

Norman: The University of Oklahoma Press, 1963

PRICE, ROSE LAMBART, (Sir). *A Summer on the Rockies.* London: S. Low, Marston and Co., 1898

REID, MAYNE (Thomas). *The Scalp Hunters.* London: H. Lea, 185(?)

ROBERTSON, FRANK C. *Fort Hall.* New York: Hastings House, 1963

ROSS, ALEXANDER *The Fur Hunters of the Far West.* Chicago: R. R. Donnelly and Sons, 1924

RUSSELL, OSBORNE. *Journal of a Trapper (1834–1843).* Edited by Aubrey L. Haines. Lincoln: University of Nebraska Press, 1955

RUXTON, GEORGE F. *Life in the Far West.* Edited by Leroy Hafen. Norman: The University of Oklahoma Press, 1959

SNYDER, GERALD S. *In the Footsteps of Lewis and Clark.* Washington, D.C.: The National Geographic Society, 1970

STIRLING, MATTHEW W. *Indians of the Americas.* Washington, D.C.: The National Geographic Society, 1955

STRONG, GENERAL W. E. *A Trip to the Yellowstone Park in July, August and September 1875.* Edited by Richard Bartlett. Norman: University of Oklahoma Press, 1968

THORP, RAYMOND W. and ROBERT BUNKER. *Crow Killer.* Bloomington: The Indiana University Press, 1958

THWAITES, REUBEN G. *Original Journals of the Lewis and Clark Expedition 1804–06.* New York: Dodd, Mead and Co., 1904–05

TOPPING, E. S. *Chronicles of the Yellowstone.* Edited by Robert A. Murray. Minneapolis: Ross and Haines, 1968

VAN WORMER, JOE. *The World of the Moose.* New York: J. B. Lippincott Co., 1972

VINTON, STALLO *John Colter, Discoverer of Yellowstone Park.* New York: E. Eberstadt, 1926

WINGATE, GEORGE W. *Through the Yellowstone Park on Horseback.* New York: O. Judd Co., 1886.

WILLARD, DANIEL E. *Montana, The Geological Story.* Lancaster: The Science Press Printing Co., 1935

INDEX